BEYOND THE FRAY

RESHAPING AMERICA'S ENVIRONMENTAL RESPONSE

BEYOND THE FRAY

RESHAPING AMERICA'S ENVIRONMENTAL RESPONSE

Daniel D. Chiras

Foreword by Roderick Nash

Johnson Books: Boulder

363.708
C 5416

Cover design by Molly Davis Gough

First Edition
9   8   7   6   5   4   3   2

Library of Congress Cataloging-in-Publication Data

Chiras, Daniel D.
    Beyond the fray: reshaping America's environmental response /
Daniel D. Chiras; foreword by Roderick Nash.
        p.   cm.
    Includes bibliographical references.
    ISBN 1-55566-067-3
    1. Environmental policy—United States. I. Title.
HC110.E5C48   1990
363.7'08'0973—dc20

Printed in the United States of America by
Johnson Publishing Company
1880 South 57th Court
Boulder, Colorado 80301

Dedication

To the earth in all its splendid glory and to those among us who journey lightly on the land with love, respect, and kindness for the gift of life.

Contents

Foreword

Friendly, or constructive, criticism occurs when the critic wishes to improve rather than destroy a way of doing or thinking. Daniel Chiras is an environmentalist, but he is not a contented one. He supports "conservation" but believes it stops far short of what is necessary to sustain the habitability of planet earth for the long haul. Modern American "environmentalism" is also tried and found wanting in this iconoclastic book. But Dr. Chiras would not have written *Beyond the Fray* if he did not believe in the possibility of improvement in the human-environment relationship.

What Dr. Chiras advocates here is nothing less than a major change in the fundamental values and basic philosophy of the life form most responsible for both endangering and protecting the only home it knows. The problem in a nutshell is that humans possess abundant power but insufficient restraint to control its use. I like to make this point with a metaphor: the three-hundred pound kindergartner. Five-year-olds are notoriously self-centered. Their ethical philosophies are inchoate, and their appetites frequently lead them into behavior that works against their long-term welfare. But there is a check on the child's tendency to destructive selfishness. He is relatively small and weak. When thity-pound Peter hits Sylvia with a toy, tears and not decapitation results. But consider a three-hundred pound five-year-old Peter. His pursuit of self-interest could destroy both his classmates and the classroom (habitat, environment). The obvious analogy is to a civilization made powerful by science and technology, but ethically unprepared to control that power.

To continue for a moment with the kindergarten metaphor, it is fortunate for both Peter and his classmates that by the time they have gained physical force they have, in most cases, also gained a code of ethics. They have learned the meaning of community (at least in its human dimensions) and understood the importance of respecting the rights of others. People like Peter certainly have the capacity to rob, murder, and rape, but for the most part, they exercise self-restraint, and the social fabric is preserved. In regard to self-interest, Peter has learned that, paradoxically, less is more. But the next level of ethical awareness, the one that focuses on the non-human members of Peter's community and the ecosystemic processes that sustain them, is much harder to attain. The failure of modern Americans to move from social to what Aldo Leopold called "land" ethics is the concern of this book.

Educators, such as myself and Dr. Chiras, have frequently pondered the problem of how to teach environmental responsibility and restrain the savage human beast. There seem to be two ways: the path of fear and the path of love. Fear is familiar to every maturing person. Control yourself, he is told, or you will be spanked, jailed, even killed. Your own self-interest warrants restraint of self-interest—the old paradox again. Environmentalists who follow the path of fear are simply extending the arena and upping the stakes. If you hurt the earth, they warn, you'll hurt yourself. The prudent course is to protect what sustains you; take care of number one. "Planet-care," Dr. Chiras states, "is self-care."

Love is the second basis for an expanded, environmental ethic. In this scenario concern is for the "other" rather than for the self. Those who love nature believe in its intrinsic value and its right to share earth with humankind. They reject a dualistic viewpoint of humans and nature as separate and contradictory for a holistic perspective, according to which human beings are members and not masters of the ecosystem. Those who subscribe to environmental ethics believe that the same restraint that Peter must learn to exercise in his dealings with people should also control his relationships to elk, redwood trees, phytoplankton, rivers, and rocks. This staggering concept, increasing numbers feel, holds the key to the long-term sustainability of all life on earth.

The book you are about to read should be disturbing. Daniel Chiras undermines the pride we have taken in many aspects of our civilization including the conservation and environmental movements. In so doing, he joins Aldo Leopold, Rachel Carson, Paul Ehrlich, and the deep ecologists who share a commitment to reformulating our relationship to nature. *Beyond the Fray* will be particularly unsettling for those conservation activists who are confident that their present efforts are leading to a sustainable civilization. But it is through critical analysis like this that the American environmental response can grow in effectiveness.

Roderick Frazier Nash
Professor of History and Environmental Studies
University of California, Santa Barbara
Author of *The Rights of Nature: A History of Environmental Ethics*
and *Big Drops: Ten Legendary Rapids of the American West*

Acknowledgments

Many people have helped me with this exciting project. My most important ally during the months of preparation was my wife, Kathleen, who listened patiently as I formulated my ideas and arguments, transcribed notes from interviews, read and commented on drafts of the manuscript, and helped research Chapter 6. For her assistance, support, patience, and love throughout this project, a world of thanks. My friend and colleague Elizabeth Otto also read the first draft and offered numerous comments that helped me in many ways. Elizabeth also provided articles and helped transcribe interviews. Her contributions are greatly appreciated. Charles Callison, long-time environmentalist and writer, read the manuscript and offered helpful criticisms, for which I am deeply indebted. Finally, I owe a great debt to my friend and colleague, Marshall Massey, who critiqued the manuscript and offered many helpful suggestions for improving it. Marshall helped me "find" my audience and find an appropriate tone. His comments, as always, were thorough, painfully honest, but right on target.

I owe a special debt of gratitude to the many people who gave so freely of their time for interviews:

Jim Abernathy, Puget Sound Water Quality Authority
David Adamson, The Nature Conservancy
Paz Artasa, Ecojustice Working Group
Thomas Atkins, Environmental Action
Jalair Box, Washington Environmental Council
Peter Berle, National Audubon Society
Steve Bonowski, Colorado Mountain Club
David Brower, Earth Island Institute
Scott Budney, U.S. Postal Service
Charles Callison, Missouri Audubon Council
Rosemary Carroll, Sierra Club
Brownie Carson, Natural Resources Council of Maine
Peter Coppelman, The Wilderness Society
Kyle Crider, The Alabama Conservancy
Larry Dieringer, Educators for Social Responsibility
David Eaton, University of Washington
Esther R. Edie, South Dakota Resources Coalition
Dave Foreman, Earth First!

Michael Fischer, Sierra Club
Anne Grady, Denver Better Air Campaign
Samuel P. Hays, University of Pittsburgh
John J. Kirk, Montclair State College
Linda Lopez, Natural Resources Defense Council
David Lynch, The Stewardship Community
Marshall Massey, Friends Committee on Unity With Nature
Suzanne Mattei, Connecticut Fund for the Environment
Angela Medbery, Colorado Pesticide Network
Woody Moore, Results
Tim McKay, Northcoast Environmental Coalition
Elizabeth Otto, Colorado Environmental Coalition
Mary Ovenstone, The Stewardship Community
Joel Plagenz, Environmental Defense Fund
Lewis Regenstein, The Fund for Animals
Craig Sarbeck, The Stewardship Community
Leon Swartzendruber, Friends of Curbside Recycling
John Turck, Marketing Communications
Paul Watson, Sea Shepherd Conservation Society
Susan Weber, Zero Population Growth

Their views do not necessarily reflect the views of the organizations for which they work or represent.

Last but not least, I would like to acknowledge and thank the staff at Johnson Books. To my publisher, Barbara Johnson Mussil, a heartfelt thanks for taking on this project and for making it possible to print the book on recycled paper. Her dedication to individual and corporate responsibility are indeed appreciated. To Michael McNierney, many thanks for his early comments, and to Rebecca Herr, a world of thanks for her careful editing and her friendly, helpful, and often insightful suggestions. I want to thank Molly Davis Gough, who designed the cover, for her time and effort and creative energies. And finally, to Richard Croog, many thanks for his interest in the project and his creative approach to sales.

Doing what can't be done is the
glory of living.

S.C. ARMSTRONG

1 | A Time for Change?

On March 24, 1989, Exxon's supertanker, the *Valdez,* ran aground on a reef off the coast of Alaska near the port from which it got its name. Operated by a third mate who was not certified to be at the controls of the ship and captained by a pilot who may have been legally drunk at the time, the supertanker had strayed off course and had lost contact with the Coast Guard monitoring station when it struck Bligh reef.[1]

The world watched in horror as oil leaked out of the gash in the tanker's steel hull and began to spread. In places, the oil slick was one to three feet thick. All told, over eleven million gallons of Alaskan crude oil spilled into the biologically rich waters of Prince William Sound.

President Bush "rushed" three top administration officials to Valdez three days after the spill, who reported that the cleanup was going better than expected. Exxon, they said confidently, had matters under control. Their announcement came just hours after Exxon executives admitted they were losing the struggle to contain the oil.

One week after the spill, the slick covered an area the size of Rhode Island. Oil had washed up on the rocky coastlines of numerous pristine islands. Sea otters and waterfowl floundered in the thick layer of oil, then succumbed, dying from exposure to the cold water. Oil collected in numerous coves, where experts feared it would remain for months, poisoning all forms of aquatic life. The spill occurred weeks before tens of thousands of waterfowl would arrive either to nest in Prince William Sound or to rest in the waters before moving northward to the Arctic tundra. By the end of September, 33,000 seabirds, 1,000 sea otters and 193 bald eagles had perished.[2] Countless others may have died without being recorded.

Most Americans were sickened by the news. A host of questions began to emerge. Why, for instance, did it take so long to begin the cleanup? Why had the consortium of oil companies that operates the port at Valdez disbanded the cleanup crew? Why, in a port that two million barrels of oil pass through each day, was there so little cleanup equipment available? Why did Exxon refuse offers of free help and equipment in the early days of the accident? Why didn't the government step in early on, mobilizing nearby oil skimmers?

When all was said and done, blame spread like the noxious oil slick. Hardly anyone was untouched. Captain Hazelwood was one of the principal villains. Exxon, the oil companies who operated the port and the emergency cleanup facilities, the U.S. Coast Guard, and the government all bore considerable blame. John Chancellor of NBC News even chided the auto manufacturers for successfully rolling back mileage standards, which drives up our consumption of oil. The American public drew its fair share of criticism as well. "Who killed the sea otters of Prince William Sound?" asks Solveig Torvik of the editorial board of the Seattle *Post-Intelligencer*. "The best way to think about it is to concentrate on the connection as you climb into your car today." A gift shop owner designed a T-shirt to commemorate the occasion. It shows a finger emblazoned with a red diagonal slash, sending the symbolic message: no finger pointing. The shirt says, "We are all responsible: Exxon Valdez, March 24, 1989."

The oil spill off the coast of Valdez came nearly ten years after the accident at Three Mile Island. It is the latest in a long list of environmental tragedies. It is no one's fault, yet everyone's. The spill is a symptom of a society that, to maintain an unsustainable lifestyle, goes farther and farther into the wilderness, often leaving its toxic debris and garbage behind.

Acre by acre, the fabric of the living planet is being torn apart to feed and clothe the world's people, a people living out of step with reality, a people so intent on the present they cannot see the inevitable results of their actions, a people that cannot seem to find a way to control themselves.

Responding to the Dangers of Modern Society

Battling against the reckless exploitation of the environment and environmental deterioration is a large and ever-growing group of folks who comprise the environmental movement. We are a diverse amalgamation of educators, writers, publishers, researchers, attorneys, activists, and government officials united by a love for the earth and a passion for other living things. No one knows exactly how many people fit into this category, but the number is undoubtedly large, for the national organizations boast a collective membership of eight to eleven million. The National Wildlife Federation alone claims a membership of 5.8 million.

Within the environmental movement opinions vary widely. Some environmentalists, for example, think that small changes—a wildlife refuge here or there, a new law, or tighter regulation—are all that's needed. At the other end of the spectrum are those who are calling for deeper changes—fundamental changes in the ways humans live. These environmentalists think that we must reduce the size of the human population and find ways of living on the earth and doing business that are dramatically different from those we rely on today. These transformationalists seek to remake society, to build a society that can endure. Between these two extremes lie a wealth of differing views.

In the uneasy aftermath of Chernobyl, Bhopal, Three Mile Island, Valdez, and a host of other tragedies that have occurred in the past twenty years, society is plagued with an unnerving realization—that human activities may be threatening our own future.

Huey Johnson, former Secretary for Natural Resources in California, believes that serious air quality problems, toxic waste problems, and toxic substances in our drinking water have put to rest a century-long debate on whether our nation and globe are threatened by environmental decline.[3] Recognizing the serious plight of the endangered earth, *Time* magazine dedicated its 1989 Person of the Year Award to the earth. In the January 1989 issue of *Time*, a panel of experts outlined the problems now facing humanity. As humans head into the last decade of the twentieth century, writes Thomas Sancton in the "Planet of the Year" issue, we find ourselves "at a crucial turning point: the actions of those now living will determine the future, and possibly the very survival of the species."

Article after article in the "Planet of the Year" issue painted a picture of despair, expressing a familiar tone of urgency—one that environmentalists have felt for well over two decades—an urgency that has largely gone unnoticed or, worse, been ignored.

The Environmentalist's Crystal Ball

Environmental educators, researchers, and activists began to warn of the dangers of the thinning ozone layer in the 1970s and pressured governments to eliminate chlorofluorocarbons (CFCs), the chemicals that destroy ozone.[4] The ozone layer lies in the stratosphere 20 to 30 miles above the earth's surface where it blocks out nearly all of the sun's harmful ultraviolet light. In the 1980s, suspicions rose even further as a result of news of a hole the size of the United States in the ozone layer over Antarctica. In 1988, a panel of one hundred scientists convened by NASA concluded that CFCs were indeed destroying the earth's protective ozone shield. Without it, skin cancer from excess ultraviolet light could skyrocket. Plant life would suffer as well, because ultraviolet light retards photosynthesis and is lethal to plant cells in high doses.

In the 1970s, environmental scientists and activists warned of the dangers of nuclear energy and its high cost to society. In the wake of the Three Mile Island and Chernobyl nuclear power plant accidents, several nations have banned the construction of new nuclear power plants. Sweden has vowed to phase out its existing nuclear plants and to make up the difference through conservation and renewable energy sources.[5] In the past decade and a half not one new nuclear plant has been ordered in the United States and many orders have been cancelled.

In the 1970s, the environmental community warned that Americans would be swimming in garbage if we didn't find ways to reduce it and recycle the valuable materials we discard each day.

Today, society is now scrambling for alternatives to the vanishing and ever-more-costly landfill. An estimated 500 to 600 cities and towns now have recycling programs in effect. Because of the rising cost of landfill space and concerns for the environment and energy conservation, progress in recycling in the next five years could easily surpass the gains of the past twenty-five years.

In the 1970s, environmentalists alerted society to the danger of greenhouse warming from pollutants generated by fossil fuel combustion. The searing droughts of the 1980s made many stand up and take notice. Pollution from human activities, it now appears, may indeed be spawning a global warming trend. Melting glaciers and the Antarctic ice cap could eventually flood 20 percent of the world's land mass. The gradual warming could destroy forests and render rich agricultural areas useless in the coming decades.[6] The destabilized climate could spawn more violent storms such as those seen in the last few years. Hurricane Hugo in the fall of 1989 caused an estimated $4-5 billion in damages along the eastern seaboard of the United States and the islands of the Caribbean—greater than the total annual damage from all floods in the United States.

Environmentalists predicted the widespread effects of unbridled population growth, here and abroad. Starvation, disease, and environmental decay were the inevitable consequences of soaring population, we said. These predictions also proved correct. Today, more than 40 million people die from starvation and diseases worsened by hunger and malnutrition *each year.* That's the equivalent of 300 jumbo jets each containing 400 passengers, crashing each and every day with no survivors. Almost half of the victims are children.

With few exceptions, environmental educators, researchers, and activists have been accurate predictors. As a result, this movement has assumed an increasingly important role in modern society. Today, there is a new and unsettling warning being sounded by people in the ranks of the environmental community: human society is on an unsustainable path. "We do not have generations, we only have years, in which to attempt to turn things around," warns Lester Brown, president of the Worldwatch Institute. Jay Hair, the outspoken president of the National Wildlife Federation, believes we have ten to fifteen years, tops. Are these predictions correct? Will the message of urgency be heeded? Only time will tell.

Successes of the Environmental Response

The environmental movement and its diverse membership have already played a vital role in effecting social and political change. Few social movements in recent history have persisted or had as great an impact on modern society. With the help of political allies in Congress, the environmental movement has turned America into a leader in environmental protection. In the 1970s, for example, Congress passed the National Environmental Policy Act, and President Nixon formed the EPA from a variety of offices and departments, creating a more unified approach to environmental protection. "These two events are the cornerstone of what is indisputably the world's most vigorous pollution control effort," writes long-time activist Barry Commoner.[7] In quick succession, dozens of new laws were passed to deal with such diverse problems as species extinction, air pollution, and hazardous wastes. Senator Edmund Muskie of Maine, one of the senate's first and most influential environmental leaders, emphasized the importance of the new laws when he remarked that "Environmental laws are not ordinary laws, they are laws of survival."

The environmental movement won a place for the environment in court in the 1960s as a result of the Storm King Case. In 1965, the Federal Power Commission was sued by a group of wealthy property owners belonging to the Scenic Hudson Preservation Conference. The plaintiffs filed suit to stop Consolidated Edison from stringing electric lines across the Hudson River at Storm King Mountain. The plaintiffs contended that the lines would mar their view and that they had a right to prevent the company from such action. The Federal Power Commission, however, asked the courts to dismiss the case, arguing that the right to bring suit was reserved only for people who could prove economic damage from another's activity.[8] A powerline across a river certainly did not impact anyone's pocketbook.

In a momentous decision, the court turned down the request of the Federal Power Commission. The court ruled that noneconomic interests were a sufficient basis on which to file a lawsuit. This decision gave environmental groups a legal standing in court, setting an incredible precedent that paved the way for thousands of similar lawsuits in the name of the environment.

Since that time, the environmental movement has gained a considerable amount of legal and political expertise and has become a major force in national politics. Governments soon learned that if they didn't listen to environmental interests early on, they would run into trouble.

The environmental movement must also count as one of its great successes its efforts to establish the Wilderness Preservation System. Thanks to the diligent labors of the Wilderness Society, the Sierra Club, and others, millions of acres of land have been set aside in the United States for future generations and for nonhuman species. Today, the United States has 90 million acres of wilderness—far more than anyone dreamed possible when the Wilderness Act was passed in 1964.[9]

Setting wilderness aside is a tribute to our legislative skills and persistence, as well as our ability to rally grassroots support—letters, phone calls, and supporters at crucial hearings. Environmental and conservation groups have done an extraordinary job in getting people interested in the wilderness and fostering an aesthetic attachment to the land. Through slide shows, picture books, and hikes, environmental organizations have built a powerful pro-wilderness alliance, which has made it possible to set aside American wilderness for permanent protection. This strategy has also been used to help save thousands of miles of rivers and streams from dams and other development.[10]

Outright land acquisition has been another area of success. Since it began in 1951, The Nature Conservancy has preserved 3.5 million acres of land, which protects threatened and endangered plants and animals.[11] The National Audubon Society and the National Wildlife Federation have similar but much smaller programs. Numerous state organizations have contributed significantly as well. Federal and state programs have also added millions of acres to the land now under protection.

"Forty percent of all of our land in this country, including Alaska, is in some form of public ownership—state, national, or local," according to Sam Hays, environmental historian from the University of Pittsburgh. Much of that land has been purchased from the private sector for protection.

The environmental movement owes much of its success to the diligent efforts of many environmental groups who have encouraged people to develop an appreciation of nature. These groups have instilled a deep desire in many people to defend pristine places. Other groups, such as Greenpeace and Earth First! have concentrated on "creative conflict" to impress on the public the need for wilderness and wildlife preservation. Still others, such as the Natural Resources Defense Council and the Environmental Defense Fund, have sought to strengthen legislation and enforce regulatory action.

But as noted earlier, the environmental movement is much broader than the formal environmental organizations. It includes college teachers who have worked tirelessly to describe the environmental problems faced by the rich, industrialized nations as well as those faced by the Third World. It includes primary and secondary school teachers who are helping raise student awareness. It includes courageous politicians who have taken the lead on important environmental legislation. It includes the thousands of scientists whose research contributes to the growing body of knowledge about the environment. It includes businessmen and businesswomen who have started recycling companies or companies that sell environmentally responsible products. It includes lawyers and scientists who work for the EPA or other governmental agencies. It includes health professionals who work for health departments or research facilities. It includes writers who specialize in environmental issues. It includes journalists who write for newspapers or work for television stations. It includes hundreds of thousands of people who drive efficient automobiles or who have installed insulation and storm windows or who have caulked and weatherstripped leaks in their homes to save energy.

Have We Failed?

Jay Hair, President of the National Wildlife Federation, proclaimed the year 1988—plagued by flooding in Bangladesh, reports of widespread tropical deforestation, reports of ozone depletion, and crippling drought—as the year the earth fought back. But I suspect differently; 1988 may in fact go down in history not as the year the earth fought back, but rather as the year the earth turned the corner. It was the year in which the environmental transgressions of many decades, the insults against the earth wrought by human society, finally caught up with us.

Fear that this may be true led to a flurry of news reports on the environment. And they, in turn, led to an encouraging outpouring of new laws and regulations and international agreements aimed at reducing the menace. Suddenly, the earth was back in vogue. That realization did not escape the environmental groups or the reporters. Nor did it escape many politicians. The plight of the planet was not missed by the man and the woman on the street either.

All this interest has brought with it some serious and much-needed introspection. Questions of profound consequence and of potentially great political embarrassment began to surface. Most important, people began to wonder if twenty years of environmental protection was falling far short of the task.

In 1987 Barry Commoner published an article in *The New Yorker* that assessed environmental progress of the previous two decades. In this article Commoner argued that, for the most part, the environmental response has failed to meet the challenge. Although certain pollutants in the environment, such as DDT and lead, have declined substantially, he says, very little progress has been made in reducing most of the major air and water pollutants. Sulfur dioxide emissions, for example, declined 19 percent between 1975 and 1985, but since that time have remained essentially the same. Carbon monoxide emissions declined by 14 percent in the same time, but have leveled off since then.

Water quality showed some improvement, but on balance, data show that gains that had been achieved by installing expensive pollution control facilities were often offset by other factors. In urban settings, for example, nonpoint water pollution (pollution from farm fields, streets, lawns, and other similar sources) that results from population growth often negates gains made by installing newer and better sewage treatment plants.

The minimal declines in air and water pollution are signs of our failure to meet environmental objectives. Ultimately, they are signs that the system is not working as many would like. However, there is an important point worth noting. From 1975 to 1987, the U.S. population grew from 216 million to over 244 million—a 13 percent increase.[12] Sulfur dioxide per capita, then, has fallen 33 percent—from 0.12 metric tons per person in 1975 to 0.08 metric tons per person.[13] Clearly, without the environmental controls instituted in the past two decades the quality of our environment would be much worse than it is today. Environmental progress is not as bad as some would have us believe, but environmental quality is far from optimum.

The environmental response to widespread population growth has had mixed results as well. While population growth has slowed in some countries, it still races out of control in a great many others. In 40 years, if growth continues at the current pace, the world population could reach 10 billion—twice what it is today. U.S. population could increase by another 50 million people before stabilizing.[14] Ninety percent of the world's growth will occur in the poor, agricultural nations of Africa, Latin America, and Asia where hunger and poverty abound. Susan Weber, who heads Zero Population Growth, notes that the failure to come to grips with population growth is as evident at the local level as it is internationally. Several groups are working on local population control measures, but efforts to stop sprawl and limit growth in the industrialized nations, by and large, are not having much effect.

One of the most obvious signs of our failure to protect the environment is acid deposition. Acids produced by industry, automobiles, power plants, and our own homes fall from the skies and wreak a subtle but far-reaching havoc on our forests, lakes, and streams with profound influences on human society. Hundreds of lakes in New York State's Adirondack Mountains are so acidic they no longer support fish. Thousands of lakes in southern Canada and Scandinavia are threatened, yet little is being done to end the menace. Acids cause billions of dollars worth of damage to buildings, crops, and forests in the United States alone.

Global warming is yet another example. Carbon dioxide, largely from fossil fuel combustion, and several other greenhouse gases threaten to change global climate, altering the face of the planet.[15] A preview of that change may already be evident. In 1988, for example, record-breaking drought cut grain production in the United States by more than one-third. The U.S. typically produces 300 million tons of grain. In 1988, however, domestic production fell to 195 million tons, just short of U.S. demand. The United States was only able to meet its export obligations by tapping its abundant reserves. The dry, hot summer made many forests vulnerable to lightning and fire. Yellowstone National Park went up in flames. Hundreds of thousands of acres of national forest in the West burned that year as well.

Time to Change

The environmental trends indicate that society's response has not measured up to the task at hand. Deeper changes are needed. Profound social, political, and economic transformations are required. The problems we face are so large and complex that they may be greater than our social and political institutions' ability to solve them. Moreover, they require solutions that traditional institutions are not philosophically equipped to provide.

Humanity is poised on the threshold of an evolutionary change. We are entering a period of incredible opportunity, an era of evolution that could broaden, diversify, and soften our approach to living on planet earth. It is time for serious reflection and self-examination. It is time for a break from the battle, to step beyond the fray to see what's working and what's not, to devise and implement new strategies. Rather than focusing on our failures, now is the time to renew our commitment and to move forward, taking advantage of the lessons we have learned along the way.

Beyond the Fray examines the environmental response. It is not an attempt to convince you of the seriousness of our problems.[16] Instead, it looks at ways that the environmental response can—and must—evolve to meet the complex challenges now facing us.

Beyond the Fray is a constructive and hopeful critique. It seeks to build, to expand and to strengthen the social, political, institutional, and personal response to the environmental crisis. This book questions cherished beliefs and actions and examines propositions that may seem utopian now, but in the long run are our only hope for survival. Most importantly, this book recognizes that all living things—all people and all species—are part of one whole and that our collective fate is in jeopardy. What we do to the earth, we do to ourselves. "The earth is one, but the world is not," wrote the authors of a report from the World Commission on Environment and Development.[17] We all depend on the biosphere to sustain our lives, but each community, each country, each individual strives separately for survival and prosperity with little regard for its impact on the whole.

To help reverse the destructive trends resulting from humanity's struggle for survival and prosperity, this book calls for unprecedented international and national cooperation as well as individual action. It advises all of us—individually and collectively—to take rapid steps to help humanity restore the balance between humans and the environment to build a sustainable society—a future that we can count on.

No doubt, this book will ruffle the well-groomed feathers of some and draw criticism from others. Individuals may disagree with some of the recommendations. In isolation, some suggestions may seem insignificant. In fact, no one solution presented here will work alone. What's needed is an approach that is diverse, comprehensive, and sustained.

This book looks beyond the present-day environmental response to what it could—and must—become. As you read, you will realize that some of the changes are already taking place. More and more environmental groups, for instance, are promoting individual actions to help right some of the past mistakes. More and more communities are recycling their refuse. More and more companies are cutting back on energy use. I am encouraged by these changes and eager for more.

*Nothing is more powerful than an
idea whose time has come.*

VICTOR HUGO

2

From Futureblindness to Visions of Sustainability

The French author and philosopher Paul Valery once wrote that "the tragedy of our times is that the future is no longer what it used to be." Gone are the immense, unsettled continents. Gone are many of the world's lush forests and many vast uninterrupted grasslands that once abounded in wildlife. Gone are the pristine oceans, the fish-filled rivers, and most of our thick mineral deposits, which have helped make economic prosperity possible. With the disappearance of these resources, the heady dreams of limitless economic growth have also begun to vanish.[1]

Humanity faces an uncertain future. Global warming, ozone depletion, acid deposition, tropical deforestation, widespread species extinction, overpopulation, starvation, and rampant desertification—to name a few—have blackened our hopes.[2]

A Tragedy of Recognition

Despite the growing realization of impending disaster, western society persists in the folly of the old ways, confused about the dangerous trends we face and uncertain about our ability to reverse them. Although the facts strongly suggest the need for new strategies, very little is being done. Modern society continues to rely on the outdated ways of our ancestors that are in large part responsible for much of the trouble we now face.

Waste managers of our cities, for example, are building incinerators instead of recycling centers to "solve" the growing landfill crisis, even though recycling programs are less costly and offer many more environmental benefits.[3] City officials continue to propose new dams to supply water for homes and businesses, despite the overwhelming evidence that conservation measures can provide the same amount of water at a much lower cost—and without the severe environmental impacts wrought by giant dams.[4] On still another front, cities continue to expand their highways to meet the growing demand, even though efficient mass transit can move far more people faster and at a lower cost. Today, U.S. timber companies (aided by our government) level forests to make paper, while millions of tons of reusable paper is discarded in landfills or shipped abroad for recycling.

These activities suggest that even though environmental realities may be tarnishing our vision of the future, many people in positions of power have failed to grasp the need to change. The tragedy, then, is not so much that the future has changed, but that few people fully recognize the change or act on it. Few understand how the industrial nations' prospects have dimmed. Few recognize that the glorious 1950s, a time when the dream of prosperity ran wild, will not be repeated. As a society, we suffer from a tragedy of recognition.

In a recent study, schoolchildren were asked about the future of the earth.[5] Sixty percent believed that the danger of nuclear war would be more severe in the next 20 to 30 years than it is today. Nearly the same proportion thought that pollution and the depletion of natural resources would be worse. Half of them believed that world population and food supply would be further out of balance than it is today. But when asked about their own future, most responded optimistically. Nearly 90 percent agreed at least somewhat that most people in the United States would be better off than they are now, exposing a kind of schizophrenia that endears humankind to its keenest critics.

Arnold Toynbee once warned that the institutions that create a civilization eventually topple it. Important as this lesson is, it is largely lost on American society. Like the schoolchildren, our politicians and many of our people tend to discount global population, resource-depletion, and pollution trends. Most people persist in believing that technological fixes and laws that support the status quo will save the day.[6]

Unbridled technological optimism is evident in Ford Aerospace's slogan: "Securing the future through advanced technology." Those who look more soberly on global population and resource trends, however, see this as a grand illusion. Surely, new technologies are needed to reduce pollution and to help us use resources more efficiently, but to think that technological innovation can save us is to ignore three key facts. First, many technological innovations are doomed in the long run because they rely on a finite resource base—fossil fuels and minerals. Second, many technologies are responsible for the problems that besiege us today.[7] Technological salvation by itself will likely lead to new troubles, as ample experience shows. Efforts to curb global warming by substituting nuclear power for fossil fuels, for example, will inevitably spawn a host of social, economic, and environmental problems.[8] Replacing some of the chlorofluorocarbons (CFCs) with some that are thought to be less harmful may help reduce the destruction of the ozone layer, but at least one substitute being considered is an active greenhouse gas. Third, technological solutions are limited. Science, for example, knows of no substitute for chromium or for the silver in photographic film. And no technological solution can bring back the passenger pigeon or the great auk.

Lincoln admonished over one hundred years ago, "As the times are new, so we must act and think anew." Caught up in the splendor of new materials, computer marvels, and information explosion, few people have begun to think anew. Few people have dared to explore the possibilities lying beyond our flashy technological era. Fewer still have begun to act anew, to begin reshaping the post-technological, post-information age.

The romantic hopes of continuing material wealth, as dim as they are growing; the blind faith that we will somehow manage or invent our way out of the mess; and the narrow personal optimism that creates future-blindness or a severe and crippling myopia—all keep us from seeing that the biosphere is rapidly deteriorating. Thus, a great many people persist in believing that their tiny sphere of influence will be left unaffected or that modern society will perform a hat trick to save the day.

A Tragedy of Mastery

Beyond our apparent refusal to come to grips with environmental realities is another tragedy. It is the tragedy of mastery. Joan McIntyre, author and environmental advocate, once wrote that "The ability of our minds to imagine, coupled with the ability of our hands to devise our images, brings us a power almost beyond our control." Unfortunately, our temporary gains in mastery over the planet have not been accompanied by equal gains in self-mastery. Our extraordinary technological competency dwarfs our powers to control ourselves and our inventions. Only rarely do industrial societies show the wisdom and foresight to curb technological muscle.

Western industrialized countries have become technological junkies, blindly dedicated to advancing technology, giving little thought to the impacts of new inventions on the finite, increasingly troubled, world in which we live. In many ways, modern society is on a technological treadmill. We solve technological problems with more of the same, in much the same way that farmers attempt to overcome pesticide resistance with larger doses of more powerful insecticides.[9] The solutions create more problems, fueling a never-ending cycle.

Technological competency fosters an unflagging confidence in the very system that threatens our own future. Solutions to our problems are left in the hands of scientists and technologists, who have, in years past, performed exceptionally well in helping society increase the efficiency of extraction technologies, automobiles, and factories, and helping society to find substitutes for declining natural resources. Our overdependence on technological fixes, however, stands in the way of profound social changes that are needed today.

Our lack of restraint and our undying optimism in technology are leading us down an unsustainable path. Technological overdependence only serves to deepen the rut we are in. Technology cannot substantially change the course we are on. What is needed are deeper, social changes: changes in the way people act and think, and wholesale changes in our way of life that will help us create a sustainable society.

These changes will come from the broad environmental movement—from teachers, environmentalists, sympathetic governmental officials, individuals, and business people. Regrettably, very little has been done to overcome the tragedy of recognition and tragedy of mastery. Very little has been done to focus meaningful attention on issues of sustainability.[10] Educators have been largely preoccupied with outlining current environmental problems. Environmentalists have been busy fighting for new laws and regulations or making sure that governmental agencies enforce existing laws. Government officials have been swamped by existing problems, so much so that they have had little time to address long-range problems and to implement long-term solutions.

Because of the onslaught of environmental problems, the environmental movement has not fully explored the issue of sustainability. It is far from developing a coherent image of a sustainable future—one that it can pass on to the general public.

What's Keeping Us from the Task?

The environmental movement in the United States has failed to develop a vision of the future for at least two reasons: its ties with conservation ideology and its reactionary roots.[11]

Ties with Conservation Ideology. The conservation movement is the predecessor of the modern environmental movement and owes its origins to Theodore Roosevelt and Gifford Pinchot.[12] Pinchot, trained in forestry in Europe, infused his friend and ally Theodore Roosevelt with the notion of sustained yield—a management term that pervades modern thinking today. Forests, Pinchot said, could be harvested without permanent damage. Indeed, carefully managed timberlands could continue to produce valuable wood products for many generations. At the time, this revolutionary new idea contrasted sharply with the shortsighted development of commercial lumber companies. In the early 1800s, timber companies cut trees mindlessly, deforesting most of the eastern seaboard. No thought was given to replanting—the continent seemed so vast. By 1870, they had reached Wisconsin and Minnesota, where they continued cutting trees with no concern for forest regrowth, leaving barren lands in their wake. By the early 1900s, the white pine stands in Minnesota and Wisconsin had been so depleted that it was no longer commercially profitable for the industry to remain. They moved south to continue the frenzy of cutting. Within a few decades most of the profitable stands in the South had also fallen.

Outraged by the reckless actions of the commercial lumber companies, Pinchot and Roosevelt began their campaign to promote forest conservation. The cut-and-run philosophy of the commercial forestry business ran counter to their belief that forests could be made to yield timber indefinitely.

The thrust of Roosevelt-Pinchot inspired conservation was management. Conservation, as they saw it, was a pragmatic matter. Its chief goal: the efficient development and use of resources.[13] The wise use of resources for the greatest good of the greatest number of people was not just prudent but right, notes historian Roderick Nash, author of *Wilderness and the American Mind*.[14]

Within the American conservation movement were two powerful dissenting voices: John Muir and Henry David Thoreau. They argued a contrasting viewpoint: preservationism—setting land aside to protect the wildlife and plants, but not just to benefit humankind. Preservationism, writes Peter Borrelli, editor of the Natural Resource Defense Council's *Amicus Journal,* is "rooted in a fundamentally different perception of humankind and nature" than conservationism. Roosevelt and Pinchot, according to Borrelli, shared an anthropocentric (or human-centered) world view. To them, nature was something to manage for human use. That often meant maximizing a single value—for example, healthy deer populations—with little concern for the welfare of the entire ecosystem.

Muir and many of his followers saw things differently. They espoused a biocentric view that recognizes humans as one of many forms of life. To them, nature has its own right to existence, and should be protected for its own sake.

The dominant view for the four decades following Pinchot's emergence clearly was the pragmatic one of conservation. Although the public was largely blind to the wisdom of conservation, restraint continued to find a place in American government well into the time of Franklin D. Roosevelt.[15] The chief enemy of the profit-minded conservationist was the private corporation—business. Adolf Berle, an advisor to FDR and chief architect of the New Deal economic policy, argued that the modern corporation should serve not just the owners or managers but all of society. Restraint continued to be the byword and efficient use continued to be the way to manage resources.

Conservation policy thrived in the post-FDR years as well. The passage of the Multiple Use-Sustained Yield Act in 1960 codified this anthropocentric view of the conservation movement. The law requires the Forest Service to manage grasslands and forests to achieve the greatest good for the greatest number of *people.*

Four years later, Congress passed the Wilderness Act. It established the National Wilderness Preservation System which sought to create an "enduring wilderness." Nature had gained a legal right to exist. Preservation had taken root in American soil. But the roots remain tenuous.

Muir's views of preservation—and more importantly his ethical stand on the rights of other living creatures—is a minority opinion in the United States and in most other countries as well. Today, judging from their oratory, most environmental supporters see wilderness in light of its benefits to society. They argue, for instance, that wilderness should be set aside to provide for the rejuvenation of harried urban residents, or that we should protect wilderness to preserve endangered species that are valuable to us, or that we should set aside forest wilderness because it protects our water supplies.[16] Anthropocentrism taints preservationist thinking, polluting the ethics that Muir championed.

The modern environmental movement is rooted in pragmatic conservation ideology that is largely human-centered. The definition of natural resources as "forms of wealth" from nature or "products of nature that promote human well-being" illustrates the fundamental bias of conservation ideology. This way of thinking stifles our imagination and impairs our moral outreach.[17] Moreover, conservation ideology promotes adjustments from within and offers human oversight and management as a means of solving resource problems.[18] Conservation holds a simple bias: that what is wrong with our system can best be fixed by improved management.

Bill Devall, author of *Simple in Means, Rich in Ends: Practicing Deep Ecology,* places many environmental supporters and many groups into a category he labels as "reform environmentalists." Reform environmentalists aim to change the world by making adjustments to laws, regulations, and basic institutions. Rarely do they question the basic social and philosophical assumptions of modern civilization.[19] The "reformers" in the mainstream environmental movement, says Devall, lack vision.

I think the so-called reformers are schizophrenic on the issue of change. Deep down inside, many so-called reformers believe that profound societal changes are needed, but their political actions don't belie their beliefs. Lester Milbrath's study of attitudes among different sectors of American society showed that nearly all environmentalists believe that nature should be preserved for its own sake.[20] They almost unanimously favored environmental protection over economic growth and believe there are limits to growth. Moreover, environmentalists were in strong agreement that the damage to the environment is so serious that society must drastically alter its ways of doing things. Unfortunately, their acts don't always reflect such attitudes.

The discrepancy between belief and action arises because many of us don't know where to begin reshaping society. The law is a convenient tool and easily within reach. Profound social changes are another matter altogether. How does one go about reshaping a society?

Conservation applies the findings of science to problems of human sustenance. David Brower, former executive director of the Sierra Club and founder of more than 30 environmental organizations during his many years of service to the environment, argues that the "practical man is a hindrance." Quoting Disraeli, he notes that "the practical man is one who has made all his decisions, has lost the ability to listen and is determined to perpetuate the errors of his ancestors." Conservationists are the practical-minded caretakers of the environment. Very little that is exciting and hopeful happens out of pragmatism, Brower argues. Things happen out of dreams and visions.

Dreams may be hard to come by, given the entrenchment of conservation philosophy and the ways this ideology precludes new ideas. A broader ethic that values the many millions of creatures that share the planet with us is especially stifled by this thinking.

In a speech at the Windstar Conference in Aspen, Colorado, in August 1988, Dr. Jay Hair, President of the National Wildlife Federation, spoke of the need to protect the world's wild living resources. He called for "radically new ideas" and the implementation of "revolutionary new plans," arguing that now was the time to "blaze a new path" to save our environment. Hair read a draft Constitutional amendment that the NWF, one of the prime movers in the U.S. environmental movement, had proposed the previous year, and plans to launch in 1990. It read: *"The people* have a right to clean air, pure water, productive soils, and to the conservation of the natural, scenic, historic, recreational, aesthetic and economic values of the environment. *America's natural resources are the common property of all the people,* including generations yet to come. As trustees of these resources, the United States government shall conserve and maintain them for *the benefit of all people."* (Emphasis mine.)

The NWF initiative could legitimize many of the environmental concerns that are currently swept under the carpet. However, the language of the amendment reflects a pervasive conservation philosophy based principally on human needs. Although other species would inevitably benefit from such an amendment, they are not bestowed rights or protection.

In September 1989 the National Wildlife Federation revised its Environmental Quality Amendment. Although the language was altered somewhat, the proposal still reflects the same human bias.[21] Far more bold would be an amendment calling for the protection of the environment for all living things, regardless of their value to human beings. Far more visionary would be an amendment that read: *"All living creatures* have a right to clean air, pure water, productive soils. *The world's natural resources are the common property of all the living things,* including generations yet to come. As trustees of these resources, the United States government shall conserve and maintain them for *the benefit of all."*[22]

Anthropocentric conservation and its gradual permeation of our thinking have sown the seeds of our current myopia—a pervasive inability to look beyond the immediate needs of humankind. Except for a small radical outcropping of the environmental movement, environmentalism has, to a large extent, become caught up in altering the system, applying band-aids to a terminally ill patient, seemingly ignoring the fact that what we have is inappropriate for the finite world we live in.

Reactionary Roots. In the 1960s the creek that ran behind my home in rural upstate New York turned brown with sewage and waste from an apple-processing plant. The creek, where we swam and fished and canoed, became a putrid sewer almost overnight. Aquatic vegetation grew so thick you could hardly get a rowboat through the channel.

The stench raised the ire of the town folks; the public outcry was near-deafening. Angry neighbors phoned town officials demanding immediate action. In two years, the creek ran clean again.

All across America outrage grew in the 1960s and 1970s. Rivers that caught on fire, putrid plumes of smoke from factories, sickly palls of pollution hovering above our cities—all spawned a storm of protest as angry citizens rallied to stop the atrocities. Environmentalists flocked to Washington to lobby for legislation. Battling against a strong and entrenched business lobby, environmentalists and citizens, working together, won victory after victory.

If legislation is a measure of success, environmentalism was exceptional. Between 1970 and 1978 came powerful new amendments to the Clean Air Act, a sweeping Federal Water Pollution Control Act, a much-needed Endangered Species Act, a vital Toxic Substances Control Act, a comprehensive Resource Conservation and Recovery Act, a precedent-setting National Environmental Policy Act, and many more. The statutory outpouring from the halls of Congress bore testimony to a simple fact: American outrage was working.

Environmental laws, however, were largely aimed at correcting wrongs, protecting already imperiled resources. Much of the legislation was reactive, designed to clean up our messes. The new laws sprang from a government still faithful to the pursuit of short-term profit, even if it was environmentally destructive.

Most democratic governments persist in the reactive mode—responding to crises rather than looking ahead and plotting strategies to avoid troubles.[23] Because the environmental response parallels the governmental response, it too remains reactionary. The halls of Congress and the front steps of the state capitols are the stages where most environmental drama is played out. The actors in this important play are the lawyers, lobbyists, and citizen activists who fight to protect the land, the water, and the soils from the shortsighted economic bulldozer we are riding.

Henry Kissinger once noted that in government the urgent often displaces the important. The same is true in the environmental movement. Continuing to wage wars with the timber companies, oil companies, and pesticide manufacturers, and with reluctant federal agencies that have failed to protect the environment, environmentalism is consumed by the urgent.[24] Our preoccupation with putting out fires has prevented us from the important long-term thinking and planning.

Because of our reactionary roots and because of our continued immersion in legal and political battles, the environmental movement has failed to become a fully activated motivating force for social change. We have consequently been forced to leave our long-term future to happenstance, perhaps hoping that the hodgepodge of ideas and actions will somehow transform our society for the better.

It is time to seek ways to transcend reactionary politics. It is time to embrace broader ethical guidelines and to begin building a sustainable future. More deliberate thought and action on the part of educators, environmental activists, lobbyists, and leaders in government and within the movement itself can help create a transition to a relationship with the earth that is sustainable.

Beyond Frontierism

To build a sustainable society, however, will require profound changes in technology, industry, political institutions, political leadership, economics, education, housing, and transportation as well as a fundamental change in our philosophy. A sustainable society must be built on a new ethic—a sustainable ethic.

Building on the Land Ethic: Sustainable Ethics. Wildlife ecologist and philosopher, Aldo Leopold, was particularly influential in widening ethical horizons during the early days of American environmentalism. He carried on the battle of John Muir, writing eloquently on the need to include nature in our ethical concerns—that is, to extend our concerns beyond human beings. Leopold called this doctrine a land ethic. It proposed that humans were a part of a larger community that included our soil, water, plants, animals—in short, the land. Leopold suggested caution and deferred rewards in our use of natural resources. We would do well to use our resources with love and respect.

Leopold first suggested the need for a land ethic in 1933. His classic book, *A Sand County Almanac,* published in 1949, acquired near-biblical status among environmentalists. In the early days of the environmental movement, Aldo Leopold quickly became the most quoted author in conservation circles, with the possible exception of Thoreau. Charles E. Little, author and founder of the American Land Forum (now the American Land Resource

Association), calls the land ethic "one of the most important ideas of the century."[25]

For Leopold, conservation required equal portions of reflection and action.[26] He called for individual responsibility in maintaining the health of the land. Leopold's view encompasses considerably more than the self-serving attitudes of Roosevelt-style conservationists and has helped to reshape American thinking. The land ethic provides the framework for a new and broader environmental ethic fashioned to modern times and modern problems.

Arne Naess, the Norwegian philosopher behind the Deep Ecology movement, notes that "A philosophy, as articulated wisdom, has to be a synthesis of theory and practice."[27] Leopold provided both, but the practical guidelines principally revolved around wildlife management.

The land ethic instructs us, in Leopold's own words, to enlarge "the boundaries of the community to include soils, water, plants and animals, or collectively: the land." The result would change "the role of *Homo sapiens* from conqueror . . . to plain member and citizen." The land ethic is a guide to govern economic activity, but is somewhat lacking in guidance for the complex modern society in which we live.

A new ethic, the sustainable-earth ethic, is emerging. It addresses the unique complexities of modern society. I refer to the sustainable-earth ethic as a sustainable ethic, because of the ease with which it rolls off the tongue and because it is after all an ethic that is sustainable. It is unlikely to be overthrown; it has staying power.[28]

Foundations of a Sustainable Society. The sustainable ethic embodies the same respect for the rights of other species and for the earth as the land ethic. It calls on us to build a sustainable society patterned after nature. The secrets of success in nature are: conservation, recycling, renewable resources, and population control.[29] These four operational principles could help us achieve a better balance and protect other species. Sustainability also requires at least two additional features: acclimation, the ability to respond to slight changes in the environment, and adaptation, the capacity to evolve in the face of change.

Sustainability does not mean sustaining what we are doing now, because in the long run that is an impossibility. Our society is spending nature's principal—depleting our bank account of natural resources—when it could be living off the interest—the abundant renewable resources.

Sustainability implies the use of energy and other resources in a particular region in balance with what the region can supply through natural processes.[30] In consuming what we can replace, we keep from robbing future generations. A sustainable society thus disposed is one that can meet its needs and aspirations without compromising the ability of future generations to meet theirs.[31]

Sustainable systems are incompatible with systems of management that optimize single values, contends Kai N. Lee, a political scientist at the University of Washington.[32] In a sustainable society, he says, a stream is not viewed simply as a source of hydroelectric power, but rather a source of fish, recreation, irrigation water, wildlife habitat, and power. A sustainable system attempts to find ways that optimize diverse ends. Ultimately, though, it is a system in which human economic objectives are balanced against biological constraints and woven into ecological cycles. It is a system in which human activities respect natural laws.

Sustainability requires a better understanding of the subtle long-term needs of the land. Artificial fertilizers, for example, meet only part of the land's needs. They do not replace many of the nutrients that are robbed by crops. Nor do they replace organic matter lost from the soil during agricultural use. Organic matter holds water and provides nutrients for valuable soil microbes.

Sustainability requires flexibility—applying different solutions to different situations. Appropriate technology—machines and processes geared to local resources and local needs—is a good example, showing the intelligence of designing with nature, rather than redesigning nature.

Sustainability requires adaptive management—treading lightly and learning from our mistakes. Human understanding of nature is imperfect, which suggests that our interactions with nature should be guided by caution and seen more as experiments that will help us write the operator's manual.[33] Our interactions become opportunities to learn from experience and find a sustainable equilibrium.

A sustainable society replaces short-term profit motives with considerations of long-term stability. It chooses to forgo potential income now for the long-term benefits of productive land.

Sustainability requires a lifetime of commitment, in much the same way that good health requires enduring care and attention. It requires individual action as well. If humanity is to persist, we must build a sustainable society—a society that perpetuates itself and yet lives harmoniously in the intricate web of life; not a society that seeks complete domination over all living things, but one that seeks a cooperative relationship. Building a sustainable society means using resources much more wisely, following patterns laid down by nature.

A new value system based on sustainability has begun to emerge in the developed world in environmental publications, in books, in college classrooms, in public schools, in the international development community, and even in multinational development banks.[34]

This holistic ethical system holds that the earth has a limited supply of resources, that humans are a part of nature, and are by no stretch of the imagination superior to it. We are just another member of an interdependent community of living things. We are a species of nature and not nature's crowning achievement. Our goal is not dominance, but rather collaboration. Sustainable ethics encourages us to redefine natural resources as those materials required by all species.

Some critics have labelled this new ethical system a "return to nature." They seem threatened that sustainable ethics, with its reverence for all life, will be translated into a return to the Paleolithic age. Others label it an elitist effort of middle-class environmentalists to restrict the progress of people who have not achieved their economic and material goals. Sustainable ethics, in which human activities are restrained for the good of the planet, is viewed as a subversion to human economic progress. Few critics see it for what it is: an attempt to reestablish balance in an era of unprecedented disorder—social disruption, economic uncertainty, and ecological destruction.

The principle concept of sustainable ethics is that "there is not always more." The earth has a limited supply of nonrenewable resources. Oil supplies are rapidly declining. World demand is expected to exceed supply in the late 1990s, or soon thereafter, resulting in worldwide shortages and sharply rising prices. Oil will cost $28 to $35 per barrel by the mid 1990s, once again raising the specter of global inflation.[35] Supplies of several crucial minerals are also fast on the decline. Chromium, platinum, tin, and palladium are examples. Without recycling, substitution, and conservation, supplies of many other key minerals will not last 100 years.[36]

Given the inevitable depletion of oil and other nonrenewable resources, it is obvious that the infinite growth of material consumption is an impossibility. Ever-increasing production based on finite resources is an environmental impossibility. The late E.F. Schumacher argued in his book *Small is Beautiful: Economics as if People Mattered,* that, to use the language of economists, our system lives on its irreplaceable capital—fossil fuels and minerals—cheerfully treating them as if they were spendable income.[37]

The second principle of the sustainable ethic is that "we are all one." Thus, humans are not apart from but rather a part of the environment and subject to its rules. In 1972, British scientist James Lovelock proposed a controversial view of earth in support of the principle of unity.[38] The earth, he said, behaves as if it is a living organism, regulating many of its biogeochemical processes to maintain conditions conducive to life. This idea constitutes the Gaia hypothesis (Gaia is the ancient Greek name for earth mother). Says Lovelock, "the evolution of a species . . . is so closely coupled with the evolution of their physical and chemical environment that together they constitute a single and indivisible evolutionary process." Together, they constitute a living organism, Gaia.

The Gaia hypothesis was drawn from Lovelock's observation that the earth's atmosphere has remained stable for millions of years, despite the fact that it contains a mixture of highly reactive gases (oxygen and methane). Salt levels in the ocean remain constant. So do oxygen levels in the atmosphere. The earth does a respectable job of maintaining surface temperature. In many ways, the earth behaves like our bodies, which maintain constant internal levels of glucose, salts, and other nutrients through complex nervous and endocrine system mechanisms.

No scientist would argue that the biosphere, that thin living skin of planet earth, contains a homeostatic system of checks and balances. How far the Gaia hypothesis can be taken, though, remains open to debate. Some scientists assert that the hypothesis is more a metaphor than reality. Whatever its status, it remains a thought-provoking and powerful idea.

In 1983, psychologist Peter Russell expounded on the Gaia hypothesis in his book *The Global Brain.*[39] According to Russell, each human being on earth is akin to a single cell in a giant organism. The individual cells, like those in many complex, multicellular organisms, form organs, functional units specialized to carry out specific functions essential to the well-being of the entire organism. Humankind, for instance, forms the nervous system of the earth superorganism. Human societies amass enormous amounts of information, store it, and transmit it from one point to the next. Our libraries and computers are the cerebral cortex of the global nervous system. Our telephone wires and microwave transmission stations are the nerves. Think tanks and futurists are the frontal lobes, peering into the future. Remote sensors and pollution monitoring devices are our receptor organs. The arts and music are the limbic system, the site of our emotions, while legislative bodies and university faculties are the association cortex, which sorts through the information and attempts to make some meaningful response to regulate the motor system—the factories, police force, and tax collectors.

The biotic components of the ecosystem serve many crucial functions. Plants, animals, and microorganisms, linked in the complex food webs, for instance, are part of a global circulatory system that serves as a conduit for the circular flow of nutrients between living things and the environment. These members of the global ecosystem form the organs of planetary homeostasis. Plants, for instance, in their role as photosynthesizers, are the main energy-gathering organs. Eaten by a host of animals, they disperse the solar energy they capture throughout the ecosystem. Plants regulate the levels of carbon dioxide and oxygen in the atmosphere and nourish the soil. Animals consume the oxygen produced by plants, keeping levels constant. Their wastes return nutrients to the soil.

Nerve cells are as important to the smooth functioning of the body as the cells of the heart. Humans, as one component of Gaia, are in no way better than any other part. Hence the third principle of sustainable ethics: humans are an integral part of the earth superorganism, on equal footing with the rest. We are not superior nor inferior. We are each unique, and by definition, incomparable.

The Ecocentric View. The emergent view of the world under the sustainable ethics is "ecocentric" as opposed to the anthropocentric view so prevalent today. "Ecocentric" as a term describing a viewpoint of life may seem contradictory, perhaps even absurd, at first glance. The apparent absurdity stems from a deeply held dualistic view of the world in which we perceive what is inside the skin as "I" and what is outside as "not I." Psychologist Alan Watts called this notion the "skin-encapsulated ego."[40]

According to the ecocentric view, there are no "not I's." We are all one—earth, wind, water, and all living things—linked inextricably together like the cells of an organism.[41]

The ecocentric viewpoint is so foreign to modern thinking that some critics laugh it off. Lester Milbrath, professor of Political Science at the State University of New York, Buffalo, and a leading thinker on sustainable futures, argues that an ecocentric value structure is a logical impossibility, because only humans value.[42] If, however, we accept that our flesh is the product of air, water, and soils, and (more importantly) allow the boundaries between the self and the world to disappear, ecocentricity is not a logical impossibility, but rather a consistent and logical outcome.

Ecocentrism is not a new and revolutionary way of looking at the world. In *The Chalice and the Blade,* Riane Eisler explores early human history. Eisler's interpretation of archaeological evidence leads her to believe that Paleolithic and Neolithic societies were based on more of a partnership between men and women. In addition, these societies had a great respect for the earth. This period lasted until about 1500 BC. In human history, Eisler argues, the anthropocentric viewpoint characterized by human domination and control may be something of a newcomer.[43]

In modern times, John Muir and Henry David Thoreau held ecocentric views. Surely Aldo Leopold held similar convictions. Today, many environmentalists embrace a broader view of the place of humans in the biosphere. For thousands of years, the writings of mystics have spoken of achieving a oneness with all of life and nonliving matter, often through meditation. This was a central tenet of Buddhism. The Taoist Chuang Tzu writing over 2,000 years ago asserted, "I and all things in the universe are one." Unity arises from achieving a deeper level of consciousness, outside of the restrictive skin-encapsulated ego.

Arne Naess, the contemporary father of the Deep Ecology movement, argues that a oneness with nature can come from a conscious process of broadening the self. William James wrote in 1890 that the self is all that we are tempted to call ours. The line between a person and what she calls hers is sometimes difficult to draw. We feel and act about certain things that are ours in much the same way that we feel and act about ourselves.

By extending the boundaries of what we call me, says Naess, we widen the self. Maturity often involves a widening of the self, which comes from extending our identifications to include other living things and the earth. In this process the interests of other beings and the earth become the interest of the self. We react to threats because they threaten our own interests. Nature programs and books on plants and wildlife widen our awareness of the diverse world around us, and can widen our ethical boundaries. Through identification "higher unities are created through circles of friends, local communities, tribes, compatriots, races, humanity, life, and, ultimately . . . unity with the world," according to Naess.[44]

Truly, in its modern form and its ancient roots, ecocentrism is a crucial element of sustainability. Adopting the ecocentric world view may not be an easy transition for everyone and may often occur in a stepwise process. By promoting unity, teachers, writers, and visionaries within the environmental movement can have a profound impact on our society and our environment. The ecocentric view of the sustainable ethic can help revolutionize modern society, but only in conjunction with the application of the sustainable operating principles—conservation, recycling, renewable resources, and population control. These actions and the philosophical tenets of a sustainable society, the directive principles, can help us create a lifestyle that is not only sustainable in the long term, but sensitive to the rights of other species.

The shift to a sustainable ethic may result in a curtailment of some of our activities with obvious benefits to future generations and other species. It could diminish our bloated sense of self-importance and bring an end to the destructive short-term view so prevalent in frontier societies. The operational and directive principles of a sustainable society are guideposts that will provide us a path out of the rut we seem to be in.

The sustainable ethic holds considerable promise for human survival. It may evolve into an overarching philosophy that unites many disparate views—for example, those of the deep ecologists with their single-minded reverence for life and the bioregionalists with their think globally/act locally orientation.

Some critics point out that one of the chief problems in the environmental movement is that there are so many competing visions.

They hinder the development of a broader view. In many ways, these seemingly disparate visions—low-tech, bioregionalism, and deep ecology, for example—are not fundamentally incompatible, but rather are parts of the puzzle called sustainability. Their existence points to the need for a unifying concept.

To outsiders, many environmental supporters and environmental groups, even the relatively mainstream groups such as the Sierra Club, appear subversive. Our views are dismissed as a hindrance to human progress. "The lessons environmentalists drive home," writes William Tucker, author of *Progress and Privilege: America in the Age of Environmentalism*, "is that since we do not understand ecosystems in their entirety, and never will, we dare not touch them."[45]

This narrow view of environmentalism illustrates an important problem: environmentalists (teachers, activists, and supporters) have no coherent and believable vision. Although the environmental movement has its share of visionaries among its educators, writers, activists, and leaders who have been thinking and writing about our world view, the movement as a whole has not grasped a common vision that unites all issues. We have fought, and rightly so, to save wilderness and land and water, but failed to expound a central unifying view that makes sense to the mainstream.

Making the Transition. The shift to the sustainable earth society is a tall order for the frontier society. Profound shifts in our political, economic, and social institutions will be necessary. But can we do it without crisis?

Crisis is the natural outcome if we preserve the status quo. By so doing, most observers would agree that we only invite disaster. Inaction is a policy of despair, a policy sure to create enormous social, economic, and political upheaval in days to come.

Lack of foresight has become something of an American tradition. While the Japanese build high-efficiency cars and recycle large portions of their municipal waste, while the Israelis install solar panels for hot water on the rooftops of their homes and businesses, and while the Brazilians convert to renewable ethanol to power their vehicles, Americans remain steadfast in defending their gas-guzzling cars, spacious homes, and fossil-fuel dependency.

The danger of inaction lies in the ways it limits our response. Given the exponential growth of population and resource consumption, it is likely that when troubles deepen Americans will not have enough time to make the changes without extraordinary hardship. The need for change in fact could bewilder our political and social institutions—indeed, could overwhelm the American public, leading to significant paralysis.

Can we respond without crisis? Yes, but we will require change that comes from at least two complimentary directions. The first direction of change is from the top down. This approach relies chiefly on governmental action—new laws and regulations and strict enforcement of the existing statutes and regulations. Top-down change will be difficult but is an essential part of the equation of change. Environmental educators, activists, and sympathizers, who are an integral part of the American political scene, can play a major role in changing our political and legal systems, as they have for over two decades.

Much more emphasis is needed on preventing problems, rather than fixing them up afterwards. Barry Commoner, director of the Center for the Biology of Natural Systems, Queens College, City University of New York, argues that environmental pollution success stories are a result of the same action: pollution prevention and outright bans.[46]

Commoner contends that pollution prevention works, but pollution control strategies do not. Only where production technology has been changed to eliminate the pollutant has the environment been substantially improved, according to Commoner. "Where the technology remains unchanged and where attempts are made to trap pollutants in an appended control device, such as the automobile's catalytic converter or a power plant's smokestack scrubber—environmental improvements are modest or nil."

The goals established by the Clean Air Act in 1970 could have been met, says Commoner, if the EPA had confronted the auto industry with a demand for fundamental changes in engine design. Had American farmers been required to reduce the high rate of nitrogen fertilizer they used, nitrate water pollution would be falling rather than increasing. If the railroads and mass transit were expanded, if the electric power system were decentralized and increasingly based on cogenerators and solar sources, if American homes were weatherized, fuel consumption and air pollution would have been sharply reduced, Commoner observes. Preventive environmental policy is needed for a great many other areas as well.

The second strategy is the bottom-up approach, a shift in attitudes of people that results in lifestyle changes and changes in government and business. As individuals embrace the doctrines of the sustainable ethics, as they develop a new world view, society will experience profound shifts in attitude and lifestyle. Unrealistic expectations will be tempered. Respect and cooperation will emerge. Restraint may become the byword.

A Roadmap for the Journey

The environmental movement and its many participants could have a significant impact on change from both levels. But first we must explore the concept of sustainable ethics, study the foundations of a sustainable society, and find ways of getting there.

Lester Brown and his colleagues at the Worldwatch Institute and Amory and Hunter Lovins and their coworkers at the Rocky Mountain Institute have done much to promote the idea of sustainability in agriculture and energy. Herman Daly has done equally impressive work on sustainable economics.[47] Several environmental science textbook writers have attempted to present this thinking in their books.[48] But more work is needed to help us develop a comprehensive view of sustainable society—one that includes all activities in our society, such as industry, agriculture, transportation, medicine, urban planning, and many others.[49] Not until that view begins to take better shape, however, will we succeed in making a transition to a sustainable state.

To explore the sustainable ethic and a new course for the world's future, the environmental community must take a breather from the battle, set aside the pressing lawsuits and appeals for a few moments—or better yet, assign people not currently embroiled in legal battles to working groups. The goal? To think creatively about building a sustainable society.[50] A joint study including government officials, business representatives, and citizens could help build a broader constituency.

Through meetings at the state and national level, the environmental community, government, and business leaders can explore the requirements of a sustainable society. In these meetings, we should not content ourselves to discuss the problems once again, but rather seek solutions—creative and exciting answers that address all levels of action: legal, technological, and personal.

"Start the meeting on where . . . you want to go," advises David Brower, former executive director of the Sierra Club. Avoid the doom and gloom. Concentrate on developing the idea of sustainability, not just in abstract terms, but in real terms. Define not just the parameters of a sustainable society, but explore the physical reality: how people will get to work, how food will be grown, how modern skyscrapers might function on solar energy, how people will take vacations, and how wastes will be handled. Envision and list the possibilities. Out of this, a consensus for action could arise.

Sustainability could begin at the state level in the United States. Other nations may want to join in by developing regional or nationwide plans. This is not an exercise merely for the rich industrial countries. It's an exercise that will benefit Zimbabwe, Guatemala, Somalia, and Hungary as much as it will help France, Great Britain, the United States, and New Zealand. The principal goal of these conferences would be to develop a blueprint for achieving sustainability.

The environmental community must explore and understand sustainability better, and it must dare to articulate a view of the sustainable future to the public, to political leaders, and to business people (Chapters 4 and 5). We must let the world know where we stand and what we stand for. In press conferences, articles, interviews, and testimonies to all levels of government we must forge an image of the sustainable future. We must help teachers not already involved in the movement see the need for building a sustainable society. We must make the image of sustainability as alluring as the "great American dream." We must impress upon our political leaders the need for a sustainable society through letters and phone calls.

Humans tend to think of themselves as apart from nature and immune to its laws. Albert Einstein once wrote that this view is a kind of "optical delusion of our consciousness. This delusion is a kind of prison for us, restricting us to our personal desires and to affection for a few persons nearest to us." Our task, then, is to free ourselves from this prison, to widen our circle of compassion to embrace all living things and the world in which they live. From this broadened view, we can build a truly sustainable society. It is time, as David Brower says, to get a "few dreams happening again."

Beyond the Chain: Tapping the Power of People

3

A friend of mine who grew up in rural Wisconsin tells a story of a terrier that one of his neighbors kept chained to the side of the garage. Under a rusting Ford pickup, the dog found shade from the searing summer sun and protection from the winter winds. Its owners fed and watered the poor animal, but left it alone the rest of the time. There beside the garage he lived his life. When one of the neighborhood children rode by the house on a bicycle, however, the dog would race from its resting spot in the shade, barking madly. The dog would dash across the lawn, but just before he hit the end of the chain, he would stop. There, bound by his chain, barking madly, the dog would turn circles. The children laughed and pedaled by.

The dog grew older, and one day its owners let him off his chain. They tried to coax him into the house, but the dog, a creature of habit, preferred to stay outdoors, sleeping under the rusting Ford pickup truck beside the garage. Even though his legs were growing weak, each time one of the children raced by on his bicycle, the dog would bolt upright, and dart after him. Precisely at the spot where he used to stop, the dog would come to a stop. There, bound to an imaginary chain, he would turn circles, barking frantically.

In many ways, our society is like the dog in this story, barking frantically at the end of an imaginary chain that restricts our imagination and our effectiveness. To solve our environmental problems we have relied principally on legal and legislative solutions—lawsuits and new laws. Caught up in legal and political battles, we are turning circles, barking helplessly, limiting our response out of habit: fighting to stop dams when we could have also been promoting widespread water conservation; passing new laws to clean up hazardous waste when we could have also been working on ways to promote environmentally responsible lifestyles.[1]

Because of our narrow dedication to legal solutions, our society is overlooking a powerful solution that could help protect the environment: individual responsibility and action.[2] For years, we have bound ourselves to an imaginary chain. We won't solve our problems until we break that chain, but we can't break it until we understand what makes up the chain that holds us back.

The imaginary chain consists of at least three links—three dominant myths of modern society. The first myth is that people don't care. The second is that individual actions don't matter. And the third is that responsible living means sacrifice.

Myth 1: People Don't Care

Society lives a lie. Teachers, politicians, environmentalists, and most of the rest of us are perpetrating a false notion: that people don't care, that people are concerned only with themselves, and that people only act when their economic interests are at stake. The myth is manifest in the private conversations of government officials. It is evident in the speeches of environmental leaders, in articles, and in the classroom. As a society, we are cynical about one another's willingness to cooperate. But the notion that people don't care is false. Nothing could be further from the truth. No assumption could be more dangerous to our efforts to widen public response.

Just because people don't act does not mean they do not care. People fail to take action, in large part, because the discussion of solutions too infrequently includes actions that individuals can take. Since Earth Day 1970, countless environmental writers have outlined the problems we face, but meager attention has been given to ways individuals can contribute personally to solving them. Newscasts, newspaper articles, and television specials do equal disservice—faithfully outlining problems but often ignoring or skimming over solutions. If solutions are discussed, they typically center on legislative and regulatory changes.

John Graham and his wife Ann Medlock travel the world in search of people who stick their necks out to stand up for what they believe in, individuals who defy authority or go up against wealthy corporate polluters to right wrongs. This work is part of The Giraffe Project, the purpose of which is to study what it takes to put caring into action and then to publicize the work of this new breed of leaders. By so doing, they provide role models for others to follow.

Graham tells a story of a speech he was giving some years ago. He had his speech typed and had practiced diligently. But as his audience filed in, he was filled with dismay. His listeners were all up-and-coming executives, young doctors and lawyers, stockbrokers, and business people. Most were in their late thirties and early forties. They were all financially successful, drove BMWs or Porsches, and dressed in expensive three-piece suits. What was he going to tell this herd from the "me generation" about bettering the world through their own actions?

As the auditorium filled, Graham tossed his speech aside. When the time came to begin, he said, "I bet I know two things about each and every one of you." The crowd silenced and leaned forward. "I'll bet that each one of you wants to love and be loved," he said. "And that each one of you, before you die, wants to do something significant in your lives to make this world a better place."

The audience was silent.

He had them. There wasn't a single dissenting voice.

I think that the same is true of most people. Despite our apparent self-centeredness, we all want to make a difference—to be part of the solution. Each of us secretly dreams of contributing to society. Unfortunately, our lives do not often provide the opportunities to fulfill these dreams. Many individuals don't know where to begin. Sitting on the sidelines, many of us live our lives patiently waiting for the right moment, the right issue to draw us in.

Myth 2: Individual Actions Don't Count

One hot summer day a few years back, a neighbor complained to me about Denver's air pollution. "It's awful," she said. "The air is going to kill us." We both gazed downtown toward the brown cloud we call air, for lack of a better term. "You'd think someone would do something about it."

I shrugged my shoulders. "Yes," I said, as she headed off to work—in her car, alone. Two blocks from her house is a bus route with service every twenty minutes to the city where she worked.

Some months later, I sat across from another friend at a Japanese restaurant. Picking up the disposable chopsticks, fashioned from trees clear-cut in the tropical rain forests, I discussed the connection between deforestation and chopsticks. He knew about the fast-disappearing tropical rain forests and seemed dismayed. He said that he wished something could be done to save them. But when I went for my fork, he picked up the chopsticks and began eating.

These two incidents illustrate a serious problem facing modern industrial society. No matter how well-meaning we might be, no matter how much we care, many of us are blind to our personal contribution to the environmental problems plaguing modern society. We've taken ourselves out of the cause-and-effect equation, and have become content to fix the blame on someone else. Environmentalists, teachers, and government officials have played a major role in propagating this view.

In the early years following Earth Day in April, 1970, environmentalists and others engaged in an active campaign to promote individual action.[3] The oil crises of 1973 and 1979 spurred continued interest in conservation, but as the price of oil stabilized and began to fall, conservation and personal action seemed to be pushed to the background. After the early days of this bold new awareness, the environmental movement seemed to depersonalize its message to the public, focusing on corporate polluters, rather than individuals. When the perils of acid deposition became widely known, environmental lobbyists descended on Washington to push for new laws and regulations. Articles on the subject pointed fingers at the utility companies. The personal connection was given virtually no mention in the environmental magazines—or in our classrooms. Little was said about the profound effects individual action could have. Little was done to start grassroots action that could begin immediately, while activists nudged government along in the slow political process of change.[4] Environmentalists targeted the electric utilities, especially those that operated coal-fired power plants, seeking regulations that would cut the burning of high-sulfur coal or require utilities to install smokestack scrubbers to remove sulfur dioxide.

Much the same happened when the threat of the greenhouse effect was becoming evident. Article after article called for new laws and regulations to improve efficiency in factories, power plants, and automobiles. But the individual was generally left on the sidelines, waiting for something to be done for him by the nation's lawmakers and regulators—that is, until recently.[5]

By depersonalizing our problems guilt is removed and abstracted. By taking the individual out of the web of cause and effect, our problems become extrinsic. If the blame belongs to someone else, then it stands to reason that our problems are best solved by regulating someone else, notably big business, municipalities, and other large organizations.[6] This brings to mind the story of the bologna sandwich told by Ken Blanchard, author of *The One Minute Manager.* A construction worker sat down to eat lunch with a coworker. Opening his lunch box, the man began to complain, "Darn it all, bologna again. This makes me mad. That's the fourth day in a row. I'm so sick of bologna sandwiches!"

His friend looked at him and said, "Harry, why don't you ask your wife to make you something else?"

Harry looked back at him menacingly. "My wife?" he grumbled, "Hell, I make these myself."

Like Harry, many of us sit around and complain about the bologna sandwiches—and we're the ones making them! We factor ourselves out of the cause-and-effect equation and wonder why the nation cannot solve its problems. Our leaders and our teachers, with a few notable exceptions, have unwittingly facilitated this process by failing to make the connection between environmental problems and our own actions and spreading the word of these connections to the public.[7]

A 1985 report, *An Environmental Agenda for the Future,* compiled by ten prominent national environmental groups, is a case in point.[8] This important work represents the first consensus reached by America's ten leading environmental groups, and presents a list of regulatory and legislative actions that could help us clean up our environment and prevent future problems. Ed Marston, editor of the *High Country News,* a highly respected newspaper that concentrates on western environmental issues, expressed disappointment in the report, however.[9] "In their reflexive adherence to legislative solutions," Marston said, "they [the authors of the report] sound like chemical companies responding to increased resistance of pests to pesticides by prescribing ever larger doses of ever more potent poisons." Marston, like other critics, was hoping for something "more far-seeing, more imaginative."

An Environmental Agenda for the Future calls for numerous much-needed changes in government policy but pays virtually no attention to lifestyle changes and other personal actions, except for grassroots political action, which has been an important part of the environmental movement since its early days. In the discussions on toxic wastes and pollution control, the report notes that citizen participation and activism are leading features of American government. For these to work, according to the authors, we need public awareness, and we need individuals who will challenge the official policies. We also need effective mobilization of grassroots efforts to pressure Congress and litigation to force government to implement new and existing legislation. The authors argue that "citizens should have the opportunity to participate in the decision-making process of government and industry in order to insure continued progress against pollution." Just as important, however, are steps individuals can take to change their own lifestyles in ways that reduce their personal impacts on the environment.

Promoting conservation and conscientious consumerism represents one of the most difficult challenges facing the environmental community. Low product durability and disposability are two of the cornerstones of our economy. The third is ever-increasing consumption, supported in large part by crafty advertising campaigns aimed at convincing Americans that whatever we have it is not good enough or new enough. All three cornerstones are unsustainable and we have no choice but to change these attitudes and actions.

The Cash Conscience. The battle to protect our environment is increasingly becoming a financial war that pits environmental groups against business groups. In so doing, however, we ignore the individual and we foster superficiality. Through direct mail, for example, environmental groups call on people to support their work. We ask for help generally in one of two ways: through donations or by writing letters to businesses or governments.

Environmental groups need money to sue and to lobby effectively, efforts that are essential to our progress. We need letters, too. But this somewhat lopsided approach to social change sends a message to people that their personal involvement need only be as deep as opening a checkbook. Lucy Blake, executive director of the California League of Conservation Voters, argues, "We're facing a real challenge, because people are operating on such a superficial level in their personal relationships and in their organizational relationships—by writing a check, for example, which says 'I support you, send me your mail' " but goes no further.[10]

The environmental movement inadvertently fosters this superficial response—the "cash conscience"—a belief that donating money to environmental groups equals environmental protection. Wendell Berry, author of *The Unsettling of America*, writes "The giving of money has . . . become our characteristic virtue. But to give is not to do. The money is given *in lieu* of action, thought, care, time."[11]

Many well-meaning environmentalists, barraged by the storm of pleas from environmental organizations, display their willingness to help protect the environment by donating money. Important as this is, it's only a part of the solution.

The Paradox of Inconsequence. The second myth of modern society, this belief that individual actions don't count and that we are, therefore, not a part of the environmental crisis, is a double-edged sword. It creates many of our problems and, at the same time, keeps us from solving them. I call this the paradox of inconsequence.

On the one hand, our sense of causal insignificance spawns much environmentally irresponsible behavior. For example, thousands of urban commuters drive alone to work each day even though carpooling, vanpooling, and mass transit are freely available and use one-fourth as much energy and produce about one-fourth as much pollution as the private automobile.[12] People persist in believing that their personal contribution to pollution and resource depletion is insignificant.

This feeling of insignificance also keeps individuals from taking personal steps to solve our problems. Anne Grady, coordinator of Denver's Better Air Campaign, said it best, "If people don't see themselves as part of the problem, they can't see themselves as part of the solution."

Christopher Leman, coordinator of the Environmental Policy and Natural Resource Management program at the University of Washington in Seattle, notes that as large polluters have begun to be controlled, automobiles and households are becoming responsible for an increasing share of our environmental problems.[13] Catalytic converters and energy improvements in gas mileage of automobiles, for instance, have helped cut back on pollution from cars in urban areas, but total emissions have increased, largely because people are driving more.

Drawing the connections won't be easy, but it can be done. Educators, writers, environmentalists, and governmental officials can clarify the links between personal actions and their consequences in ways that empower people to change instead of becoming mired in guilt and hopelessness.

Given the size of our society, the rampant growth of material consumption, and the prevalent notion that individual actions do not matter, many people will resist the idea that individual actions can be brought to bear on the problems we face. The environmental movement can counter this resistance by publicizing examples of ways in which individual action has helped solve environmental problems. The National Wildlife Federation has taken a lead role in this activity: by publishing regular articles on people who make a difference, they are helping to show ways that ordinary citizens from all walks of life can make important contributions.[14] In 1989, PBS aired a National Wildlife Federation program called Champions of Wildlife, which showed the efforts of individuals to help make this world a better place for wildlife. Other groups and individuals are also helping to spread the word.[15]

Behavioral changes can have many unanticipated benefits as well. Social psychologists, for example, tell us that behavioral changes can cause subtle shifts in one's attitudes.[16] People who become recyclers, for example, often become more interested in environmental protection, and their interest often translates into additional actions. By inspiring people to recycle or to become more conscientious consumers, we may let loose a powerful cascade effect.

To many people, inside and outside of the environmental movement, the solutions to our problems are generally seen as political or legal ones—passing new laws, instituting tougher regulations, or suing somebody. The central thrust has been one of imposed restraint. As a result, our approach to change has been adversarial instead of inclusive. Our society continues to rely on this approach in large part because passing laws makes a difference—or many people think it does. Humanity, however, is at a point in its social evolution where alternative strategies could be brought to bear on our problems. Surely we cannot manage everything by voluntary programs, but we can find a healthy mix of voluntary cooperation and imposed restraint.

Duane Elgin, author of *Voluntary Simplicity* summarizes the issue nicely. He points out that "The clothes that we wear, the work that we do, the technologies that we employ, the transportation that we use, the manner in which we relate to others . . . the energy systems that we develop, the learning systems that we acquire, and many more are vital to well being of the totality of life on this planet." He adds, "In our highly interdependent, increasingly vulnerable world . . . we can no longer be oblivious to the impact of our way of living on the rest of the world." People are ready for a change; people are tired of traditional political solutions and tired of being told what to do. Moreover, people may be beginning to see the effectiveness of collective action and the need for government that operates on a softer path.

Myth 3: Conservation Is Sacrifice

The third and final myth is that conservation is sacrifice, that living responsibly means giving up pleasure and comfort. Like the two other myths, this is a problem of mind-set. It is a manifestation of a bankrupt national ethic that puts the concern of the individual above concern of the whole. It stems in part from constant media advertising that panders obsessively to consumer comfort, vanity, and pleasure. It stems from a blindness to a simple, but elegant truth: that planet-care is self-care. It stems from a society that seeks material satisfaction to salve internal feelings of inadequacy and perhaps even fear.

In our search for happiness and self-affirmation, many of us turn to excessive consumption. The bumper sticker that reads

"When the going gets tough, the tough go shopping" expresses the need to counter life's trials and tribulations with possessions. Material possessions bring short-lived happiness, but in the long run, they are ineffective in filling up the internal emptiness. The things we buy ultimately end up in the dumps, along with our feelings. As a result, many people become locked in a wasteful and destructive cycle, seeking more and more *things* to fill the voids we feel in our lives. Giving up the things that are supposed to make us feel better about ourselves exposes us to the cold reality: self-affirmation must come from within.

Nancy Newhall, conservationist and writer, once said that "conservation is humanity caring for the future." In this light, individual acts of kindness are not sacrifices but rather gifts to future generations, gifts to our fellow creatures, plants and animals, and gifts to the generous earth that supplies us with everything we need and much we really don't need. In giving gifts to those we care about, we are not diminished but made richer.

The root of the word *sacrifice* means to "make sacred." Conservation, therefore, is sacrifice that is giving *to,* not giving *up.* In giving love, we are not diminished, but made richer. Loving the earth and all its richness is empowering.

Clearly it is time to counter the three erroneous myths that hold us bound to our chain. People do care. Individual actions do matter. Giving is not sacrificing, but enriching. But there is a lot to be done.

Getting the Message Across

Over the past decade and a half, I have been watching programs on environmental problems, looking for positive and constructive suggestions for solutions. With few exceptions, solutions are ignored in most of the magazine articles on the environment, the television news, many articles in environmental publications, and classroom lectures. All in all, the media and the environmental community seem content to inform their audience to death and seem stuck in the analysis phase.[17]

The more we talk about problems—and there are many—without outlining solutions that empower people, the more people close down. Overwhelmed by the barrage of stories on environmental ills, people often feel powerless and become increasingly cynical about change. (This is where the myth of public apathy be-

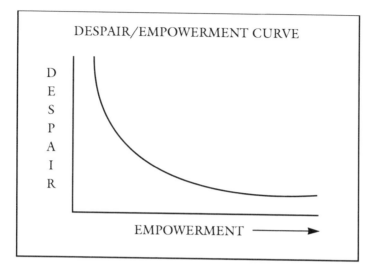

DESPAIR/EMPOWERMENT CURVE

comes apparent.) Little constructive change takes place when we see only danger or solutions in which individuals have no part. People become paralyzed with fear on the one hand and inaction on the other.

The overriding sentiment among most Americans is that our environmental problems are too big to solve. That sense of impotence and the despair many feel over the rampant destruction of our environment keeps people from acting. By leaving the individuals out of the equation for change, teachers, government officials, and environmentalists are unwittingly contributing to the paralysis gripping many of the world's people.

The encouraging news in all of this is that we *can* break out of the cycle of despair and inaction. How? Through individual empowerment—people taking action. Despair and empowerment can be plotted on a graph. As illustrated above, despair is shown on the vertical axis and empowerment on the horizontal axis. The graph shows us that as people take action—become empowered—despair falls. In other words, when people stop letting themselves be powerless and begin making changes in their own lives, despair quickly fades.

As people are drawn into creating solutions and taking actions, we will find a renewed vigor in this country. The process will not be entirely smooth. Bouts of depression or occasional despair are likely to occur, and to expect anything less is to ignore the fundamental nature of the human animal. But empowerment will begin a positive upswing with many benefits.[18]

Educators, environmentalists, and responsible governmental officials can begin by teaching people that they *are* part of the solution—that the answer involves more than an occasional signature on a petition or a check to the legal defense fund of a national environmental organization. We can communicate this idea in newsletters, articles, television shows, classrooms, and conferences. Instead of simply recounting the ills of an environmentally crippled nation, hoping that this will stir people to action, we must suggest effective individual actions.[19] (See Appendix A for a list of individual actions that can help build a sustainable society.)

Several encouraging signs have appeared in recent months. In June 1989, for example, the Greenhouse Crisis Foundation launched a campaign listing 101 do-it-yourself steps to help curb the greenhouse effect. The National Wildlife Federation has also begun to publicize the connections between individual action and environmental problems and is helping show people ways they can contribute to solving these problems.[20] As part of the celebration of Earth Day 1990, the National Wildlife Federation launched a nationwide project that called on college students to implement ways of reducing global warming on campus and in their communities. The NWF's theme for Earth Day 1990 was "Earth Day Every Day." In September 1989, the Sierra Club sent out a list of eight actions individuals could take to help fight global warming. The Union of Concerned Scientists published a pamphlet "How You Can Fight Global Warming: An Action Guide." Numerous state environmental organizations have also devoted more of their newsletters to individual actions. Even banks are chipping in, sending their customers lists of actions.

This sudden flurry of activity is encouraging. I think it is a manifestation of a dramatic realization that individual action is needed and that it has been sorely overlooked in the past 20 years. Nature programs, articles, speeches, and classroom lessons can support this new consciousness. New hope is arising, inspired by the recognition that individual actions, multiplied by those of many others, can bring about enormous changes.

It is not enough simply to suggest that people can make a difference. It is not enough to encourage people to conserve, recycle, use renewable resources, and help control world population. We must also *prove* that individual action really works—that individuals working together can and do make a difference. Our newsletters, magazines, press releases, speeches, and classroom lectures must present the evidence.

Better Air a Better Way: A Model of Citizen Involvement

Fortunately, there are many examples that show the vast un-tapped potential of individual action.[21] The Australian government, for instance, is promoting changes in land use to help fight the destruction of agricultural soils by salinization (salt deposits caused by application of excess irrigation water to arid soils). The government provides trees, incentives, and information to the public, which then supplies free labor.

The city of Denver has engaged individuals in combating its chronically polluted air. In 1984, the Colorado Department of Health proposed a program to help the Denver metropolitan region comply with federal air-quality standards. The plan called for the establishment of a voluntary no-drive day during the high-pollution months.[22] Citizens would be asked to leave their cars at home one day each week from November to the end of January or February, and find some alternative way of getting to work.

The plan was controversial from the start because it was based on voluntary action. The last digit on the license plate would be used to determine an individual's no-drive day. If your license ended in a 0 or 1, you were asked to leave your car at home on Monday, and so on.

The media were skeptical about the program's chances for success, and some members of the media attacked the idea as impractical and doomed to failure. Who in Denver, they wondered, would leave their cars at home one day a week to improve air quality? The regional office of the EPA and the state legislature were equally skeptical. Virtually no one in these institutions thought a voluntary program would work. The overriding sentiment of the Better Air Campaign critics was that you have to force people to do something to get them to change lifestyle—especially to cut back on driving. The public was skeptical as well. Polls by the Colorado Department of Health showed that most people thought that their own driving made little difference to the Denver's pollution.

The EPA refused to approve the idea, in large part because it was a voluntary program, not mandatory, and also because it had never been done before and because the agency didn't think it would work. The Health Department, however, set up a public hearing on the program and invited people to give opinions. The response was surprising. Despite widespread skepticism, Denver mayor Federico Peña and Colorado governor Richard Lamm both showed up to testify in favor of the program. Numerous citizens testified that they supported the program and would cooperate to make it work. So did the environmental community and many people in the business community. As a result, the EPA agreed to let the health department give it a try.

One of the first things the department did was to hire an ad agency. Since it would be a voluntary program, the department decided it would use marketing strategies—advertising and public relations—to persuade people to join in. It was a far cry from typical governmental approach.

Some health department officials had proposed naming the program the Episodic Share a Ride Program. The first thing the ad agency came up with was a more appealing name. They called it the Better Air Campaign and immediately launched an aggressive advertising campaign.

Through numerous television, radio, and newspaper advertisements, the Better Air Campaign began extolling individual action. "You hold the key," the ads claimed. In carefully worded advertisements, the Better Air people asked citizens to leave their cars at home one day a week on "their" no-drive day. One of the most effective strategies was introduced in the second year of the campaign. Officials received permission from Paul Simon to use his hit song, "Fifty Ways to Leave Your Lover." "It was a catchy tune. People loved it. It really sort of hit our target market," said Anne Grady, coordinator of the Better Air Campaign. More importantly, the program emphasized ways individuals could participate. The Paul Simon song told people to "Drop off the keys, Lee" and "Hop on the bus, Gus." Ads offered additional suggestions.

Certainly, the program was popular, but did it work? Because of difficulties determining the vehicle miles traveled in a large metropolitan area, officials were unable to report any significant decline in traffic.[23] However, surveys and other research showed that many people were leaving their cars at home and joining carpools or riding the bus on their designated no-drive days. Others were merely cutting back on driving by combining trips or walking when they could.

A.B. Dick, a manufacturer of printing presses, asked its sales force to stay in the office one day a week to cut back on driving. This policy was so successful that the company has asked their employees to continue the policy throughout the year. By combining trips, employees have become more efficient in the use of their time.

Many people who take to the bus or join carpools during the high-pollution season continue these activities. This is called the carryover effect. For two years, approximately 7 percent of all drivers in the metro area who participated in the Better Air Campaign the year before continued carpooling or riding the bus, which they started during the program. A follow-up survey conducted after the 1988–1989 campaign showed an even higher carryover effect: 13 percent of the people who had participated continued riding the bus or carpooling. In addition, over one-third of the people phoned in a random survey of 2000 citizens said they continued some kind of gas-conserving behavior started in the campaign—for example, consolidating trips or walking to stores nearby.

Bus ridership statistics during the 1988–1989 campaign showed a definite increase. In November and December of 1988, for example, there were 116,000 additional boardings. Carbon monoxide, a pollutant produced chiefly by automobiles in the Denver metro area, has been dropping steadily in the region for a number of years. The Better Air Campaign no doubt helped play a role in this decrease.

Perhaps one of the greatest accomplishments of the program is a dramatic increase in awareness of the need for individual action. Polls show that a substantial number of people in the region now support individual actions such as this to solve the air pollution problem in the region.

One of the unanticipated benefits of the Better Air Campaign, according to coordinator Anne Grady, has been a rapid change in public attitude. Research showed that within the first year, people had changed their views on individual action. They quickly realized that they *could* have an impact on air quality. The campaign also increased general awareness of air pollution and made it easier to rally public support for clean air legislation at the state level.

Throughout the Denver metropolitan area, tiny savings here and there are adding up. The program demonstrated that people who care can be enlisted to help solve environmental problems and that individual actions can be effective. Thus, the psychology that creates many of our problems and that has traditionally prevented us from solving them—that pervasive sense of inconsequence—can be overcome.

At the end of the first year, the EPA officially approved the Better Air Campaign's plan for voluntary no-drive days. "They've been going around the nation ever since, telling other cities to do the same thing," says Grady. Today, Colorado Springs has a program modeled after Denver's, and Phoenix started one several years ago as well. Programs are up and running in Los Angeles, New York City, Albuquerque, and Philadelphia—a wonderful tribute to the power of people.

Business participation in the Better Air Campaign increased over the years. For example, in the survey taken after the 1988–1989 campaign, nearly 30 percent of the respondents said their employers were doing something to promote better air. A survey a year earlier showed that only about 8 percent of the businesses were actively promoting better air.

Individual Action Is Catching On. Citizen involvement spurred by government is catching on. In 1989, Washington's King County sponsored Recycle Week 1989. The Solid Waste Division of the county, home to Seattle, scheduled seven days of educational events, aimed at increasing public awareness and stimulating individual responsibility and action. Citizens were offered tours of recycling centers and tours of landfills to see what happens to unrecycled waste. The county sponsored a household hazardous waste collection and offered workshops on composting yard waste and household organic wastes. A short grocery store tour showed individuals how to choose environmentally sound packaging, how to reuse packaging, and offered practical tips on incorporating recycling into shopping trips.

A Recycle Week 1989 brochure offered tips on ways to start the recycling habit. For a government agency, the ideas were revolutionary. On Monday, for instance, they suggested that people think "recycling" when they shop. The brochure recommends buying durable, reusable goods, and products made from recycled and recyclable products. On Tuesday, they ask citizens to "think before they toss." The brochure asks citizens to think about giving their waste a second chance or finding someone who will.

The County offers compost bins and suggests that instead of tossing the brochure, which was printed on recycled paper, that people tear it up and add it to their compost pile, or use it as a wrapping paper.

The Better Air Campaign and King County's Recycle Week are models of how government can work to change individual behavior through cooperation and inspiration rather than compulsion. Environmental groups can help promote the concept of governing through cooperation in newsletters, magazine articles, and by lobbying governments. National environmental organizations may want to launch programs of a similar nature of their own.

Throughout America voluntary groups are working to build trails, refurbish streams, and plant trees on barren soils. These programs represent another good start at engaging people in the solution of environmental problems. David Adamson, former executive director of the Volunteers for Outdoor Colorado, which has carried out dozens of such projects, makes an interesting point about membership in his organization. "Membership," he says, "stresses what you give, not what you get. Human nature is such that when people work on the land, they develop a sense of pride and ownership, and, ultimately, take better care of it."

In 1986, Volunteers for Outdoor Colorado completed eight projects on public lands with 1,000 volunteers. The work would have cost federal agencies $250,000. VOC did it with a $50,000 budget and a cadre of volunteers. Similar groups now exist in Florida, California, Washington, New Mexico, and Pennsylvania. Volunteer groups can widen the ambit of action by stressing that weekend volunteer work is just the beginning of a lifetime of dedication, a commitment that begins at home—a message that must be heard far beyond the community of like-minded environmentalists.

In Perryville, Arkansas, an eroded hillside was recently transformed into a demonstration farm thanks to the Heifer Project and a dedicated group of volunteers from a nearby high school. The students planted trees, terraced the land to reduce erosion, and have gradually made the land productive again. The two-acre farm is now a test site for sustainable agricultural practices, and small farmers from all over the world come to learn about sustainable agriculture.

Throughout America volunteers are flocking to build new trails, repair damaged ones, and refurbish stream beds choked with debris and sediment to restore fisheries. These programs have at least two added benefits: they show people how working together can make a difference and they help people become invested in protecting the environment.

Operation Outreach. To help spread the message of individual action, environmentalists and environmental educators may want to mount an Operation Outreach. In such a campaign, members are asked to take time to talk to friends, relatives, and neighbors about ways they can conserve, recycle, and use renewable resources.[24] In Operation Outreach, we can help people emerge from the sidelines and find ways to alter their lifestyles in ways that contribute to solutions.

Petra Kelly, a long-time member of West Germany's Green Party, points out that "the threat as well as the solution are not 'out there.' They are within us. Taking responsibility for our personal behavior is the only thing in the world over which we have complete control." Solving the problems depends on people adopting caring lifestyles. These notions can be the central thrust of our outreach.

Tapping the Power of People

In 1988, the Environmental Defense Fund launched an ambitious project in cooperation with the nonprofit Advertising Council, the folks that brought us such unforgettable slogans as "Only you can prevent forest fires" and "A mind is a terrible thing to waste." The EDF project is designed to promote recycling in America. "If you're not recycling," the slogan goes, "you're throwing it all away." Through radio, television, newspapers and magazines, the EDF is hoping to spread this message to the American people, helping to effect long-term changes in peoples' attitudes and habits.[25]

The International Decade of the Environment. On February 16, 1989, James Gustave Speth, president of the World Resources

Institute, called on the world's nations to establish a decade-long program to protect the environment.[26] The project, he argues, could create a way of life that is sustainable. It would be a gift to the new century.

"Today's environmental problems are closely interlinked," says Speth. "They cannot be addressed issue-by-issue or by one nation or even by a small group of nations acting alone. They will not yield to modest commitments of resources."

As a starter, the national environmental groups in conjunction with many others could begin a nationwide campaign that identifies a problem, such as global warming, that will affect a great many people. Droughts and food shortages make this a highly visible problem that could be the focus of a decade-long effort aimed at promoting lifestyle changes—to bring American life in line with ecological realities. Global climate change will help reinforce the notion that we are all one, that energy waste in Europe affects people in Africa and that pollution in the North Sea impacts an Eskimo village in the frozen Arctic Circle.

Participants in the Decade of the Environment project must first outline the dangers—both in the short run and the long run. Then, and more importantly, they must outline strategies that engage individuals: tree planting, energy conservation in the home, recycling, carpooling, and so on. Through carefully worded advertisements, we can begin to reshape American society.

In the Decade of the Environment, massive tree planting in cities and suburbs could help offset global warming and beautify our cities and highways. Urban trees absorb atmospheric carbon dioxide but also provide summertime shade and wintertime wind protection, thus reducing fuel bills and cutting back on carbon dioxide pollution. We could set a nationwide goal of cutting carbon dioxide emissions by 20 percent nationwide through the combined efforts of tree planting and energy conservation in homes, automobiles, and factories. Individual actions, added to governmental efforts to reduce carbon dioxide, could greatly reduce global carbon dioxide levels.

Surely, our efforts must span the globe. When our program is up and running, we may want to instigate an International Decade of Environmental Improvement. National and international campaigns must include people from all sectors of society: children and adults, the rich and the poor, the religious community, the minorities, and so on (Chapter 4). They must engage our governmental leaders. They must see that laws and regulations are not the sole output of government. The campaign must include businesses as well. They must be brought in early in the planning stages.

The International Decade of Environmental Improvement project must engage the media to reach deep into the heartland of America. It will be essential to stress the need for sustained change—permanent change—a lifetime commitment to cut back on fossil fuel combustion and to reduce unnecessary expenditure and waste. People must be reminded that a clean environment is akin to good health. It can't be achieved by an occasional action; it can only be ensured by a lifetime of attentiveness and action. Earth Day every day!

Our campaigns must be carefully crafted and skillfully executed to work. We will be most effective if we avoid the feelings of guilt and despair—and the paralysis they create. We can find ways to help people make their lives structures of fulfillment. We can find ways to evoke a sense of challenge, rather than despair and hopelessness.

Drawing the connections between our own actions and environmental problems can backfire on us if we are not careful. It can disenfranchise otherwise receptive audiences, unless skillfully done. Our message must not be mixed with indignant self-righteousness, but must be filled with a spirit of helpfulness, and, at the risk of sounding quaint, love. We can avoid the language of exclusion, verbiage that supports a view of "us versus them." Edmund Burke once said that "nobody made a greater mistake than he who did nothing because he could only do a little." Let this be our rallying cry!

New Concepts of Leadership. Many of us tend to sit back and wait for someone else to take charge. We want leaders who will lead, people to inspire us to make changes. But leadership rarely comes from the top.[27] It more often comes from individuals. In many cases, community leaders are not necessarily the mayor or city councilpersons, but individuals who take responsibility to do what needs to be done. They are people who take on a leadership role even though they are not in a leadership position. In effect, people become leaders because they take actions out of conviction. A community leader, for example, might be a person who pushes for an ordinance requiring the city to purchase recycled paper or to ban styrofoam. Or it might be a person who inspires people on her block to recycle or to eliminate pesticides. It can be a person who organizes a community garden. Our elected leaders, in contrast, often find it easier to shift like weather vanes in the winds of public opinion than to take charge, and because of this you and I must become the leaders. We must become the heroes and heroines of the twentieth century.

Our campaign to champion individual action can be a forum that promotes the concept of multilevel leadership. It's an idea that could serve our country and our environment for many years to come.

Do We Dare to Change Ourselves?

The resource demand of our society is enormous, the waste mind-boggling. The result? Destruction of epic proportion: air pollution, tropical rain forest deforestation, habitat loss, wildlife extinction, and so on. To make matters worse, Americans have become consumers of frivolous gadgets and throw-aways that waste important resources and have no earthly value except to amuse us a little. It seems unconscionable but, as one Denver EPA official said, "we rip apart the fabric of life because there is a demand for rags."

It is time we began to teach a simple lesson: that environmental problems are created by individuals and can be solved by people who dare to take action. Individual efforts multiplied many times—this must be a part of our solution, just as much as new laws, regulations, and technologies.

Surely, a single recycled aluminum can or a well-insulated house or a gas-miserly car on the road will not save the world, but these single acts, multiplied by millions of others in this country and throughout the world, will translate into tremendous savings of energy and other natural resources. Individual actions multiplied by many can make significant inroads into habitat destruction, resource depletion, and pollution, just as individual waste and disregard create the dismal list of problems we now must address. "The character of a society," writes Duane Elgin, "is the cumulative result of countless small actions, day in and day out, of millions of persons." That character can be regenerative and kind just as easily as it can be wasteful.

We have the brainpower and the technology to reshape our future, to build a sustainable society. But do we have the leadership to tap into the enormous reserve of caring individuals? Do we have the presence of mind to stop making bologna sandwiches? Do we have the will to dare to change ourselves?

Sir Edmund Hillary once wrote that our environmental problems are really social problems. They begin with people as the cause and end with people as one of the chief victims. It is time that the entire environmental community came to grips with this truth. It is time to spread the word: that environmental problems can be solved by people who dare to take action. It is time for small changes to become great contributions by the collective actions of many. Individual action is a new frontier of activism. It's a new step in the evolution of human social change. Charles de Gaulle once said, "Going to the moon isn't very far. The greatest distance we have to cover lies within us." It is time we began the journey.

The loftier the building
the deeper the foundation must be laid.

THOMAS A. KEMPIS

The Minds of Many: Making Environmentalism Mainstream

4

By most measures, America has become a nation of environmental sympathizers. Poll after poll shows that environmental concerns rank high in the national psyche. "From corporate chief to schoolchildren, the concern is becoming unanimous," writes Huey D. Johnson, former secretary for natural resources in California.[1]

Lois Gibbs and Karen Stults, of Citizens Clearinghouse for Hazardous Wastes, express a similar sentiment in an article on grassroots environmentalism in *Crossroads: Environmental Priorities for the Future:* "For the first time in years—perhaps the first time ever—there is a public consensus supporting efforts to protect and improve the environment." This conclusion stems, in large part, from a Harris Poll showing that 92 percent of the American public believes that hazardous waste is a serious problem.[2] This poll also shows that a large percentage of the American public views acid deposition, water pollution, radioactive wastes, and air pollution as issues of concern. "The numbers," Gibbs and Stults claim, "show a new consensus for the environment."

Beyond the Polls

Environmental issues are of great concern to the world's people thanks in large part to an outpouring of media reports showing the startling signs of breakdown—the oil spill near Valdez, the hole in the ozone layer in Antarctica, dying seals in the Baltic, and barges of rotting garbage that can find no home. American interest in the environment seems to have peaked once again.[3] Environmental groups, environmental educators, and scientists have also played a crucial role in raising awareness.

While the polls reflect concern and growing fear, stemming from the increasing visibility of the problems, they may not necessarily indicate full-blown public *support*. Dr. Leon Swartzendruber, a social psychologist and environmental activist, agrees.[4] He thinks that we may be reading more into the polls than is really there. Concern for issues is one thing, but a public consensus supporting efforts to protect and improve the environment is quite another.

"One of the things that social psychologists . . . have been concerned about," says Swartzendruber, "is the big gap between attitudes and behavior." Being concerned about a problem with a high public profile is a far cry from being willing to do something about it—to change one's lifestyle or to support legislation that will control the problem, especially if it costs money. "Just knowing what somebody's attitude is," says Swartzendruber, "isn't necessarily a good predictor of their behavior. Right now, it's socially acceptable to say that toxic wastes are a problem."

Is the American public solidly behind the environmental movement? "In words, yes. In deeds . . . that's questionable," according to Swartzendruber. Can the level of interest expressed in the polls be translated into political action? "I think so, provided the people do not see it as an economic threat to themselves or a threat to their lifestyles," he claims. The concern expressed in the polls is paralleled by a dramatic increase in membership in environmental organizations and a growing interest in environmental science courses in colleges and universities.[5] But the 1970s illustrate that the attention of the American public is fickle. Its interest turns quickly from one issue to the next.[6]

We must be cautious in how we interpret polls and the potentially growing body of support for our concerns. We must read them for what they are: a crack in the door of the national psyche.

Peter Berle, the amiable and articulate leader of the National Audubon Society, says, "One of the things that I worry about is whether people who are involved in the environmental game can capture the current rising tide of public concern." If we accept the poll results as an expression of interest, the challenge is threefold: First, we must find ways to deepen the public's interest and turn it into commitment. Second, we must find ways to convert commitment to action—both individual and social. Third, we must find ways to sustain public concern.

The door of public concern opened in the early days of the environmental movement, but for one reason or another seemed to close again. Many supporters seemed to lose interest. The public turned its attention to other concerns, particularly the economy. In the late 1970s and much of the 1980s, college students reflected the shift in social concern. College enrollments in engineering and business courses skyrocketed while many environmental science courses shrank. Why did the intense interest generated by Earth Day in 1970 fade? Or perhaps more important, why did environmentalism not spread more broadly and deeply into society?

Messages of Gloom and Doom. Perhaps one of the key reasons was that the environmental movement did not articulate a vision of its goal, as discussed in detail in Chapter 2. Educators, activists, and others may have spent too much time talking about problems and not enough outlining solutions, especially those involving individual action (Chapter 3). The public became wary of environmentalists who seemed to stand in opposition to almost everything that society had come to view as a manifestation of progress. The public couldn't see where environmental writers, educators, and activists were aiming and feared that the movement was a knee-jerk reaction against technology and perhaps even society itself.[7] Michael Fischer, executive director of the Sierra Club, notes "This is a complaint that people have always raised about the Sierra Club. 'You're against everything, you don't make it clear what you are in favor of.'"

Over the past two decades, environmentalists have tirelessly uncovered a wide range of problems. In meeting after meeting, press release after press release, article after article, we have expounded the atrocities of the modern technological society, railed against pollution and habitat destruction, and grumbled about the depletion of finite resources, such as oil and natural gas. Too little attention has been directed to solutions—except those that necessitate new laws and regulations. This is not to say that the environmental movement has not talked about solutions and proposed some meaningful ones. Groups like the Citizens Clearinghouse for Hazardous Waste (and others) have made it clear from the outset what they oppose *and* what they support. The problem is one of degree. There has just not been enough talk about solutions—especially individual solutions—in classrooms, magazine articles, speeches, and television specials.

The environmental movement has not broadened and deepened as much as it could for other reasons as well. Perhaps even more significant than the lack of proposed solutions is the fact that the environmental community confronts people with issues that they would just as soon not have to think about. We have been forcing attention to issues that create discomfort, anxiety, and feelings of helplessness. Discussions of species extinction, finite resources, and burgeoning population growth, to name a few, overwhelm and depress many people. Since we haven't provided nearly enough information on ways out of the seemingly hopeless traps, people turn off to the message.

Michael Fischer propounds a thesis that "everything we [the Sierra Club] say we are against is simply another way of defining that which we are in favor of."[8] But that is not enough. People can't be expected to extrapolate.

The environmental movement's obsession with problems creates an atmosphere of gloom and doom.[9] That leads to a sense of helplessness. The bad news may roll off our backs like so much water off a duck's back, but it can create denial and paralysis in others. Humorist and syndicated columnist Dave Barry tells how he deals with the problem of global warming: each time he sees the words in print, he squints his eyes until the words disappear. The public may be doing much the same. Educators, environmentalists, environmental leaders, and writers have played an unwitting role in this process.[10]

By spending more time expounding solutions, environmental educators and the rest of us in the environmental community can build a more positive image of environmentalism and help ease the paralysis that grips our nation. We can show that environmentalism is a social force that has the society's well-being in mind. Environmentalists care about trees, animals, birds, *and* people. Through our policies and actions we seek to build a sustainable relationship in which humans can survive alongside other species. Rather than evoking guilt and apprehension that lead to helplessness, we can arouse excitement and challenge. Instead of turning people away, we can rally support for positive changes. To do so, we could devote as much as half of each television special we sponsor, each speech we deliver, each article we write, and each book we publish to positive solutions. Such actions could begin to focus attention on where we need to go and what people can do individually and collectively.

Negativity and Self-Righteousness. The environmental movement may have lost some supporters because of a simple personality problem. David Adamson, Colorado field representative for The Nature Conservancy and former executive director of Volunteers for Outdoor Colorado, says, "The major problem with the environmental movement is its negativity. There are a lot of negative and self-righteous people in the movement. Negativity and self-righteousness are the two Achilles' heels of the environmental movement."

According to Adamson, environmentalists are often very right-or-wrong oriented. Many are torn by feelings of despair and hopelessness. At the same time, they are a remarkably dedicated and faithful group of people. They have kept the environmental movement alive for two decades and we owe much to them. Unfortunately, the negativity, self-righteousness, and "I'm right, you're wrong" attitude of some is alienating. Has it hurt the movement? Probably.

Self-righteousness hinders efforts to enlist broader support. "Many more people would be active in environmental groups," says Adamson, "if we only had a more positive attitude."

Many environmental leaders interviewed for this book argued that the environmental movement needs to reach a much larger constituency to build a broader base of support. But we won't reach a larger constituency with negativity, despair, and gloom and doom.

Our challenge, then, is to make the environmental cause interesting and exciting and promising. The Windstar Foundation, founded by John Denver and Thomas Crum, is an extraordinary example of such efforts. Something of an amalgamation of new-age philosophy and environmental activism, Windstar preaches personal involvement. It engages a wide range of people who might not otherwise become involved in environmental action because it eschews negativity and self-righteousness. It merges love for one another and love for the planet in a way that is not only inspiring but empowering.

Bound by Tradition. Another reason the public interest in environmentalism has not broadened has to do with image. Some of the larger, most visible organizations, such as the Sierra Club, are bound by tradition. The celebration of wilderness, mountain climbing, native species, and rare and endangered habitats have been the principal focal points of the Sierra Club. This long-standing tradition, however, may be one reason why the Sierra Club and other groups have not been received by a much more diverse audience.

The Sierra Club's long-standing and continuing interest in wilderness issues creates an impression in the minds of many people that environmentalists are a special interest group with a narrow preoccupation, even though the Sierra Club and other groups have greatly expanded their work in recent years. Environmentalists have been typecast by critics such as William Tucker and Ron Arnold as an elite group of obstructionists.[11]

Our perceived narrow interest in the out-of-doors, a concern far removed from the lives of many Americans, especially the poor and the minorities, may serve to set us apart from American society. We're viewed by some as a privileged few that can afford to backpack and cross-country ski, a group that's content to impede progress (such as mining and timber cutting) to enhance its own outdoor escapades.[12]

Steve Bonowski, former president of the Colorado Environmental Coalition, argues that the environmental community has not effectively countered the claims of developers (and others) who view us as "a bunch of elitists who want to lock up our resources."[13] In the past, says Bonowski, "we've allowed development interests to paint us as elitist backpackers with big bucks who want to shut off land to multiple use."

The environmental movement has fallen short in selling the public on the need for wilderness and river preservation. But that is beginning to change. By pointing out economic benefits of wilderness and free-flowing rivers, for example, environmentalists help the public realize that the out-of-doors is valuable not only for the protection of other species, but also as a sustainable economic resource for human welfare. We're letting small communities throughout the nation know that their long-term interests are often best served by catering to outdoor recreation—a land use that is frequently compatible with species preservation. Anglers, backpackers, river runners, and cross-country skiers generate enormous amounts of money in small communities throughout the United States. As a rule, they don't use up the resource. "Somebody going fishing is going to spend a lot of money over the years in small towns," says Bonowski. "That's a renewable economic resource. A clear cut, on the other hand, creates jobs. But once the timber is gone, so are the jobs and so is the recreational opportunity."

The recent rash of environmental disasters may also be helping the general public realize that the environmental movement does indeed have the best interests of society in mind. More and more, the public may be beginning to be perceive environmentalism as a *public* interest movement, and not just a group of elitists.

The environmental movement can do more to demonstrate that the general public is a beneficiary of environmental protection. By spreading the word, we can dispel the notion of elitism. By offering alternatives to costly and environmentally harmful projects, we send a message to the American public that we are working for the public interest by protecting sustainable recreational resources and protecting against short-term economic folly.

The effort to prevent construction of the Two Forks Dam on the South Platte River southeast of Denver is a good example of environmental commitment that could help protect valuable wildlife habitat and an important public recreation site and save money as well. The Denver Water Department and city officials from outlying suburbs have, for many years, coveted a beautiful river canyon 20 miles southwest of Denver. A few years ago, they filed for the permits to build a 500-foot dam. The dam on the South Platte River would flood 35 miles of incredible whitewater, fishing stream, and wildlife habitat. With the diversion projects that are needed to supply water to the new reservoir, the project would cost of over $1 billion, perhaps as much as $2 billion.

The Two Forks Project is the crown jewel in the Water Department's multidam plan that most environmental leaders—even most of the national leaders—see as unnecessary and environmentally costly. Environmentalists opposed the project for several reasons. Its need was based on inflated population growth projections and water demand and the project is costly. Furthermore, it would destroy an exquisite canyon. Water impoundment might dry up the Platte River in Nebraska during part of the year, threatening the nesting habitat of several endangered birds. Finally, environmentalists knew there were other, cheaper, less-damaging alternatives.

Instead of just standing in opposition, though, the environmental community put together a sophisticated plan that would provide water, when needed, much less expensively and without the impacts. Environmental support brought hundreds of angry citizens to hearings to protest the economic and ecological folly of the Two Forks project and to support alternative means of supplying water to the sprawling Denver region. Public sentiment, as shown by polls, aligned against the project as a result of environmental opposition. Says Bonowski, "We showed [the public] that we're not a bunch of nay-sayers. We weren't saying no to more water, but were saying . . . let's find cheaper and less-damaging ways to get it." Environmental plans are a benefit not just to society, but to all species.

This example is the kind of public image-building that benefits the environmental movement.[14] Press releases and articles that outline viable, economically feasible solutions also help. Headlines could read: "Sierra Club proposes cheaper and less damaging alternatives to . . ." "Wilderness Society suggests economical, environmentally safer alternatives to supply paper . . ."

The public is becoming increasingly aware of the economic benefits of a clean environment, in part, thanks to the recent efforts of the environmental community. But we are only in the first hundred yards of a road that's a mile long. Polishing the public image of environmentalism will help us broaden our constituency and probably gain new dues-paying members as well.

Private Conversations. Despite millions of dollars spent each year on direct mail, the environmental message is largely a private one. Through mountains of environmental magazines and newsletters, the environmental message is spread through a tightly knit community of environmental advocates. Thus, the message travels primarily to like-minded people. (The "preaching to the choir" syndrome.)

"I don't mind us getting the message to each other," says David Brower, who now heads the Earth Island Institute.[15] Why? "We are so confused and need to consolidate our thinking and try to get the rough edges off and get better and more useful thoughts going among our own. But certainly we have to reach far beyond that," says Brower.

Susan Weber, executive director of Zero Population Growth, argues that we may be spending too much time "talking among ourselves."[16] There is not enough effort, she says, focused on swaying the general public, on "winning a constituency of broad support." That's no easy task, but it must be done. Important as it is to educate our constituency, we need to reach far beyond the environmental community to shape public attitudes and actions. A massive public education campaign as part of the Decade of Environmental Cooperation (proposed in the previous chapter) might be a good start. A consortium of state and national groups, for example, could work together, spreading the costs and burden. Education however, must go considerably beyond current efforts.

Public education, for many groups today, is subsumed by the direct-mail campaigns, claims Paul Watson, founder of Sea Shepherd Conservation Society—the oceanic counterpart of Earth First! "In most organizations," says Watson, "education . . . means direct mail, so it's actually fund-raising and education become one." His view was substantiated by several others I interviewed. Fund-raising masquerading as education isn't enough, for it reaches only a small fraction of the public. And of them, only a tiny segment ever reads the material.

Carefully worded radio and television campaigns would probably be far more effective than direct mail pieces sent to people already sympathetic with our cause. The African Wildlife Foundation, for example, aired a radio advertisement telling of the destruction of over 70,000 African elephants in 1988 by poachers to feed the growing demand for ivory. Jimmy Stewart narrates the ad, asking the American public in a raspy voice to do their share to stop the slaughter of elephants by not buying ivory. It's a simple message, but forceful. It lets people know that they're part of the problem and can be part of the cure.

This kind of public education may prove more effective in the long run for rallying public support not just to join groups but to take active measures. This type of advertising is costly, but arguably more effective than the direct mail route. To reach a broader constituency and to help bring about the necessary transformation in society, we must get our message to the general public. We can make the messages short and clear. We can delineate the problem accurately and honestly, then describe ways people can be part of the solution. Television, radio, and newspaper spots may not be appropriate (or affordable) for all environmental groups, but will help the movement become mainstream, by building a broad and committed following. Free public service announcements may work just as well, especially if they are aired during prime time.

Suzanne Mattei, executive director of the Connecticut Fund for the Environment, says "My feeling is that things always go better for the environment when there is citizen involvement, and . . . anything that forecloses that . . . hurts the environment." Negativity, righteousness, gloom and doom, narrow focus, and our private messages hinder public participation, but we can change our ways.

Making Environmentalism Mainstream

Lois Marie Gibbs and Karen Stults of Citizens Clearinghouse for Hazardous Waste wrote that the environmental community has "learned the hard way that there are only two sources of real power: people and money. Since we [environmentalists] will never be able to muster the kind of money-based power the polluters have, we should focus on the most effective means to build people power."[17] The key to meaningful change in national policy and personal lifestyles hinges on building a real consensus for environmental protection. It hinges on values that lead to action. It hinges on environmentalism becoming mainstream.[18]

Until the environment becomes an issue of international priority, however, much of the movement will remain trapped in the trenches. "Where we need money to solve millions of acres of soil problems," says Huey Johnson, "we will continue to have only a few shovels and lots of hopes." Increased power will come as we enlarge the circle of individuals and nations who support environmental protection and enhancement. But who do we need to reach? At least these four overlooked segments of society: minorities, senior citizens, the religious community, and children.

Reaching Minorities. Thomas Atkins, who works for Environmental Action, argues that the minority community— blacks, Hispanics, Native Americans, and poor whites—receives little attention and little assistance from the environmental organizations. Yet minority communities are disproportionately impacted by pollution and other environmental problems. In some cases, minorities are engaged in a battle to save their lives. In Louisiana, says Atkins, children are dying of lung cancer and emphysema because of industrial pollution. In New Mexico, Native Americans and Hispanics are devastated by toxic wastes. Large corporations from all over the world are thinking about dumping their toxic wastes in the rural south where people are too poor to put up much of a fight. Minority communities are viewed as sacrifice zones.

The Reverend Jesse Jackson summed it up well in a recent issue of *Greenpeace* when he wrote: ". . . environmentalists can no longer afford to ignore the crucial determinants of race and class in the environmental crisis. Toxic waste is not deposited in Beverly Hills or Chevy Chase. It is stowed away in the middle of the night in poor communities in places like Arkansas, Louisiana, and South Carolina." Jackson adds that "after a decade of cutting back public health programs and a decade of cutting a break for corporate polluters, personal health is fast becoming an elite consumer item hoarded by the rich."[19]

The difficult part of this problem is that minority communities, who suffer disproportionately, are often dependent on the factories and the industries that are poisoning them. But the residents of these communities have their hands tied. "They are damned if they do anything, because they will lose their jobs. If they don't do anything, their children are going to die," Atkins argues. Outside involvement would help to provide a voice for people caught in a bind.

"The environmental community does not see that a clean environment is a civil right," says Atkins. Almost without exception, everyone I interviewed on the issue of broadening public support said that the environmental movement must reach the minorities. "We need the widest possible ethnic diversity in our audience," said Michael Fischer of the Sierra Club. Peter Berle, President of the National Audubon Society, agreed and outlined a program sponsored by the Society, which is now underway in many U.S. cities. It is designed to instill an appreciation for nature among inner-city children.[20] The program introduces children to the rudiments of ecology and prepares them to deal with environmental issues.

Reaching adult members of the minority groups is also necessary. Since many environmental problems occur in inner cities or in depressed rural areas, showing ways that environmental issues affect their lives will not be difficult.[21] Reaching minorities, however, will require concerted efforts on the part of what has been a largely mid-to-upper middle class white movement. Recruiting more minorities like Atkins into environmental organizations as staffers may be helpful in building bridges between these separate but interconnected worlds. Recruiting more minorities into environmental education efforts would be helpful as well.

The names of blacks and Hispanics rarely appear on mailing lists, one of the environmental movement's chief access points to the public. This makes it more difficult for environmental groups to reach minorities, but certainly not impossible. Minority civic leaders, clergy, business owners, politicians, and other professionals who are sympathetic to environmental protection serve as a vital link between the environmental movement and minority communities. Environmental groups need to find ways to work with these groups to help bring the message home. Neighborhood leaders may emerge from public meetings and become catalysts for change among the urban and rural poor.

Minorities *are* interested in environmental issues. Black leaders in Congress vote consistently in favor of environmental legislation. According to Atkins, Native Americans, blacks, and Hispanics care about the environment as much as they do about education and other pressing issues. But they often lack political clout, legal acumen, and scientific expertise. The environmental community can help provide some of the necessary ingredients for change.

Gray Power: Reaching Senior Citizens. America is home to 30 million senior citizens—men and women 60 years of age and older.[22] Like minorities, they are a group that has been overlooked by the environmental community. "Senior citizens are segregated . . . out to pasture," complains David Brower, who remains active despite his seventy-plus years. "In nursing homes, they talk to one another about the way things used to be, practically never about what needs to happen and what they can do. What are they going to pay back to the earth that's given them sixty, seventy, eighty years?"

Brower dreams of going on a senior-citizen circuit to rally support for the environment. Environmental groups could help by launching a nationwide campaign to mobilize this politically powerful group. We could form a coalition of environmental groups interested in the project in order to avoid duplication of effort. By identifying issues of concern to senior citizens and by identifying older citizens who are interested in environmental issues and are willing to lead their cohorts, we can build a much wider base of support.

The Coalition of Seniors for the Environment can offer information and financial support. Working together, senior citizens and environmentalists can set an agenda for action involving personal and political changes. We can help identify and delineate crucial environmental problems and their solutions. We can explore the concept of a sustainable society and work collectively to find ways to help build it. Through such actions, senior citizens can become a useful part of society once again, bringing their wisdom to bear on important issues.

Senior citizens have wisdom and experience in abundance. America's senior citizens grew up in a time before plastics, a time when product durability and quality were more than mere advertising slogans. They grew up in the pre-disposable age and many participated in nationwide recycling during World War II. In short, senior citizens have a lot to share with the environmental community. They could become an important source of inspiration as we go back to the future.

Reaching the Religious Community. "Environmentalism suffers from being too resolutely secular," says Marshall Massey, co-founder of the Friends Committee on Unity with Nature. Massey points out that there are 100 million adults on the registers of American churches. Many of these people, he says, have little knowledge of environmental issues.

The religious community represents a huge pool of people that is not being fully reached. These people define what is good and what is bad, what is right and what is wrong on the basis of their religious thinking. The environmental community—its educators, leaders, and activists—could help broaden that view, ushering environmental concerns into the churches. Unfortunately, the environmentally concerned clergy are a small minority of the religious leaders. They often feel isolated and have trouble getting the attention they want for environmental issues.

Because of growing interest in environmental issues within the religious community, the time is ripe for building creative partnerships with the churches. The environmental community could form a national coalition of religious environmentalists. The coalition, in turn, could form an outreach group to work with the religious community, facilitating individual and political action at local, state, and international levels.[23]

Clergy, churchgoers, and environmentalists can meet in conferences to clarify the issues, discuss ways of integrating environmental and religious messages in Sunday services and draft solutions to environmental problems. Conference participants can develop strategies to promote political and individual action. Massey warns, however, that environmentalists must avoid the "we-know-better" attitude and must be prepared to engage in a give-and-take process with representatives of the religious community.

Several encouraging programs are now underway in the United States and abroad. The Ecojustice Working Group of the National Council of Churches, for example, is an interdenominational committee formed nine years ago. Ecojustice stands for both ecological and economic justice. The chief goal of this group is to disseminate information (for example, environmental information for Sunday schools) within the various member denominations and congregations.[24] The group also sponsors conferences and hearings and works on legislation. A year and a half ago, they invited community organizers to join to provide the group with first-hand experience on issues. Through their environmental stewardship network (called IMPACT), they reach approximately 10,000 contact people in local churches for a variety of social and environmental issues. Through these connections, they work to inspire individuals to get active politically.

On another front, since June 1987, the United Nations Environment Programme has proclaimed the first Sunday of each June as the Environmental Sabbath: Earth Rest Day.[25] The program's goal is quite simply "to change attitudes, to save the world," according to Dr. John J. Kirk who founded the program and teaches at Montclair State College in New Jersey. The lesson clergy are encouraged to give is that our planet is our primary shelter and its care and maintenance is our responsibility, both collectively and individually. Many churches throughout the nation now observe this special day.

In 1987, the Interfaith Council for the Protection of Animals and Nature in Ann Arbor, Michigan, published a booklet entitled *Replenish the Earth: The Bible's Message of Conservation and Kindness to Animals,* which discusses religion, the protection of nature, and the threat of present activities to human survival.[26] Through activities such as these and a greatly expanded effort to create ties with the religious community, environmental advocates may be able to build a much stronger base of support.

Teach Your Children Right. Expanding the environmental movement to include senior citizens, minorities, and the religious community is an important first step. It can help us make immediate changes, but it is a short-term solution. How can we ensure long-term success?

The answer lies in educating our children about the value of a clean, diverse, and healthy environment—and the value of other species. We must teach our children sustainable ethics and sustainable lifestyles. In short, we must begin building future generations of responsible citizens.

Educating children is the preventive medicine of environmentalism. This does not mean that education is *the* answer to our problems; rather, it is an integral part of a much larger set of changes needed to become more effective in creating lasting solutions to our environmental problems.[27]

Sam Hays, an environmental historian and author of *Beauty, Health, and Permanence,* a study of environmental politics in America from 1955 to 1985, agrees, "I think we've done a very poor job on environmental education. Most of what passes for environmental education is just nature education. If you look at the programs that have developed under the rubric of state environmental education, you'll see almost nothing that deals with issues." Although that's beginning to change, for years educators have spent little time driving home the point that the fundamental problem facing modern society lies in the relationship between humans and the limited environment within which we live, says Hays. For years there has been very little in primary and secondary education—even in colleges—that encouraged students to think about individual choices, about how those choices are made, and the ways our choices affect the environment.

Children have a natural empathy for animals and plants, says Craig Sarbeck of The Stewardship Community, an international organization dedicated to sustainable living. Nature lessons comprise much of what passes for environmental education, and they help unleash children's natural affinity and empathy for other living things. Nature education, says Larry Dieringer of Educators for Social Responsibility, helps raise awareness of the existence of a natural environment and it raises awareness of species interconnections.[28] But traditional nature programs aimed at teaching students the names of common plants and animals in their community are not enough. Students are bombarded by the press with information about environmental problems and don't know how to analyze them. They need information on issues and skills to analyze them critically. Thus, nature education, while essential, is just the first step in a much larger process of educational change.

Nature study can help teachers teach their students the principles of ecology and, most importantly, how these principles relate to human society.[29] The lessons we glean from our study of nature can show us a better way to live. Classroom lessons can, therefore, begin with a study of nature and progress to a study of human society. By showing how human society is affected by natural forces and bound by ecological principles, teachers can touch their students' lives. Educational programs can provide direction, showing ways to correct the ills that plague our society and showing how to ensure permanence through sustainability.

Effective environmental education, especially for younger children, must grapple directly with issues. Without a broader, more issue-oriented curriculum, "we're missing opportunities to make a difference in student's lives," according to Dieringer.

By discussing the impacts humans have on the environment and the ways our impacts often come back to haunt us, teachers open the classroom to the real world. Such lessons are as important as history and English classes, health and physical fitness, and trigonometry and algebra. Creative teachers can find ways to integrate basic knowledge—lessons in reading, history, English, science, and mathematics—with environmental issues in ways that make lessons more interesting to students. These integrated lessons can provide students with information and skills they will use throughout their lives.

It is not enough simply to describe the environmental crisis, we must teach our children the ways out, including personal actions students can take to minimize their impact on the earth. Educators can find ways to teach students about sustainable ethics. Some teachers may be uncomfortable with teaching ethics, but with time and experience, the awkwardness and discomfort will subside.[30] Without an understanding of the complex interaction of modern society and the life-giving environment, without an appreciation of the delicate balance of life and our responsibility to build a sustainable society, students may grow up naive, feeling out-of-place in a world of rapid change and great personal and political challenge. These are not ordinary lessons; they are lessons on survival.

Fortunately, many important changes in environmental education are under way. The state of Washington, for example, recently published guidelines for environmental education in the public school system. This project results from interest on the part of the state legislature and the State Board of Education in making environmental education a topic of instruction in the public schools. The booklet outlines four basic goals and shows ways teachers can help achieve them. The first goal is to develop knowledge of the environment. The second goal is to develop an appreciation of the importance of nature in our lives and our economy. The third goal is to teach students how individual actions can affect the environment, positively and negatively. The fourth goal is to develop the knowledge and skills students will need to work with others to protect the environment.

Educators can also help students deal with environmental issues by teaching critical thinking skills, which are often missing in public policy debates and in the media.[31] Critical thinking requires individuals to examine the immediate and long-term impacts of human actions, helping us develop anticipatory thinking. It requires us to examine ecological relationships, thus helps us think holistically. Critical thinking demands a broader view of cause and effect. Critical thinking examines the importance of understanding bias when interpreting information we are given by scientists, teachers, the press, and others. By teaching students to become more critical thinkers, educators will help develop a more enlightened public debate and better public policies. (See Appendix C for an elaboration on critical thinking skills.)

Educators for Social Responsibility, headed by Larry Dieringer, is one of the groups helping to teach students ways to analyze local and international issues and ways to affect the decision-making process. ESR began in 1982 to help introduce nuclear war and peace issues in American classrooms. Since then, the focus has expanded to include a variety of environmental issues. ESR is committed to encouraging a healthy interchange of ideas. The group believes that there is too much polarity around issues and that it is important for students to learn to work with people who disagree on important issues. ESR teaches students to understand that many different perspectives arise on each issue. Students are taught to ask questions and especially to question deeply held assumptions and biases. From this it is hoped that students will develop a deeper understanding of issues.

A study of the environment is incomplete if it deals just with the sciences, for the decision-making process is also based on values and emotions. To be truly effective in teaching our students to grapple with real-life issues, students must find ways to clarify the role of both values and emotions in public policy.

A study of the environment will inevitably touch students very deeply. Some students will be dismayed, depressed, and overwhelmed by the issues. Some will feel hopelessness and despair. Left unattended, these emotions can lead to apathy and inaction, described in the last chapter. Avoiding this emotional dead end is a necessity; teachers must find ways to instill realistic hope that leads to action, just as the environmental community must find ways of breaking the cycle of apathy and despair in the public.

On a final note, the study of the environment must be a fusion of the heart and mind. A dispassionate recitation of facts and figures about the environmental crisis is simply not enough. Slide shows, videos, and stories of environmental disasters, such as the tragedy at Bhopal in 1984 and events at Chernobyl in 1986, illustrate the impact of human actions and touch emotions deeply. The environmental crisis is, in large part, the result of a failure to care deeply for the environment. In the name of progress, our emotional attachment to the land, air, and water and all other life forms is often denigrated. "Tree huggers" and "animal lovers" are the labels applied to those who show compassion for our only home, the earth. To deny deep feelings, however, is to repudiate our humanity, to artificially separate the mind into two distinct and warring factions: feelings and logic. It is to make us less whole and integrated. To teach about the environment in such a vein is to foster an artificial separation that is, in many respects, responsible for the mess we have made of our environment.

Our emotions are the root of our virtue. To separate power from virtue is to ensure that power will be without virtue, and that virtue will be powerless, according to Marilyn French, author of *Beyond Power: On Women, Men and Morals*. The good of humanity will fall to greed.

Sustainable ethics, described in Chapter 2, encompass the need for a sense of compassion that reaches to the entire earth. Facts alone will not convince the student of the need for dramatic change. Emotion, such as love and unconditional respect, will.

Along the Rouge River in Detroit, dozens of high-school students regularly take water samples, which they test in their chemistry class for nine pollutants. Students from different schools monitor different sections in this collaborative effort. Water quality analyses allow students to detect illegal dumping and to discover leaks in sewer pipes, which they bring to the attention of public officials. The project is an example of environmental education at its best. Not only does it teach science, but it shows how students can play a role in their own lives in protecting their environment.

Changing People's Lives

Environmentalism has largely set its sights on the law. We've engaged primarily in a series of costly and time-consuming legal and legislative skirmishes aimed at passing new legislation and enacting new regulations. In recent years, our efforts have largely focused on getting the laws that were passed in the 1970s enforced.

Clearly, it's time to broaden our compass. It's time to expand into the public arena to find ways to promote individual responsibility and action, creating real consensus for the environment.

Steps to Transformation. The road to a sustainable society is a long one, made more rugged by years of destructive social influence that stresses personal pleasure and a kind of *laissez faire* ethics that says, "Whatever happens happens, so don't get upset."

Anne Grady, of Denver's Better Air Campaign, believes that the path to personal change follows roughly a five-step process, each dependent on the preceding one: (1) awareness, (2) understanding, (3) attitude change, (4) intention shift, and (5) participation.

Raising people's awareness is the first important step in deepening the level of commitment and bringing about social change. First of all, says Grady, you need to get people's attention. You can't do anything unless people are aware. This is relatively easy, given the nature of environmental problems. It's made easier by dramatic symbols like the Valdez oil slick that poisoned wildlife and fish, and homeless garbage scows like the Islip barge that wander the globe looking for a receptive port, giving off the foul smell of rotting trash.

Next, people have to understand what the issues are and what they are being asked to do. They need to understand the benefits of action as well. What will they get out of changes personally? How will their children and future generations benefit? George Bernard Shaw contends that "a man's interest in the world is only the overflow from his interest in himself." Our job is to make the two interests seem as one, as described in Chapter 3. Our job is to instill the notion that planet care is a form of self-care. What's also important at this stage is that individuals recognize that they *can* make a difference.

With an understanding of the issues and possible solutions, individuals next must change their attitude about a problem and its solution. They must say, "Yes, this is a problem and yes, it can be solved these ways." If environmental writers, activists, educators, and leaders have done a good job helping people understand the problems and solutions, an attitude change is very likely. But a huge gap exists between attitude and behavior.

Even if people believe that what they are doing will have an effect, they must truly intend to change. In short, they must commit to change. That's where many people get stuck. Commitment is such a dubious thing. We want to commit, but just can't. Without a commitment to change, people will not reach the fifth and final stage in this long, but important process: participation.

Between our good intentions to participate and our actual participation many of us get lost. "People make excuses," says Grady about the program's voluntary no-drive day. "They couldn't find the bus, they stood up for the bus, the bus didn't come, they didn't get the right information."

Participation of the Environmental Community. At each stage in this progression of changes, the environmental community can play an important role. Too often, though, we seem to be caught up in the first two stages—awareness and understanding. Our newsletters, our lectures, our magazine articles, our speeches, and our press releases describe the frightening problems, perhaps with the blind hope that awareness and knowledge is enough to get people stirred into action. While it works for some, it's not enough for many others.

The environmental community can help people change attitudes, the third stage in transformation. By showing how problems affect individuals and especially ways individual actions can help solve our problems, the environmental community can help people through stage 3. By opening the possibilities, we open the door to change. "Yes, I can see how global warming will affect me. And yes, I can see how ozone depletion will affect me and my children. Yes, I can see how I can make a difference." All that can help topple the skeptical barriers that keep people from changing their behavior.

The intention shift poses the biggest barrier for public interest groups. A decision to do something requires commitment. If the stakes are explained well and if the role of each individual—either in supporting legislation or in changing individual lifestyles—is clearly outlined, and if people see others making changes, they are more likely to make a commitment.

Pleas for financial support by environmental groups could be reworded in ways that call on people to commit. Environmental groups can ask for money but should also inspire individual action. In September 1989, the Sierra Club sent postcards to its members listing eight actions that people can take to help fight global warming. Seven of the eight involved personal actions: writing letters, adding insulation, switching to natural gas for heating, taking public transportation, and the like. The eighth was a plea for money to support the Sierra Club's Global Warming Action Campaign. This is a good example of the way environmental groups can get both messages across, the need for individual responsibility and action and the need for money to support political campaigns. As noted above, however, we must also find ways to get these same messages to the public.

Environmental educators, writers, and activists can help the process of change by starting to talk more about commitment.

The Better Air Campaign aired radio ads describing carbon monoxide pollution, noting that the average automobile produces approximately one pound of this colorless, tasteless, but highly poisonous gas every eleven to seventeen miles. The ad ends by asking citizens, "What are you going to do about it?" In all the hoopla over Earth Day 1990, the twentieth anniversary of the first Earth Day, the National Wildlife Federation reminded many that Earth Day should be every day. Commitment must run deep. Without it, our long-term future will only be a dream.

Educators and public speakers can help. Environmental groups can help train leaders at all levels in techniques that inspire people to commitment and action. Local and national leaders can attend workshops that focus on commitment—especially ways to inspire commitment in others.

Participation is the final step. It depends on the previous steps and yet is not guaranteed by intention. We can help bridge the gap between intention and action by providing opportunities for change, by providing suggestions, by gentle prodding, and by providing feedback on the successes of others. And, we as individuals and groups can set a good example. By using recycled paper, by reducing wasteful direct mail, and by whatever other examples we can find, the environmental community can serve as a model for commitment. David Adamson of The Nature Conservancy says, "The message that all groups have to give is that in our individual consumption we make a difference. By conscientious buying decisions we can help reduce the need to extract resources. That lessens the overall load on the world." Most important, says Adamson, "It's a lesson we've all got to start broadcasting . . . and living."

Conventional Morality Caves In. One of the chief stumbling blocks to personal change is a kind of a national obsession with satisfying our pleasures. Erich Fromm, world renowned for his books on social psychology, said that the concern in this society is mainly with physical things and with money.[32] Money is even thought to be a measure of your social value or your self-worth.

If you're rich, says social psychologist Leon Swartzendruber, then you're somebody who amounts to something in the eyes of most people in this society. If you're poor, somehow you've missed the boat, you're a failure. That's the conventional morality that dominates American thinking. With personal worth linked to materialism, it might seem that there is little room for social justice, environmental concern, and a belief in well-being based on psychological health and other nonmonetary attributes. "I can't say that I had a lot of success, nor do I know of any other psychologists who have good methods of getting people concerned about principles instead of conventional morality," says Swartzendruber.

"Conventional morality means that you accept the moral standards of the people around you regardless of what those standards are; regardless of whether they're consistent or not," he explains. "I think today that the conventional morality is that it's okay to consume as much of the planet's wealth as you want, because that's the American dream. I think that's going to have to be changed." Consumption is almost a religion in this country. We are facing an uphill battle, but it's a battle that must be waged and won.

But what we can do, according to Swartzendruber, is get the 20 to 25 percent of the population who are generally concerned about principles to set a public example. They can serve as role models, and each of us, in turn, can influence the behavior of people around us. As environmentally responsible behaviors become socially acceptable, more people will become concerned about them and, quite possibly, will change their lives. Individuals can become agents of social transformation, changing society from the bottom up, while litigators and lobbyists (with the help of public pressure) create change from the top down.

"You're not going to do much by yourself," admits David Brower, "but you can be an instigator. You can be a catalyst. Get the reaction going, but don't let it burn you up."

The estimated 8 to 11 million environmentalists in the United States are catalysts for change.[33] Lester Milbrath of the State University of New York calls them a vanguard of a new society.[34] If each lives consistently with his or her values and changes the lives of ten people—friends and relatives—we have reached one-third to one-half of the U.S. population. And if each of these people reaches another ten people, the problem is licked.[35]

Environmental Media

In years past, the environmental community has had to rely on the whims of television, magazines, and newspapers, but public environmental education cannot remain solely in the hands of the media. For one, they're a fickle lot, chasing sensational stories sometimes at the expense of the more important ones. Global warming wasn't an issue on national news, for instance, until farmland started to dry up and crops withered on the parched landscape. Ozone and trash didn't make the news much until disaster had struck. Even in 1988, a year when environmental problems such as ozone depletion, improper medical waste disposal, and global warming became household words, the environment ranked thirteenth out of eighteen categories on the evening news, according to a study by the United Nations Environment Programme. Natural disasters, crime, wars, terrorism, drugs, and sex were just some of the issues that received more news time.

This lack of coverage suggests the need for our own reporting system. Some groups are already tackling the job. The Northcoast Environmental Center in northern California, for example, publishes a monthly newsletter that is sent to members and also distributed free to the community. The Center also sponsors a public affairs program on a national public radio station. The program is one-half hour long, and airs twice weekly. Tim McKay, executive director of the group, also broadcasts environmental commentary on a local news and information station, which airs every other week. David Moore, the executive director of the New Jersey Conservation Foundation writes weekly environmental editorials for newspapers in his state. Many local groups could follow suit. David Brower believes that the environmental community needs a weekly newspaper for the general public. By covering peace, justice, and environmental issues, he thinks, we garner a sizable audience—large enough to make it work. Local environmental groups may want to publish weekly or monthly newspapers and distribute them to the public at least on a limited basis. The national environmental organizations could join forces to produce a national newspaper—or to convince major newspapers to publish a daily section on the environment.

After a dramatic outpouring of books on the environment in the late 1960s and early 1970s, many mainstream publishers suddenly became disinterested. Interest in the environment waned in the late 1970s, eclipsed by the rising cost of oil and a crippling inflation rate. Diet books and books on ways to get rich quick became the mainstay of many large publishing companies. Throughout the 1980s, publishers continued to shy away from environmental titles.

In this vacuum, Island Press arose. Island Press, a nonprofit publishing venture of the Center for Resource Economics in Washington, D.C., produces books that New York publishers typically shy away from, for fear of low returns on investment. Island Press publishes timely and authoritative books on many urgent topics. Their books and catalog are printed on acid-free recycled paper. Working with many of the leading environmental groups, they are bringing new and useful information to the public. Island Press' 1990 catalog lists 159 books on a variety of subjects, including sustainable agriculture, land planning, biodiversity, and toxic waste management.[36] Many of the books in their catalog are produced by other publishers, thus permitting wider distribution. All in all, the founding of Island Press is one of the single most important events in the history of the environmental movement. In 1990 an independent group began publishing *E Magazine*.[37] It could also become an important contribution to environmental reporting.

Some critics believe that we have a need for a TV environmental journal, a television weekly that discusses important environmental issues and solutions. Public television now broadcasts a fair amount on the environment. A weekly program on public television sponsored by the environmental community might help deepen the debate. Public television, however, represents just a fraction of the audience that we need to reach. "A way of getting beyond the public broadcasting system needs to be invented," says Brower. "Somebody has to invent it." Ted Turner's weekly cable television program, Earthbeat, may be a start.

Brower thinks that arousing corporate environmental consciousness could help. As corporations realize that they have to operate in ways that are consistent with the earth's limited and often abused life support system, they might help sponsor environmental documentaries that could be aired during prime time television, thus helping us reach a larger audience.

But Brower isn't very optimistic. He thinks that the environmental community needs to build its alternative communications system. "The media are pretty much pre-empted by the Fortune 500," argues Brower. "Whether we like it or not or whether they admit it or not, their editorial policy is . . . determined by their advertising revenue. They can't operate without advertising revenue. They can't attack the big advertisers and get the ads. And there they are trapped. They'll say the editorial department is not influenced by the advertising department, but don't believe it. It has to be or they're out of business."

We have to find a way to discuss issues and alternatives in a meaningful way. We can't continue the glib and superficial coverage so common today in the newspapers and television media. Vladimir Posner, a Soviet citizen who grew up in the country was asked a question at the Choices conference sponsored by the Windstar Foundation in 1988. He, former Colorado governor Richard Lamm, and Atlanta mayor Andrew Young were asked the same question: "If you had a minute and you had all the world listening to you on radio and television, what would you say?" When it came to Posner, he said, so you've got the most important question in the world and you're giving me a minute. Forget it.

We are talking about life and death issues. The one-minute answer is inadequate. It encourages simplistic thinking and even simpler solutions. As H.L. Mencken once remarked, "There's always an easy solution to every human problem—neat, plausible, and wrong."

Somehow we've got to break through the simple lines of cause and effect. We've got to supplant the capitalistic dream of continuing economic growth with sustainable practices.[38] That will help us keep from falling into the Mencken trap and help us move from a nation of environmental sympathizers to a nation of environmental protagonists who live their lives in accordance with the demands of a finite world.

Every reform was once a private opinion.

RALPH WALDO EMERSON

5 | The Third Wave of Environmentalism: Beyond Reactionism

President Ronald Reagan was both the best and the worst thing that ever happened to the environmental movement. In his years in office, Reagan systematically fought to dismantle the EPA, gut the Clean Air Act, hamper efforts to solve acid deposition, and to clean up hazardous waste sites. To assist in this task, Reagan appointed a mob of environmental henchmen to key posts in the EPA and Department of Interior. Under the banner of reducing red tape and federal bureaucracy, and with the assistance of his loyal following of antienvironmental bureaucrats, Reagan tried to pull the rug out from under the environmental gains of the previous decade. Reagan's anti-environmental agenda succeeded in many ways. It did not seem to matter that many of the hard-won gains bore the stamp of earlier Republican administrations, notes Doug Wheeler, vice president of The Conservation Foundation and former executive director of the Sierra Club.[1]

The Reagan years were also a boon to the environmental movement. Reagan's blatantly antienvironmental policies, for example, became the focal point of significant public attention. Even many Reagan supporters were appalled by his lack of sensitivity to environmental issues. The administration's obstinacy on environmental issues, observes Wheeler, is probably more responsible than any other single factor for the growth in the environmental movement in the 1980s. Few tragedies could have stirred so much proenvironmental sentiment. As Reagan's policies went into effect, membership in national and state environmental groups skyrocketed. Sierra Club membership climbed from 100,000 to 500,000 in eight years.[2] Audubon membership hit the half-million mark and Greenpeace grew to over three million members.[3]

Lessons from the Reagan Era

The horror of Ronald Reagan's antienvironmental policies was soon replaced by action, as activists dug in their heels for what would be a long and costly battle. "It is almost miraculous," says Peter Coppelman, vice president of The Wilderness Society, "that we have fought Reagan to a draw on most issues, and even managed some major advances—for example, reauthorization of the Clean Water Act and the Endangered Species Act, and the addition of ten million acres to the National Wilderness Preservation System."

Still, the fighting took its toll. "It has taken all of our resources, creativity, power, and influence," observes Coppleman, "to stave off the environmental disaster so ardently sought by the Reagan administration." A tremendous amount of resources were consumed in those years, trying to hold the line against Reagan's actions. Important opportunities to move this nation to a sustainable lifestyle were lost.

The Reagan years taught us an indispensable lesson, something that many had feared all along: environmental laws are useless without regulations and enforcement. For years, environmentalists have spent incredible resources to pass new laws. But they have not paid enough attention to their implementation. Cynthia Wilson, former executive director of the Friends of the Earth, argues that the regulatory process that follows a law's enactment is less glamorous and considerably more tedious than the work required to get a law passed.[4] The regulatory process requires in-depth knowledge of resource management, pollution, toxicology, and government regulations. Because of these factors and others and because of the rapid pace with which new problems unfold, environmentalists often move on to new legislative battles before the ink from the President's pen dries on a law. Perhaps a bit naively, many of us trusted that the government, given its instructions from the Congress and the President, would do as it was told. But we were wrong—dead wrong in many cases. The Reagan era showed us that regulation and enforcement were matters of extreme importance. Without them, lawmaking was almost meaningless. Without follow-up, we are wasting our time.

During the Reagan years, environmentalists displayed their political muscle. The Environmental Defense Fund, working with several other groups, for example, successfully sued the EPA, forcing them to draft standards for a whole host of recycled products, such as office paper, that could be used by the federal government to help stimulate demand nationwide. The guidelines, required by the Resource Conservation and Recovery Act, came more than 12 years after the EPA had been instructed by Congress to write them. Without the lawsuit to force compliance, it's safe to say that we would not have the standards today!

The Natural Resources Defense Council, Friends of the Earth, and other groups have also won numerous lawsuits to tighten the regulatory noose. Under the citizen-suit provision of the Clean Water Act, says Wilson, these groups have brought numerous lawsuits against industrial polluters in New York and New Jersey and have won fines on average four times greater than the EPA and Justice Department were awarded in comparable cases.[5]

The environmental movement successfully fought the administration over its plans to dismantle the environmental gains of the 1970s. But at the same time, the environmental community must bear some responsibility for the stagnation that prevailed in the Reagan era. According to Doug Wheeler, a more effective Clean Air Act had been a first priority of the environmental movement throughout the Reagan years, but no bill reached the president's desk. Wheeler also notes that there had been no substantial progress in reducing indoor air pollution, protecting groundwater supplies, reducing the threat of pesticide misuse, cleaning up toxic waste dumps, preventing degradation of wildlife refuges and national parks, cutting back on soil erosion, protecting dwindling wetlands, safely disposing of toxic and nuclear waste, or tempering the adverse effects of urban sprawl.

"To be sure," says Wheeler, "environmentalists cannot be expected to make headway on each of these increasingly complex issues in the face of strong opposition from the Reagan administration on nearly every front." But even leaders of the environmental movement suggest that progress is not what it might have been. Michael McCloskey, former executive director of the Sierra Club acknowledges that "In the late 1980s, the environmental movement is under attack for having delivered lots of laws and words but not enough results when it comes to improving the physical environment." Wheeler is partly correct in laying blame on failing bureaucracies and government, but there is also considerable evidence that the environmental community has failed to make optimal use of its own rather substantial resources.

In the coming years, environmental groups will need to continue to hold the line against congressional backsliding. We will need to continue monitoring state and federal agencies to ensure that they are enforcing existing laws and regulations, and we will need to continue to put pressure on government and the corporate sector to obey the laws. Without a doubt, new laws and major overhauls will be needed. More than anything, however, environmentalism needs to move out of the trenches and needs to become more of a proactive force.

Broadening Our Approach

For many years, environmentalism has been something of a knee-jerk reaction to troubles. When a new problem was uncovered, we flocked to Congress or state legislatures to pressure governments to pass new laws. Our lawyers flocked to the courtrooms to file injunctions to halt harmful activities or to sue offenders. Still others among our ranks set out to protest, calling public attention to important issues.[6] Laws, lawsuits, and protests have been the cornerstone of environmental response and have played a key role in our success in the past two decades.[7]

Breaking the Dependency. "The dependence upon legal approaches," says Dave Brower, "has been forced upon us. You've got to go to the Courts. That's the only reason we haven't had an environmental disaster with the eight Reagan years."

Paul Watson, founder of the Sea Shepherd Conservation Society, the oceanic equivalent of Earth First!, agrees. "Environmentalists have been forced into fighting rear-guard actions," constantly responding to oil spills, toxic waste dumps, and the wholesale massacre of animals.

"It is because of the proliferation of these brushfires . . . and always having to spend time putting them out," says Watson, "that it is very difficult for many environmentalists to actually take the time to project future problems and to deal with those problems before they develop."

The sooner we reverse the situation and decrease our dependency on reaction, the better off we will be.

Lawsuits and legal actions are only part of a bigger, comprehensive plan of action to solve our nation's growing environmental problems. The previous chapters have outlined the need for an articulated vision of sustainability, individual action, and a broader constituency. We are not, however, going to accomplish much within the western economic, political, and spiritual system, which is largely anti-earth and anti-nature. What's needed is a major transformation of modern society making it pro-earth and pro-nature. Broad-scale changes in ideology and commitment can help us foster this change.

David Adamson of the Nature Conservancy sums it up well. "The environmental movement hasn't articulated a vision of how humans and nature should work together. We haven't articulated the ways to build a sustainable society. I think we are working on that, but the environmental movement has been sort of a palliative or a stop-gap, a way to redress the most serious ills of this industrial society. I think there's a much broader and deeper issue here which is how do humanity and nature work together? That's the next stage."

The Next Wave of Environmentalism. The next stage of environmentalism may already be under way. All across America environmentalists, environmental educators, and governmental leaders are beginning to seek alternatives—ways in which humans can work with nature.

One of America's leaders in proactive solutions is the Environmental Defense Fund. Although best known it for its legal action, EDF has become a major player in the reshaping of American society through its efforts to present alternatives to environmentally harmful projects. The Rocky Mountain Institute, the World Resources Institute, and the Rodale Foundation are also important participants in developing and promoting alternative technologies and lifestyles.

Frederic Krupp, director of the Environmental Defense Fund, believes that U.S. environmentalists must embrace a major shift in tactics.[8] Environmentalism, he says, is entering a constructive third stage in its evolution.

The first stage of environmentalism, according to Krupp, was a reaction to decades of rapacious exploitation of natural resources. President Theodore Roosevelt was among the first to announce his outrage. This reaction spawned the National Audubon Society and was instrumental in transforming the Sierra Club from an outing club to a more politically active organization.

In the 1960s, people began to realize that they were also becoming victims of environmental abuse. Thus arose the second stage of environmentalism. It gave birth to the Environmental Defense Fund and other similar groups, which fought to ban the use of DDT and other environmental contaminants. "The EDF's original vision—to present the evidence of environmental science in a court of law—proved to be an effective strategy to halt and even reverse environmental damage," writes Krupp. Lawsuits, lobbying, peaceful protests, and other direct actions were the chief expressions of environmental concern during this era.

"Most environmental organizations still emphasize this form of reaction, but a new age of environmentalism may be dawning," notes Krupp. The "New Environmentalists" Krupp envisions hold that we cannot be effective simply by opposing environmental abuses. We must seek alternative ways of meeting the legitimate needs of society, replacing ill-advised projects (dams, for instance) with environmentally compatible ones (water conservation).

By opposing environmental abuses and not finding environmentally and economically sound alternatives, we are treating only the symptoms of problems, which are bound to surface again and again. By satisfying the needs of society in environmentally safer ways, we are helping to find lasting cures that foster the transition to a sustainable society.

Meeting the legitimate needs of people through environmentally and economically sound alternatives helps build a resourcewise infrastructure in the rich as well as the poor nations of the world. Environmental educators, activists, leaders, and governmental officials would be well advised to continue promoting population stabilization.[9] Unwieldy growth is one of the root causes of all environmental problems. Not until we achieve a stable population can we reach sustainability. In the meantime, here are some examples of work that is helping pave the way toward a more sustainable society.

Convincing the California Utilities to Find Renewable Alternatives. In the late 1970s, Pacific Gas and Electric Company, one of the nation's largest utilities, presented plans to build a number of coal-fired and nuclear power plants to meet projected demand for electricity in California. The various projects would have cost an estimated $20 billion. The environmental impacts would have been enormous.

"Forces on both sides," says Krupp, "were strong and deeply entrenched. Then, an EDF team—a lawyer, an economist, and a computer analyst—developed an unprecedented package of alternative energy sources and conservation investments . . ." They argued that their plan could meet the projected demands for electricity *and* do so at a lower price for consumers. Surprisingly, their proposal would also yield higher returns for stock holders and promised a healthier financial future for the company itself. After some careful thought and analysis, the company agreed and adopted the plan.

EDF's plan had several effects. It blocked construction of the polluting plants, and helped illustrate the folly of the bigger-is-better mindset so prevalent among electric power planners. It was one of the first and truly most important steps the environmental community has made in beginning to reshape American society and build a sustainable economy.

Alternatives to Colorado's Two Forks Project. The Environmental Defense Fund joined with a number of environmental groups in Colorado to form the Environmental Caucus. They waged a battle against Colorado's highly controversial Two Forks Project, a large dam and reservoir project southwest of Denver, mentioned in the previous chapter. The project would turn a beautiful canyon, visited by tens of thousands of people each summer, into an ugly reservoir whose water levels would fluctuate hundreds of feet, creating an unsightly, barren shoreline. The project also would threaten the habitat of sandhill cranes and endangered whooping cranes in Nebraska. The river in Nebraska could dry up in the summer, allowing vegetation to take hold on sandy islands now used as nesting sites for several endangered birds. Predators would have easier access to nests as well. Fish in the Platte River would die as a result of falling water levels and endangered least terns and piping plovers would have inadequate food supplies for their young.

The Environmental Caucus (a coalition of 15 environmental groups) assembled a group of engineers, economists, and water experts to draw up an alternative plan that would meet the water needs of the Denver metro area with a minimum of environmental impacts. The plan called for conservation, water exchanges, water reuse, and the construction of several smaller dams, to be built as needed.

Their work helped convince ex-real estate developer, now-governor Roy Romer, to urge similar alternatives to Two Forks.[10] In the summer of 1989, EPA regional administrator Lee De Hihns announced plans to veto the project, in large part because of the many alternatives available to Denver. Water conservation measures in the Caucus plan, in fact, have become the blueprint for Denver's new water conservation program.

Investing for Prosperity: New Levels of Cooperation. In 1978, Huey Johnson, Secretary for Natural Resources for the state of California began a program called Investing for Prosperity. It was the first of its kind, a monumental achievement in natural resource conservation. Diverse interest groups, including industry, banks, agriculture, labor, and environmental groups, joined forces to convince the state legislature to spend $400 million over four years to carry out the program.[11]

One of the projects provided money to help Californians revegetate private forest land. The state of California has 13 million acres of timberland, but only about 8 million were forested at the time. The remaining acreage needed planting, but the owners, for one reason or another, could not afford to borrow money to do it. Under the program, the state provided $5 million to replant this land, turning barren hillsides highly susceptible to erosion into productive forest. The money is also being used to ensure that the forests are managed on a sustainable basis.

Besides the environmental benefits of regenerating forests, this project also provides a sustainable income to many local communities. A recent study, in fact, showed that over the next 50 to 75 years, the $5 million investment will return more than $400 million in timber sales and $100 million in tax revenues. If these estimates are correct, the project must be considered an overwhelming success in forest management. Moreover, it is a model for other states.

Agendas and Blueprints. In recent years, the environmental community has begun to take a more active role in public policy by drafting environmental agendas and blueprints. *An Environmental Agenda for the Future,* published in 1985 by Island Press, was a fairly comprehensive proposal for new environmental legislation and policy. The Agenda, discussed in previous chapters, represents the views of ten leading environmental groups. Although it ignores personal contributions to environmental problem-solving and doesn't outline a vision of a sustainable society, it is an important step in the environmental movement's evolution—a process that could turn the movement into a more proactive force for change.

The Agenda was followed by a more ambitious project called *Blueprint for the Environment,* published in the fall of 1988. *Blueprint* was a list of recommendations to then President-Elect George Bush from 18 environmental groups, drawing on the resources of twice that number. It presents over 700 recommendations for federal action and offers ready assistance to implement them.

Blueprint is available in three forms, making it more accessible to a wider audience. There is a booklet of about thirty pages, which outlines the major problems and recommendations. The document is also available in a 300-page paperback, which describes 300 of the issues. Finally, the complete recommendations are also available on disk, which contains a considerable amount of background material on each issue and is equivalent to 2,200 printed pages.

Opinions of the *Blueprint* vary. Sam Hays, an environmental historian from the University of Pittsburgh, thinks it is a positive change. Dave Foreman of Earth First!, on the other hand, thinks it's just so much fertilizer. "It's madness," he says. "We have to recognize that we are on a collision course right now. That modern society is not sustainable. That we are in a crisis and that we've got to change our way of living," says Foreman. The report sends the message that "we can maintain our American standard of living and our growth economy and our preeminence in the world and still save natural diversity."

The vision of *Blueprint* may be too mainstream. It may fail to challenge the blindness that is causing our problems. It may suffer from a lack of understanding of the true dimensions of the environmental crisis, but it is an important work for at least two reasons: First, it is the product of unprecedented cooperation, of numerous groups working together. Second, it spells out in great detail the environmental position and offers numerous suggestions for structural change. Many changes could help bring about a sustainable society.

Rekindling the Fires. All across America, it's happening. Environmentalists are taking a more active role in developing proactive solutions. Nonetheless, there are dangers lurking in our midst. One danger is that in our efforts to become team players, we may be giving up too much. We may be losing our vision, and our solutions may fall short.[12] We may, in fact, have become overly compliant and prone to expediency as we wend our way through political channels.

Angela Medbery, long-time environmental activist and co-founder of the Colorado Pesticide Network, says "I see a lot of leaders who are very interested in being a member of the bargaining table. They have sacrificed being bluntly true in what's going on to the point that they may even not be telling themselves what's going on."

The political softening has put us in the position of "rearranging the deck chairs on the Titanic," according to Dave Foreman. We hire staff more political than environmental, people who don't have the "fire in their bellies anymore." Joy Williams, novelist and essayist, published a satirical essay called "Save the Whales, Screw the Shrimp" in *Esquire*.[13] In it she notes that environmentalists must be calm, rational, reasonable, and willing to compromise, otherwise society won't listen to them.

In our desire to remain credible and to be part of the mainstream, says Foreman, environmental groups are compromising before they need to. RARE II identified 80 million acres of roadless areas suitable for wilderness, but The Wilderness Society and the Sierra Club set their sights on 35 million acres, even though "we would have liked all of it," says Foreman, who spent nearly a decade working in the mainstream of environmental movement including the Wilderness Society before cofounding Earth First! When the negotiations began, the groups had pared down their request, asking for only half of the 35 million acres "to appear more reasonable," says Foreman.

What did they get? "Fifteen million acres of rock and ice."

Foreman thinks that groups like Earth First! have helped the mainstream groups to start talking with more vision, and still remain in the mainstream. "You're seeing . . . more visionary proposals than you once would have seen from these groups," he says. Sierra Club is starting to ask for what they want. Earth First!, Greenpeace, and the Sea Shepherds may be helping to rekindle the fires!

In the 1970s, society badly needed environmental action groups and public-interest law firms to meet the problems of the time. "Today," writes EDF's Frederic Krupp, "the need is for these institutions to envision solutions and to assemble new coalitions—even coalitions with former enemies—to bring about answers to environmental problems." Krupp warns against softening, however. "The third stage of environmentalism is in no sense a move toward compromise, a search for the in-between position. We will still need skillful advocacy—even in court—against narrow institutional vision or vested interest in the status quo." In the same paragraph, however, Krupp notes that "What the American public wants . . . is both to expand our economic well-being and to preserve our natural resources and public health. It is up to us as environmentalists to prove this is no paradox and find the innovative ways to do both."

Polls by Lester Milbrath, of the State University of New York at Buffalo, tell a different tale.[14] His surveys of the American people in the early 1980s show that the thrust for continued economic growth comes principally from the business community. The data from his survey showed that the American people choose environmental protection over economic growth by a ratio of 3 to 1. Surveys showed the people of West Germany preferred environmental protection by a ratio of 2 to 1 in 1982, and in Great Britain the ratio was nearly 5 to 1.

It would appear that many people are more concerned about a healthy environment than a growing economy. Our business leaders, however, may be perpetrating a myth. They have convinced government that economic growth is the central preoccupation of the public.[15] The environmental community cannot afford to buy into this myth. It's the in-between position that Krupp warned about earlier, but seems to endorse when he sanctions continued economic growth.[16]

A more appropriate message might be that it's up to the environmental community to show the American public that we can live in closer harmony with the natural world, that individual actions to make a better world add up, that sacrifices for the good of the whole will have to be made, but that people can live comfortable and, indeed, enjoyable lives. We ought to promote the need for a healthy economy and a healthy environment. Health implies stability, not endless growth.

Environmentalism has to go beyond reactionism, beyond just saying "you can't do this, you can't do that." We in the environmental community—teachers, group members, writers, scientists, and activists—have to look at ways in which we can help meet the legitimate needs of a society and preserve the ecological health of the planet. It's (almost) as simple as that.

Building a Healthy Economy

At times, many of us in the environmental community seem to forget why we are involved in protecting the environment. "It's for the love of life on the planet," says Nature Conservancy's Adamson. "It's for the love of people, as well as the endangered animals. It's for the love of quiet places, for mountains and wildflowers."

Environmentalists are concerned about the shape of the world in 50 years, 500 years, 5000 years, asserts Paul Watson of the Sea Shepherd Conservation Society. But in our rush to protect the environment from ourselves, however, our rhetoric is often misanthropic or boiling with an undercurrent of contempt for humanity, technology, and narrow economic pursuits.[17] Many of us in the environmental field view economic activity as something of an evil necessity. We perpetuate the notion that what's good for the economy is bad for the environment. Indeed, much of our economic growth has been based on unsustainable resources—oil, for instance—and unsustainable practices: overfishing the seas, overharvesting forests, overgrazing rangeland and pasture, and overfarming land. Human economic progress often forecloses on the environment, justifying concerns of environmentalists the world over. Dams along the Columbia River and its tributaries, for example, provided cheap electricity that helped the Pacific Northwest develop economically, but devastated the salmon fishery, reducing the number of salmon in the watershed from 10 to 15 million per year to about 2.5 million. In this instance, economic development not only harmed the environment, but impeded other economic sectors—notably the fishing industry. Deforestation of Brazil's rain forests to provide rangeland for cattle to supply America's fast-food restaurants is another example.

My contact with the business community and my reading of Ron Arnold's biting antienvironmental book, *Ecology Wars: Environmentalism as if People Mattered,* suggests a profound fear on the part of the business community, a fear that environmentalists are out to end business. Ron Arnold suggests that the central question to American industry is this: will business be allowed within a decade or two?

Although environmentalists are more sensitive now to job issues, it seems to me that in the past we have been a little too hasty to dismiss the need for employment and a respectable income.[18]

We can help end the environment vs. economy conflict by finding ways to demonstrate that a healthy economy and a thriving ecosystem are compatible. The important goal of industrialized society is economic health—not development or growth, which both imply a continuation of unsustainable practices. Sustainable economics disputes the need for waste and destruction. It disdains "growthmania," a term coined by the economist and chief proponent of the steady-state economy, Herman Daly. It scoffs at the ideology of the cancer cell—the obsession with unlimited economic growth—in a world of limits, instructing us that this belief is an invitation to disaster. But economic reform will not be easy.[19]

In response to the economic dilemma western societies now face, many leaders in and out of government have jumped on the sustainable bandwagon, endorsing the vague concept called "sustainable development." But to many observers, sustainable development is just a way of doing what we've been doing all along, but a little less obtrusively. It still embodies continued economic growth. Unlimited growth is impractical and antienvironmental. It's a river flowing against the stream of life. What we need is an economy that is healthy and vigorous, one that meets our needs, and does not trash, but rather enhances, the environment.

Ending the Obsession with Economic Growth. Environmental educators, writers, politicians, and leaders can help end our obsession with economic growth. One way is to begin substituting the term "healthy economy" for "growing economy." Secondly we had better define "sustainable development" more carefully and find ways to practice it.

My home state of Colorado, like many states, has been guilty of a shortsighted obsession with economic growth for decades. Waving the banner of jobs and economic prosperity, Colorado's leaders have blindly pursued a host of big-ticket items to create jobs and economic growth. The state, for example, has actively courted lucrative government projects, including the superconductor-supercollider and space technology research center. When Colorado lost the superconductor-supercollider to Texas in 1989, the governor tempered the defeat by announcing his optimism over other pending "big-ticket" items—plans to recruit Sears and other corporations to Colorado. Economic planners were quick to remind the public that a convention center soon to be under construction and a new airport would help end the economic malaise that had set in when the price of oil fell several years ago.[20] Both projects, government officials assure the public, will create construction jobs and increase business in Denver. The airport will also help stimulate international trade by easing access to foreign markets. Clearly, Colorado had lost the superconductor-supercollider, but hadn't lost hope.

In all of the hoopla over recruiting big-ticket items, however, Colorado officials—like their counterparts in dozens of other states—seem to have lost track of one important thing: what society wants from economic development. For example, do the citizens of Colorado really want more businesses if it means additional congestion on our highways? Do people want more money in the economy if it means dirtier skies and more restrictions on automobile driving? Do citizens want more housing developments that block scenic vistas? Do anglers want to stand elbow-to-elbow at their favorite trout streams because the state has recruited thousands of new residents in its mad scramble for the almighty dollar? Probably not.

Most people want a healthy economy. They want a job they can count on to earn a decent living. They want stability. What they don't want, though, is to destroy the environment to get it. But that's what our economic planners, government officials, and business leaders are doing to sustain economic growth. Most economic thinking today consists of finding ways that will continue this cycle of destruction.

What is happening here is happening just about everywhere. Business economists and government officials look to growth to cure ailing economies the world over. Many of us may be buying into the logic. Economic growth, however, is the root of our current economic and environmental turmoil. Prescribing more growth is like administering testosterone to a boy in puberty.

First Steps in Building a Healthy Economy. The challenge in all of this is to look at the economy and the environment as parts of one whole. The challenge is to explore economic health, not growth, and find ways to balance economic needs with environmental requirements—clean air, clean water, and a healthy environment. In a truly sustainable system, economic concerns will need to be tempered to provide for the needs of the species that share this planet with us.

As a first step, let us study the goals of traditional economic development strategies and examine ways that these goals can be met without more growth. In the broadest sense, economic development is based on a desire to increase wealth. For most people, wealth is metered by the size of a bank account. To a business owner, wealth means more spending money and, possibly, business expansion. To the jobless, business expansion means employment. One person's wealth is another's job. For the government official, a thriving business means healthy tax revenues. And jobs mean a lower unemployment rate.

In theory, economic development is supposed to make everyone happy, but it doesn't. Citizens who value pristine clean skies and safe drinking water are often troubled by the ecological backlashes of economic development. To such people, a healthy economy is too often gained at the expense of the environment. Uncontrolled growth, of the kind that has plagued western states for over a decade, has created a crowded and unhealthy atmosphere. But is there any alternative? Can we have a healthy economy and a healthy environment? Are traditional economic development plans that rely in large part on importing big-ticket items the only way to go?

I think that we can have a healthy economy and a healthy environment, but we must examine other avenues of economic activity. We must set aside our interest in big-ticket items to look at two environmentally and economically lucrative strategies.

The first strategy is aptly called plugging up the leaks. It's a strategy you might employ in a leaky lifeboat. Plugging up the leaks means making existing communities more efficient in how they use energy, water, and other resources. It's a concept developed, in part, by the folks of the Economic Renewal Project at the Rocky Mountain Institute in Snowmass, Colorado.[21]

By using their resources more judiciously, business owners, for instance, can improve the bottom line. The more money they have, the more they can afford to spend to expand their businesses. Increased profits means more jobs, making the jobseeker happy. Increased profits means more tax revenue, to the delight of government officials.

Plugging up the leaks should be the first line of defense in any strategy that seeks to build a strong and healthy economy. It's a way of stopping the outflow of dollars from a business. If an entire community joins in, incredible amounts of money can be kept from flowing out of a regional economy. Reducing the outflow of money can help foster regional stability. Before the 1973 oil embargo, a dollar used to circulate 26 times in the United States before leaving the country. Now, it circulates fewer than 10 times, largely as a result of our increased dependence on foreign oil and foreign imports. Plugging the leaks stops the unnecessary outflow of currency.

Entire communities can pursue ways to cut water, energy, and other resource use. Increased efficiency in transportation, housing, and government, for example, will help retain dollars within a local economy. Every dollar we save is a dollar that stays. Increased efficiency also helps reduce air pollution, water pollution, hazardous waste generation, wilderness destruction, and so on. Thus, economic health and environmental protection go hand in hand.

The Japanese understand the benefits of plugging up the leaks—at least from an economic standpoint. Japanese manufacturers, for example, use energy more efficiently than their U.S. competitors. The U.S. currently spends 11.2 percent of its gross national product on energy. Japan, on the other hand, spends only about 5 percent. This relative inefficiency in fueling industry costs the United States $220 billion a year. The cost differential gives the Japanese an economic edge on everything they sell to the United States and other countries.[22]

Energy waste is still prevalent. About half the energy used in the United States and in most Western European nations is wasted. Somewhat less than 50 percent is wasted in Japan and considerably more than 50 percent is wasted in the Soviet Union.

Testifying to the incredible potential of energy conservation, the World Resources Institute believes that the world could meet most of its energy needs through the year 2020 simply by making more efficient use of the energy now available. Even though world population may double between 1980 and 2020, only a 10 percent increase in energy production will be needed if the existing energy-efficient technologies are adopted, according to the World Resource Institute Report.[23] Among the energy-efficient products already on the market or under development are superinsulated houses, cars that get 98 miles per gallon, and long-life fluorescent light bulbs that fit into incandescent sockets and use approximately one-fourth as much energy as the incandescent bulbs they replace.

The second economic strategy involves ways to find hidden opportunities. Here's an example of what I mean. Over 300 million tires are discarded each year in the United States, according to Lawrence Musgrave at the Hazardous and Solid Waste Resource Facility in Broomfield, Colorado. Today, only about 4 percent of the tires are recycled.

A single tire contains the energy equivalent of 8 gallons of oil. Tires can be ground up and burned for energy or added to asphalt. Their use in asphalt, Musgrave says, increases the cost of road building, but substantially decreases road maintenance. Rubber makes asphalt watertight, which in turn, decreases water penetration and cracking. Clearly, used tires are a waste we can build a business or two around.

Recycling is another business opportunity just ripe for the picking throughout the nation. A study published in the New York

State Recycling Forum shows that recycling 10,000 tons of trash in a curbside program produces 36 jobs.[24] Landfilling that much garbage creates only six jobs and incinerating it creates just one job, according to the study.

Americans can find ways to make use of our municipal waste. State and local governments can help by pointing out the hidden opportunities for business and perhaps fostering their development. This strategy, like the first, relies on local labor.

As a final note, if communities must import business, the environmental sector can encourage them to invite clean businesses. That means businesses that don't pollute the air, water, and land, businesses that don't produce hazardous wastes—or if they do, reuse and recycle them so they don't end up in landfills. Clean businesses are conservation-minded. They're businesses that use resources, such as water, efficiently. They're businesses that promote carpooling or vanpooling among employees and help employees find homes close to work. Finally, clean businesses would include those that produce environmentally responsible products, not wasteful throwaways.

In summary, economic development is viewed too narrowly. We need to develop strategies to build economic strength by plugging up the leaks and finding hidden opportunities. Wherever possible, recruit clean businesses. The environmental dividends could be enormous. We can encourage our political leaders to rethink economic development plans, to set aside their business recruitment strategies for a while and give these simpler and more profitable strategies a fair shot. The environmental community can develop plans for such actions and make them public. These efforts will be an important step in building a sustainable economy.

It's Healing Time on Earth

America has entered a new era, a time of restoration and repair.[25] It is a time to rebuild and reshape American society. Restoration is also occurring in China, Africa, Australia, Thailand, and Central America.[26] Clearly, it's healing time on earth.

The environmental community can play a substantial role in the healing process. The first step in healing is to work actively with all levels of government to find cheaper and environmentally more responsible alternatives to new dams, powerplants, landfills, clear cutting, and automobiles used for commuting. Frederic Krupp notes that "if conservationists worry about the impact of a dam . . . they better address the water-supply or power-supply problem the dam was proposed to solve. They must concern themselves with the science and economics of environmental protection." Moreover, "Jobs, the rights of stockholders, and the needs of agriculture, industry, and consumers for adequate water and power—all of these issues must become part of the new environmental agenda." At the same time we should offer guidelines to achieve a simpler, lower-impact lifestyle.

Greening the Corporation. Another important healing project has to be efforts to change the corporate conscience. "We have to green the corporate movement," advises Dave Brower. "We have to green all businesses that operate without ecological conscience."

One attempt is the National Wildlife Federation's work to develop a college class curriculum on the environment for business majors.[27] NWF's staff is working with college faculty at several major universities to teach environmental policy and environmental management. Several schools offered a pilot course in the fall semester of 1989.

On another front, in 1989 environmental groups, working with several public pension-fund managers, drafted guidelines for corporate conduct, which they called the Valdez principles. The Valdez principles call on corporations to minimize and eliminate pollution, practice sustainable resource use, use energy efficiently, reduce risk to workers and the public, and repair previous damage. They also call on businesses to appoint at least one board member who is qualified to represent environmental interests and to conduct annual self-evaluations to assess progress in implementing the guidelines. It is hoped that the Valdez principles will be adopted by American companies and will help them redirect policy and management.

The National Wildlife Federation's environmental course for business majors and the Valdez principles are important first steps in greening American business, but much more is needed to heal the corporate wound.

Brower suggests additional changes. His approach would be to work with sympathetic corporations to get major changes in the law, mandating better business. I call it the Corporate Environmental Responsibility Act.

The first provision, says Brower, would be one that allows a corporate CEO to bypass opportunities for profit without being sued by the shareholders. "Right now they can't," says Brower. A corporate CEO should be able to say "no thanks" with impunity to a proposed project that would have unacceptable impacts on the environment. Such a provision would allow the corporation to function more as an integral part of society—rather than within the narrow profit motive.

Secondly, to help inform shareholders about the impacts of their investments and to appeal to their better conscience, Brower suggests that environmental impact analyses be required in all offerings for investment. If you want to invest in a company, you should see the impact statement. If you want to invest with ecological conscience, you can. Impact statements and reports on the wastes, pollution, and environmental destruction a company creates could help the corporation, its officers, and its shareholders become more environmentally responsible. To avoid cheating and bias, independent reports would be necessary.

The third provision, says Brower, is an impact statement on all takeovers. With the "current insane rage of takeovers," he says, "we need environmental impact statements. Right now, all kinds of money is being spent, just passed around on sort of a musical chairs in the corporate world, where nothing new is produced. It's just a shift of ownership and their resources are spilled and wasted."

The best example is Pacific Lumber Company, described by Brower and others at one time as the most environmentally conscious lumber company in America.[28] Before 1986, Pacific Lumber managed its redwoods on a sustainable yield basis, a remarkable feat when you consider that redwoods live 1000 years and more.[29] In January 1986, however, Pacific Lumber was purchased by Charles E. Hurwitz. To finance the takeover, the company issued junk bonds—bonds with tantalizingly high yields, but low credit ratings. The interest alone on the bonds came to $83 million in 1989. To pay off its debt, the new owners abandoned sustainable harvesting practices. Today, trees are being harvested at a rate that jeopardizes the forest's future. One Pacific Lumber worker said, "They're just leveling everything . . . They're destroying the future, leaving nothing for the next generation." Pacific Lumber has more virgin redwood forest than any other company, but not for long.

A legal instrument to help green corporations and prevent repeats of the Pacific Lumber story would be an important step in the right direction. But what else can be done? First, by reaching a broader audience and instilling in them the need to be a part of the solution, environmental groups can help reshape the marketplace (Chapters 3 and 4). In 1988, the Council on Economic Priorities, a nonprofit group based in New York, published *Shopping for a Better World*, a guide to socially and environmentally responsible products in America's supermarkets.[30] In 1989, Canada instituted a labelling system for environmentally benign or environmentally beneficial products, much the same as the health labels on American food products. These labels identify green products and let the consumer decide whether he or she wants to spend a little more to help promote environmentally responsible companies by purchasing their products.

Conscientious consumerism is a marketplace vote for environmental responsibility and action at the corporate level. In November 1986, Californians overwhelmingly approved Proposition 65, a major experiment in toxic chemical control.[31] Under the new law, the state of California sets acceptable public health standards for chemicals in various products. For carcinogens, the state has established a threshold level that would produce one excess cancer per 100,000 exposures. Manufacturers who violate these standards must print warnings on their products noting that the product contains chemicals at levels that the state deems unsafe. Thus according to the law, excess exposures are legal, but proponents of Proposition 65 hope that market forces will inspire manufacturers to minimize exposure or eliminate potentially harmful chemicals from foods altogether. Two similar products sitting on the shelf side by side may compete fairly equally in price. The one bearing a cancer warning, however, would probably have an unfavorable market position.

California's regulators worked quickly and feverishly to produce health standards. In a single year, they produced more standards than the EPA has managed to create under the Federal Toxic Substances Control Act in the past decade and a half.

California businesses have had a year to look over the information and to decide when necessary whether to reduce the exposure or to print a warning on their packages. While some businesses object to this approach, others consider it a step in the right direction. Chevron's chairman, George Keller suggested in a recent speech that it might be in an industry's interest to take initiative in controlling toxic chemicals before legal action takes place.

Environmentalists, citizen activists, and government officials can use a variety of means to make inroads into the corporate conscience. In Chapter 7, I describe some ways that environmental groups and state officials have worked successfully with corporations.

Underestimating the Business Community. The environmental community largely underestimates the business community—in much the same way that society underrates the willingness of people in general to take action. This is not to say that business is without reproach. Corporate polluters remain of serious concern. For corporate officials who knowingly violate emissions standards, putting workers and the public at risk, stiff penalties and even jail sentences are needed. But many companies have shown a willingness to help clean up the environment without the threat of punitive measures. And many companies are finding that pollution prevention pays. The 3M Company, for instance, has taken the lead in reducing air pollution at its plants. The company has reduced air pollution emissions from its factories by more than 110,000 tons per year; in the process, it has saved millions of dollars. In its Northridge, California plant, for example, the company replaced a solvent-based chemical used in a coating process with a water-based chemical. This switch cost the company $60,000 but saved it $180,000 in pollution control equipment that would have been required to prevent the solvent from escaping into the atmosphere.

As another example of corporate responsibility, in the 1988–1989 pollution season, for example, Denver's Better Air Campaign (discussed previously), offered an award to the company that did the most to reduce air pollution by reducing driving.

Much to the surprise of many, the winner was the Total Petroleum Company, the parent company of Vickers, whose gas stations dot the Denver metro region. Vickers gave away free coffee to carpoolers and free round-trip bus coupons to area residents who filled up in their station. All told, Vickers handed out over 200,000 bus passes in the 1988–1989 high-pollution season and 125,000 of them were used. The previous year, they distributed 120,000 coupons, 60,000 of which were used. Vickers also sponsored an employee program aimed at reducing driving, which boasted a 52 percent participation. They cosponsored a contest with the *Denver Post*, offering a $10,000 award for the individual with the best idea for reducing vehicle miles traveled in the Denver metro area.

What's a company that profits by selling gas doing trying to reduce automobile traffic? They're helping Denver clean up its air. Who among us environmental skeptics would have imagined that a company would take action that seems so contrary to its own interest? Yet, during the course of this program, Vickers was able to increase its market share by 7 to 8 percent.

In 1989, Denver's Better Air Campaign changed its name to Clean Air Colorado and announced that it would be working much more closely with business. The governor appointed a Blue Ribbon Committee comprised of seventeen CEOs from some of the largest and most influential businesses in Colorado. Their role is to make recommendations for ways that businesses can help all employees cut driving. It is hoped that they'll spread the word to other area businesses as well. The Better Air Campaign is also looking at ways that small businesses can help, for they employ 60 percent of the people in the major cities on the eastern side of the Rockies. The Blue Ribbon Committee is part of a comprehensive plan that is aimed at cutting all forms of air pollution in the Front Range—a region extending from Fort Collins to Denver to Colorado Springs. In years to come, the program will also focus on global warming. It will work with businesses, government agencies, and schools. The object, says Anne Grady, coordinator of Clean Air Colorado is to work "with the business community as partners, not as a government agency telling them what to do." Other goals are to help businesses develop emission reduction programs and to create a menu of strategies that individual businesses can implement, including subsidizing bus passes for employees, paying for parking for carpoolers, purchasing more efficient vehicles, or powering vehicles by alternative fuels, such as propane. The Deep Rock Water Company, for example, has already changed its fleet to propane to reduce emissions, and has also developed a computer program that rescheduled deliveries to reduce driving. The efforts help cut pollution and save the company money.

Clean Air Colorado is developing a computer program that businesses can use to estimate their contribution to air pollution. The group can then work with businesses to find strategies to cut

air pollution and get a commitment to reduce the company's contribution to air pollution. "I want to be able to give . . . a little
business that employs ten or twenty-five people a sense that not
only do they contribute to the problem, but they can materially
contribute to the solution."

What Are We After Anyway? Environmental sympathizers may
find it advantageous to work more closely with businesses and
business organizations like the Chamber of Commerce. Forming
alliances with the business community will pose an enormous challenge for a movement that has traditionally viewed, and still views,
the corporation as evil. Cooperation is made all the more difficult
by markedly differing views of progress. For such an effort to be
successful, we may benefit from the experience and example of a
Washington, D.C.-based group called Results, founded by Sam
Harris.

The purpose of Results is to create the political will to end
hunger. "Their secondary purpose is to empower individuals . . .
to help individuals realize they make a difference," says Woody
Moore, a regional coordinator for Results.

Results has had incredible success in the political arena. Their
methods could be applied in other areas, especially in our dealings
with government and business. Their secrets? "We're completely
positive . . . That is to say, we don't get into making a legislator
look bad, or wrong . . . we don't do score sheets. We're assertive,
but not adversarial."

Results maintains a minuscule central office in Washington,
D.C. Here, Sam Harris and coworkers provide guidance and information to a cadre of dedicated, forward-looking people working in
cities throughout the nation. The Washington staff trains the regional representatives, showing them the best ways to approach
legislators, and teaching ways to work constructively with legislative staff. By providing factual information and by making repeated, congenial contacts, Results whittles away at the opposition.
They become reliable resource people. And they get their way!

Results also fosters friendly relationships with editorial page
writers and, over time, provides them with information that often
makes its way onto the newspaper editorial page. They use these
editorials as support for their case. A friendly letter to a decision
maker with a copy of an editorial or two can have an enormous

impact. It's a signal that someone's concerned about an issue. If it makes the editorial page, it must be important.

The larger environmental movement could benefit immeasurably from the Results model, which provides a way of dealing more effectively with the government as well as the business community. The positive, personal approach could generate many benefits.

A central tenet of the Results philosophy is that there are no enemies. Many people want to get involved in social change, but find the alarmist rhetoric of environmentalists and the negativity too overwhelming. They are attracted to the soft path of change proffered by Results. "I think most people prefer it," says Moore. "I know it [discovering Results] was a great relief for me. I wanted to work on hunger and I heard about Results and I heard about the effectiveness and I thought okay, let's go do it. And when I realized, somewhere along the way, that they don't do negative stuff, I thought, how wonderful that I can do this work and be effective and not have to be negative."

"I have a personal thing about the importance of operating out of love and operating out of unity rather than separation," says Moore, echoing a sentiment common among the people he works with.[32] Results works, and the group is willing to "give away" its secrets to anyone who asks. It is important to recognize the importance of finding common ground with people that we don't agree with. That approach may sound crazy, but so what? "Why use that as an excuse not to make the world work?"

It is time for the environmental community to come together. What do you do when you're face to face with a polluter? "Look for his or her commitment . . . because that is one place that we all are common. We all have commitment." People involved in the world of business, government, and in social change are unified by commitment, even though they may be isolated by differences in vision. Thus, although we may not agree with the direction of the commitment or its by-product, we must recognize and acknowledge the common bond of commitment.

When we look at our "adversaries" to see their commitment, we see different people. What we see are sensitive, caring, intelligent people. We must remember this as we go about remaking America.

Green Century Project. In an article in *Crossroads: Environmental Priorities for the Future*, Huey Johnson proposes that the environmental community create a nationwide hundred-year plan of resource recovery. It would start with a team from a national organization that would assist each state in defining its own hundred-year plan. He calls it the Green Century Project. The ultimate goal would be to create a healthy environment and to preserve natural resources to pass on to future generations. Similar to the Investing in Prosperity program Johnson headed in California, this project must assume nationwide proportions. Its success would hinge on all of the changes discussed so far, and would require the same kind of cooperation from business, government, and environmentalists that characterized the California program.

The money for the project could come from defense expenditures, Johnson suggests. The Green Century Project would establish a policy in which a share of the national assets are invested to recover lost resources—eroded hillsides, denuded forests, and polluted streams. Lester Brown and his colleagues at the Worldwatch Institute believe that $774 billion is needed during the last decade of this century to reverse the dangerous global environmental trends now evident.[33] That's about $80 billion a year, a small fraction of the world's *annual* defense budget.

This whole modern age has lacked a future. We've been tied up in a race to conquer space with little consideration for our own home. Caring and protecting the earth has fallen by the wayside. A Green Century Project could touch off a spirit of hope, helping stimulate a new ethic that values the future as well as other living things. It will help us eliminate our short-term economic vision, replacing it with a more long-term outlook. It may help us abandon short-term planning and adopt more realistic 100-year-plans that outline roads to a sustainable future.

Building a Sustainable Society

"We are all ready to meet together and decide what's gone wrong and who is to blame," says Dave Brower. But what we're not very good about, and we have to get good at, is establishing where we want to go and establishing a course of action.

"We want the human race to stay on the planet as long as the sun keeps it warm enough," says Brower. And many of us want to preserve the diverse web of life into which our lives are woven. "But we are headed right over the edge. And the people are turning down the warning signs." By offering positive, realistic plans that involve individual action and more widespread cooperation, the environmental community can counter apparent widespread apathy and help America begin to build a sustainable society.

Surely, we have a great distance to travel. We're not going to reach our goals just by adversarial relations. We're not going to get there by spreading fear, preaching doom, and standing in opposition without offering alternatives.

We have a choice to make. We can be effective, offer a vision that other people want to join. We can work together with others. We can be flexible and entreat others to add to the emerging vision. Or we can continue along the narrow path that we have been on, failing to reach our full potential.

Be great in act,
as you have been in thought.

WILLIAM SHAKESPEARE

In Thought and Action: The Missing Connections

6

Albert Einstein spent a great deal of time in his later years pondering ways to end the proliferation of nuclear weapons. One thing he concluded from his musing was this: you can't solve a problem with the same logic that created it. Einstein argued quite simply that we can't make the world safer by building more bombs.

Environmentalists take heed. In the battle to build a better world, to end the waste and pollution that are turning our skies into ugly smears across a congested landscape and turning our rivers into putrid running sores, many groups have fallen victim to—even come to endorse—Madison-Avenue sales tactics and their underlying logic. Madison Avenue is the home of many of the nation's advertising agencies who, through cleverness, hype and mild deception, help make it possible for American business to hawk its wares, driving our wasteful, throwaway economy. Madison Avenue is the hub of the advertising industry with spokes extending throughout the world. The consumer passion fanned by advertising that comes from Madison Avenue and its many outposts is responsible for much of the environmental crisis we now face.[1]

The signs of the submission to Madison Avenue sales tactics within the environmental movement are alarming. One of the most obvious symptoms of submission is our heavy dependence on direct mail.[2] To finance costly environmental battles and to recruit new members to replace the high rate of dropout, many national environmental groups have come to rely heavily on direct-mail appeals to raise funds.

The flood of direct mail, however, violates the senses of a growing number of supporters for several reasons.[3] The first is sheer volume. The second is a qualitative matter. Until very recently, much of the environmental direct mail has come to us on nonrecycled paper. Much of it is packed with inserts that few of us ever read. Most of it has for years sidestepped issues of personal responsibility and promotes the "cash conscience," described in Chapter 3.

Another sign of our alignment with the Madison Avenue logic is the "environmental credit card," offered by many of the national groups. In addition, catalogues offering consumer goods, giveaways offered as enticement to join groups, and phone solicitation are part of the growing efforts to raise money. Some efforts are admirable; others violate the very principles for which environmentalists stand.

This chapter takes a more narrow focus than earlier ones, focusing principally on the environmental organizations themselves—and their membership. It is about consistency of thought and action in the environmental movement and, ultimately, about consistency in our own lives. It describes the dangers of disassociating the two and the need for environmental groups to align more closely with their principles.

Environmental Direct Mail: The Missing Connections

Environmental direct mail is a contagion. Join one group and within a few weeks come pleas for more money and pleas from other groups that have gotten your name, asking *you* to help *them* save wilderness, forests, or wildlife or to put a halt to toxic wastes, acid deposition, and leaking underground storage tanks. The contagion spreads because environmental groups at all levels actively swap their membership lists. This practice allows them to reach a wider audience and helps groups garner support. However, when individuals join a group it is not to have their names traded or to be inundated with requests for more money. Many environmental groups will honor an individual's request not to have his or her name traded and will even honor requests not to send additional appeals for more money. However, this option is not offered on membership forms or during phone solicitations.

Opinions of Direct Mail. There are over 61 billion pieces of third-class mail delivered in the United States each year, totalling over 7 billion pounds—or equal to about 50 million trees. All told, that's over 300 pieces of direct mail for every man and woman over the age of 15. No one knows exactly how much of this is from environmental groups. Nonetheless, national environmental groups are a significant contributor. The national environmental groups annually send 4 to 30 million direct-mail pieces each *just to acquire new members.* The Sierra Club, for example, sends an estimated 12 million pieces a year to replace the 100,000 or so members who drop their membership. Greenpeace sends an estimated 20 to 30 million pieces. The Wilderness Society sends 20 to 25 million. The National Wildlife Federation sends 30 million.

In addition to these mailings, national environmental groups send millions of pieces of mail to members asking for additional contributions to support issue work. The National Wildlife Federation alone sends 20 million house mailings each year—in addition to the 30 million pieces seeking new members.

In a survey of its members, the Environmental Defense Fund found that each of its members on average actively supports six other environmental groups. Since many national and local groups send out an appeal for money every month, their members may be receiving six to seven pieces of direct mail every month. For people who are more active, hardly a day goes by without an appeal.

Opinions of environmental direct mail vary. I think that many people are really upset with direct mail from environmental groups. Paul Watson, one of the cofounders of Greenpeace, agrees and so did many other environmentalists (both leaders and members) I talked to over the past year while researching and writing this book.

Says Watson, "Although the direct-mail approach is certainly effective in increasing membership, I don't think it is something the public is really very receptive to . . . I've heard nothing but complaints about the number and the volume of junk mail that people receive from so-called environmental organizations." My personal experience is much the same.

Michael Fischer, executive director of the Sierra Club, disagrees that their mailings have become excessive and wasteful. "Frankly," he said, "I think you are focusing on nits. I don't think [direct mail] is a substantial problem. I hear an awful lot of complaints from where I sit, get a lot of mail in my in-box, making suggestions or raising complaints, and frankly [it doesn't] register very high on that particular Richter scale."

The Escalating Game. Direct mail, like all advertising, is something of an escalating game, a game of one-upmanship. Environmental groups—some say by necessity—have become caught up in the game, inadvertently contradicting the very principles they support. Consider one example.

The Sierra Club recently switched the format for many of their mailings. To make their appeals stand out among the crowd, they are now mailing appeals in 8½-by-11 envelopes, instead of the normal letter-sized envelopes. These appeals waste more paper, but no doubt help the Club create a stronger presence in the market. The larger format undoubtedly increases visibility, but it drives up the cost of doing business.[4] One has to wonder whether the benefits of this strategy are worth the price of the resources and pollution that result. In the textbook industry, as in most others, outdoing the competition is the way companies stay competitive. It is the reason why a textbook now comes with a teacher's guide, a text bank, a student guide, overheads, free videos, and calendars and a whole host of other giveaways.[5] The extras help drive up the cost of doing business and waste resources. Some environmental groups have succumbed to the same logic.

Greenpeace has followed the Sierra Club's "lead." Conservation International. which is working to save tropical forests from destruction, followed suit in 1990. No doubt others will join. A group called Handgun Control, not an environmental group but part of the same direct-mail battle, may have added a new dimension to the competition. Their mailing in the spring of 1989 came in a poster-sized (13 by 17 inch) envelope—twice the size of the Sierra Club's and Greenpeace's—with letters of equal size to match. Will the Sierra Club or Greenpeace up the ante soon?

The Personal Connection. A great many people I talked to are dismayed by direct mail from environmental groups. Appeals featuring pictures of forests about to be decimated by loggers plead for money to protect them. These and other mailings are justified by a belief that the paper and resources used to print and distribute these pleas are more than offset by the environmental benefits.[6] The important point here is that excessive appeals squander our forest resources unnecessarily and contribute to pollution. Moreover, we can find other ways of funding environmental work that are consistent with our values.

Discussions with direct-mail people suggest that the reason for the excess is, quite simply, that it works.[7] A two-page letter receives a better response than a one-page letter. But a three-page letter is even better. It may be heresy to suggest, but I think we can do the job more efficiently. We can find ways to raise the money we need and reduce the waste in the process.

NRDC's executive director John H. Adams called direct mailing "the fund-raising medium that people love to hate." Like Adams, many leaders of environmental organizations and their direct-mail people are concerned with this necessary evil, but the flood of direct mail gives the appearance that the groups don't care. It gives the appearance that the groups are overlooking their connection to deforestation and the growing American waste stream to advance an important goal. When I explained my frustration with their mailings some years ago, the solicitor explained that the organization only spends 5 percent of its annual budget on direct mail. But that misses the point. We need direct mail. It helps groups develop and maintain membership. It provides broad-based funding, so groups are not dependent on a few sources of money. Surely, we cannot do without it. The point is, however, that the quantity—the sheer waste of resources in each appeal—troubles a great many people. Moreover, critics say, environmental groups need to look not only at the impact of their own actions, but at the collective impact of all groups.

A Greenpeace appeal sent in the spring of 1989 illustrates my point about the dissociation of environmental direct-mail appeal and personal responsibility. Inside the 11-by-17-inch envelope was a survey, some colorful wildlife stamps, a two-page letter, a decal, and a return envelope. The letter from Greenpeace's executive director says that "The only way to achieve everyone's goal of clean air, clean water, and clean soil is to end the generation of toxic wastes *at the source.*" (Emphasis added.) Surely, environmental direct mail is part of the source. Paper and ink production produce hazardous wastes, and mailings require energy to produce, print, and deliver, resulting in additional pollution.

The Greenpeace letter goes on to say, ". . . the issue of toxics, like all of our shared environmental concerns, matters to everyone. And we can't wait for legislators and bureaucrats to come to our defense." His remedy is simple. "*You and I* must seize the initiative and show them what needs to be done." (Emphasis his.) Few would disagree. But shouldn't we begin at home?

Despite their good intentions, environmental groups often equate personal responsibility with donations. In their zeal to increase membership, many environmental organizations have succumbed to waste-generating tactics.

"The direct-mail approach that we are taking we see as education," says Sierra Club's Michael Fischer. "We are communicating the club's mission, the club's purpose, and attempting to recruit like-minded folks to our ranks. For those . . . people who read but do not respond to the letters, well, they've got at least a subliminal message. But I think much more than that." Those who don't even open or read the mail, Fischer contends, also receive subliminal messages. "They see the club active in the world that touches them through their mailbox," he explains. "I think that it can't but have a positive response."

NRDC's executive director John Adams expresses similar feelings in a recent newsletter. "Direct mail," he writes, "enables NRDC to get important environmental messages out to millions of nonmembers every year—thus raising the visibility of key issues." According to their own surveys, NRDC members rely on direct mail as a primary source of credible news about environmental issues. Direct mail, he adds, has helped mobilize grassroots pressure for important national issues.

But not everyone views direct mail as favorably. "I think a lot of people have been boiling over the excessive junk mail for years," counters Dave Foreman. "I think a lot of people are . . . numbed by it." The numbing, in fact, may explain why the Sierra Club receives so few complaints about the direct-mail overload. Moreover, some like Dave Foreman fear that the Sierra Club and other groups are filling their ranks with people who fail to make the connection between personal waste and environmental despair—or haven't had it explained to them adequately.

Frank Schumann, a physician and environmentalist, who lives in Seattle, belongs to a number of environmental groups. He complains, "The junk mail's become overwhelming. I can't read it. I don't have the time. It piles up on my desk and never gets read. There ought to be a way to give a donation and not get the junk mail . . . a box to check on the yearly membership that says, 'Yes, I support your efforts. Here's my donation. Put it to good use and don't waste it on further appeals." As it is, he worries that his donations get frittered away. "It's all eaten up by appeals for more money that I'm too busy to read. I can't help but think that my money's being squandered. I want it put to good use, then I see it wasted. It makes me want to quit." It also makes him wary of joining new groups.

The key question is not whether direct mail is good or bad, but whether we can wage our battles and build membership more efficiently. I think we can. I think we must.

Some of the Problems with Environmental Direct Mail

Before looking at ways to increase membership and broaden our base of support through less wasteful methods, consider some more problems associated with direct mail.

Direct mail is the one of the few effective ways environmental groups can communicate with a larger audience, because for the most part, we don't access the media to publicize our message. The mail is almost the only way to find people. In recent years, however, the competition for money and members has become fierce for a couple of reasons. First, the job continues to grow bigger. More and more problems are coming to a head. Second, federal government support for many nonprofits has decreased drastically. A lot of organizations that were once funded by the government have lost that support and have turned to the public.

Important Issues Are Sometimes Ignored. Some groups shape their agenda around the flashy issues, claims Suzanne Mattei, executive director of the Connecticut Fund for the Environment.[8] She argues that the biggest danger of this fund-raising approach is that some environmental groups may not be selecting issues that are the most serious.[9] A good example is solid waste. Until recently, there was little interest among environmental organizations in the issue. But when the wandering Islip garbage barge hit the news, groups throughout the nation sprung up. The eye-catching issues are the ones that are often addressed, in large part because they're the ones that can generate revenue and keep a group going.

"I think that air pollution has been really ignored by a lot of groups," says Mattei, by way of example. The problem with air pollution as an issue is that it just isn't as dramatic as dying whales or hazardous wastes leaking into groundwater.[10] "You just don't get the kind of large gifts in response to an air pollution appeal because it is not tangible. If you show people a river and say this is going to go if you don't help us, they can relate to that," says Mattei. "To say, look at the sky today and look at the sky tomorrow, the change is so gradual, that it is hard to communicate. So as a fund-raising item it is harder to use."

If acid rain were not killing fish, Mattei argues, people would not be using it to raise money. For some groups, issues that are easier to organize fund-raising around become major issues, when they are not necessarily the most important issues. The environmental movement should not be shaped by the amenability of an issue to fund-raising in the same way that a business product is shaped to satisfy the fancy of the consumer.

This raises issues of ethics and management. Groups that have a very strong board of directors, committed to establishing goals based on environmental needs, develop their fund-raising programs around environmental necessity, not fund-raising convenience.

Soft Members. One of the more troubling problems that stems from such fund-raising is the *kind* of membership it creates. The new members drawn in by direct-mail campaigns of this nature are typically "soft" members. They are interested in the issue for a while, but when press coverage dies, their interest wanes. Soft members have a low renewal rate, according to Dave Foreman. When an organization stages its fund-raising around the issue of the day, it is invariably successful, and the additional funds result in expansion. This results in an organizational infrastructure that, once started, must be maintained. To maintain that level of activity, the groups have to initiate more direct-mail campaigns, creating a vicious circle.

Samuel Johnson once wrote, "The chains of habit are too weak to be felt until they are too strong to be broken." The direct-mail habit chains may be closing in on some of the largest environmental groups. Some fear it's already too late to break the bonds. "Many . . . large organizations are bogged down in a bureaucratic nightmare of paperwork and administrative details," argues Paul Watson. "Much of the money is spent on . . . administration as well as fund-raising activities. Those fund-raising activities ironically consume vast amounts of resources," he notes. Collectively, the major environmental groups, with some important exceptions, send out *millions* of direct-mail appeals each year. The National Wildlife Federation, in fact, has a warehouse that houses its gargantuan direct-mail operation. Many national groups mail seven or more appeals a year to their members. Says Jalair Box, former assistant director for development of the Washington Environmental Coalition, "That's not what membership is about."

Unnecessary Waste. Junk mail creates other problems, besides the cycle of dependency. One of the most obvious is the waste, which I alluded to earlier. The standard mail piece is a two-page double-sided letter with short paragraphs and the phony underlining and the phony personal messages scribbled in blue to catch the reader's eye. Then there are the little pieces of paper that fall out and the pamphlets that come along with it, and then there are the letters from celebrities that accompany the president's many-paged rambling. There are the phony surveys. All this is designed to give you the idea that whoever is asking for money is working hard and deserves your financial support. Direct-mail people argue that this strategy works, and we take their advice. No matter that there's way too much paper in each mailing, which adds to the energy and materials required for printing and mailing. No matter that junk mail is partly responsible for the growing demand for paper and the resulting deforestation that threatens the ecological vitality of the planet. Deforestation accounts for about one-fourth of the carbon dioxide added to the atmosphere each year.[11] Although some environmental groups have begun using recycled paper for their direct mail, the volume of waste is still significant.

Disenfranchising Supporters. "The direct-mail people have . . . taken over the environmental movement, and every kind of social change movement," says Dave Foreman. And with them comes the attitude that the more that's in a direct-mail piece, the better—a notion that the environmental community has long accepted.

One of the chief troubles with direct mail is that it is disenfranchising many ardent followers, especially the supporters who understand the connection between individual consumption and environmental degradation, people who take the bulk in bulk mailing very seriously.

Direct mail *costs* members. Good members. Members who strive to live consistently with their ideals. More than one person I talked with said they let memberships lapse because they were tired of being inundated with direct mail. Others said they wouldn't join another group because they just didn't want to get flooded with more mail.

Brownie Carson, executive director of the Natural Resources Council of Maine, is an example. He and his wife gave up membership in Greenpeace because they grew tired of the appeals. Others I talked to abandoned support of The Wilderness Society for similar reasons. Greenpeace "does some good things," says Carson, "but I decided that my $25 is probably more than eaten up in the mail they send me. We give the extra $25 to NRDC [Natural Resources Defense Council] or one of the other groups." Why the switch? "You get a few extra solicitations from those groups, but I think by and large the top-flight groups that are carrying the weight of the substantive work are sensitive to that sort of thing. We don't get 16 appeals a year from NRDC trying to get us to join."

Putting an End to the Problem

We're each a maze of conflicting ideas and emotions. Environmentalists are no exception. Our lives are lived inconsistently with our ideals; it's inevitable in modern society. Environmental groups are partly to blame for the chasm between sentiment and action, having all too often taken the individual out of the cause-and-effect equation. Moreover, in our zeal to protect the environment, we are unwittingly setting a bad example.

Jan Silver, the managing editor of the Northwest Environmental Journal says, "Environmentalists are often people who tell *others* what to do." We rail against society's wastefulness, we condemn corporate polluters, we denounce deforestation, and we exhort people to use recycled products. Perhaps it is time to bring the environmental cause more in line with its own beliefs.

Duane Elgin, author of *Voluntary Simplicity*, argues that the example of a person's life, much more than his or her words, speaks with power. "Simplicity of living, if deliberately chosen," says Elgin, "implies a compassionate approach for life. It means we are choosing to live our daily lives with some degree of conscious appreciation of the condition of the rest of the world." The same can be said of the examples set by the environmental movement. Environmentalism can strive for a higher degree of appreciation—a consistency of thought and action.

Giving Members Some Options. Many environmental groups will honor requests to protect your name from trade or sale. This option, however, is not publicized. It's only if you write them and request that your name be guarded that they will do it, and even then accidents happen.

Environmental groups could be more forthright in offering to protect one's name from being traded with other groups. In addition, groups could offer an option that would free them from additional appeals. You join, pay your annual dues, maybe receive a newsletter, but are left alone the rest of the year. The "no-frills membership" is an option that appealed to a great many people I talked to. It's not for everyone, but it's a choice many of us would like. Critics of wasteful mailings would be delighted and support for many groups could conceivably increase. So, why not offer members a no-trade option—the choice of whether they would like their name sold or swapped—and a "no-frills" membership?

When asked if such a policy would be feasible for the Washington Environmental Council, Jalair Box hesitated, saying it would probably reduce flexibility. WEC, she said, is very sensitive to the use of its list, and addresses the problem at other levels. The executive committee, for example, reviews individual requests for the use of the WEC membership list. WEC receives many requests each year, she says, but the group rarely sells or trades its list, partly to protect members and partly to reduce competition for funding. In 1988, WEC released its membership list to a coalition fighting a new highway, says Box, but "that was like pulling teeth."

Direct-mail people note that the no-frills options can backfire. If people don't receive mailings from the organization, they say, members are often left with the feeling that the group isn't working hard enough. Many members drop out. That's a problem, however, that could be easily remedied. When sending a renewal notice, include a list of the previous-year's accomplishments.

The Rocky Mountain Institute (RMI), founded by Amory and L. Hunter Lovins and renown for its work on energy efficiency, advertises on membership forms that it does not trade names. Its members receive a quarterly newsletter and are not inundated with appeals. RMI is housed in a solar-powered facility in Snowmass, Colorado, and uses state-of-the-art technology to cut energy and water consumption. In short, it's an organization that practices what it preaches. I joined in 1989, knowing that my money will be well spent.

Cutting Back on Waste. The environmental movement might benefit from a joint resolution similar to the federal government's Paperwork Reduction Act. It's purpose would be to cut back on waste by eliminating the unnecessary and superfluous material in mailings, using recycled paper, limiting appeals to single-page letters without all of the extra material that is only occasionally read, avoiding glossy stock, and using envelopes with windows that can be recycled. We can set a better example.[12]

Direct-mail people warn that cutting the size of our mailings won't work. Tests show that the present format (packed with all the extras) is the most effective. But I think that the environmental movement is behind its constituency on this one. Rising discontent over environmental direct mail may render the results of earlier studies obsolete. It may be time to retest our hypotheses. Moreover, it may be time to do a little education to counteract the thinking that compels environmental groups to stuff our appeals with unnecessary material. Environmental organizations can draw attention to the issue, for example, by letting members know how much money is being saved by more economical mailings and how they plan to put that money to use. Many people are wary of donations that end up fueling additional mailings and overhead, detracting from the programs. It's likely that many people will welcome the change to a more economical and less wasteful format.

Next, environmental groups may want to look for ways to cut back on the frequency of their mailings.[13] How do groups such as the Environmental Defense Fund and many state groups operate so effectively without burying us in appeals? The Washington Environmental Council, for example, sends a renewal letter and two appeals each year to members asking for special donations and that's it. Despite this, the group is successful on many fronts with an annual budget of $250,000. Their money comes from three principal sources: membership, grants, and appeals. WEC also prints its appeals and letterhead on recycled stock and uses recycled paper for all office copying. Since five other environmental groups share the copy machine, they have an even larger effect.

Workplace Solicitation. One possible way of reducing direct mail is through workplace solicitation—a program similar to the United Way. United Way solicits donations for a number of charitable organizations by approaching workers once a year through their places of employment. Employees who participate make a small donation from each paycheck.

Workplace solicitation, says Jim Abernathy of the Environmental Fund of Washington, is ultimately one of the least costly and most productive methods of fund-raising for charitable organizations.[14] The cost of workplace solicitation is much lower than the cost of direct-mail or door-to-door appeals. If an employer allows workplace solicitation, he or she also encourages employees to give. People also tend to give more money through workplace donations. A direct-mail or door-to-door solicitation, for example, might earn a group $10 or $15, perhaps a bit more, but workplace solicitation is likely to yield a $40 or $50 payroll deduction. A $1 per weekly paycheck deduction is hardly noticeable, but adds up to a healthy annual contribution.

The Environmental Fund of Washington began workplace solicitation in the fall of 1989, so it is too early to determine its efficacy. But similar groups in California and Oregon solicit funds in private and public workplaces and net the environmental community a sizeable income. Some national organizations have been successfully involved in this type of fund-raising since the late 1970s and early 1980s through the Combined Federal Campaign, which solicits from federal employees.

Workplace solicitation could help us reduce the number of direct-mail appeals and cut the waste, saving the environmental community millions of dollars a year and helping it align more closely with its principles of conservation and wise resource use. It is not a panacea, just another avenue that seeks to support essential work by less impactful means.

Cutting back on direct mail won't come easily. "The argument you would get from any group," says Dave Foreman, "is that they are in competition with all the other groups." If one cuts back without all the others cutting back, then people think they will lose the competition. Dave Foreman likens the problem to the tragedy of the commons. "The mailboxes . . . are the commons," he says. Environmental groups "try to graze that commons as much as possible." Each grazing accrues great individual benefit, but we are now in danger of overgrazing. A summit meeting of environmental leaders may be in order to address two principal questions: Can we make direct mail more consistent with environmental values? Can we find cleaner options of garnering support?

The summit meeting can be used to find ways to cut back on direct mail. What we need is for all of the national environmental groups to sit down and work out a code of direct-mail ethics, an agreement that they will all cut back to some agreed-upon level.

There was a time when The Wilderness Society's field representatives were ordered to get more column inches in the newspapers than Sierra Club field representatives, says Foreman. That competition is still alive, but it is now being waged on the direct-mail battlefield. In the meantime, the forests are falling and the waste dumps are bulging, much of it from wasteful direct mail, a good portion of it ours.

An Environmental Agenda for the Future, published in 1985, which has been discussed in earlier chapters, notes that the challenge of our economic system is "to find and implement the means by which a complex industrial society can function and grow without destroying or depleting the ecosystems that sustain it." If this is true of society, is it not true of the environmental movement?

The Personal Approach. Ann Beckenhauer, an environmentalist who is perturbed with direct mail, raises an interesting question,

"Whose message is going to be heard if the environmentalists cut back? Won't the merchandisers and all the other direct-mail interests reap the benefit?" Would the environmental movement's unilateral partial withdrawal from the direct-mail battle be equivalent to the unilateral reduction of nuclear arms some Americans fear? Will the NRA and other powerful groups reap unprecedented advantage?

Perhaps so. But maybe not. My sense of it is that environmental groups will able to maintain the current level of funding by economizing on their mailings and pursuing other options that are not so wasteful—such as workplace solicitation. One of the most effective ways of raising money is to ask for it personally, one-on-one, asserts Brian O'Connell, president of Independent Sector, an organization of foundations, volunteer organizations, and corporations that promote public philanthropy. "There is a great temptation to say that a personalized letter going to 500 people is better than trying to see ten or 25 people personally, but don't you believe it." The Sierra Club, following this advice, is trying to encourage existing members to recruit friends and neighbors.

Phone solicitation is another method that turns out to be incredibly successful in raising money. Linda Lopez of the Natural Resources Defense Council notes that it is clean and two to five times more effective than direct mail. Solicitors beware, however; many people I talked with called it "telephone nagging" and were particularly dismayed by the increase in this activity. "Perhaps it is because I am old-fashioned," says Charlie Callison, long-time conservationist and a former executive of the National Audubon Society, "but the long-distance begging annoys me the most. They always call at dinner time, an hour calculated to find people at home." By simply asking people if they object to being called and gracefully hanging up if the respondent says yes, however, phone solicitors could alleviate some of the annoyance.

The bottom line is this: We need to investigate other options besides direct mail to get our message across, and use all of our creativity to raise money in ways consistent with our ideological foundation. Those who are numbed by wasteful direct mail or are unaware of the problems it creates might sit up and take notice. People who refrain from joining groups whose work they admire for fear of becoming inundated with direct mail might be more likely to participate if approached in other ways.

Living off the Interest. To help meet operating expenses, and to reduce periodic budget crunches, some groups have begun setting money aside in endowment funds, accounts whose interest will later be used to support the group's activity. Endowment funds can be built slowly by diverting a small portion of a group's annual revenue or through special appeals. Over a ten-year period, a fund of $100,000 or more can be accumulated. By investing in environmentally and socially responsible companies, environmental groups can earn as much as 16 percent a year.[15]

After a fund is built up, part of all of the interest can be used to help support day-to-day operations or, perhaps, to support new work. A portion may be reinvested to allow the endowment fund to continue to grow. Ultimately, endowment funds may help reduce fundraising activities, so that activists may spend more time on issues and less time on the onerous task of raising money.

Opinions of endowment funds vary, and opponents will raise a number of objections. Perhaps one of the major obstacles is concern over the diversion of money from a group's operating expenses to an account that is, for all intents and purposes, unavailable. Why, they ask, when money is so short, should we be setting it aside? Won't it impair our effectiveness?

Given the urgency of many issues and the need for money, setting aside money for an endowment fund for use ten years down the line, may seem ridiculous. In some cases, a 5 percent diversion would be troublesome; in others, it may have no effect whatsoever. By finding creative ways to cut waste in the office or in direct-mail appeals, however, groups may be able to find the money in the existing budget. Separate appeals can be made to members for the express purpose of supporting the endowment. Many members will be willing to support a fund that will help promote economic stability and will reduce future fundraising efforts.

Given the high rate of return on many environmentally sound investments and the need for long-range economic stability, the endowment fund has an important place in most environmental groups. It's not a panacea, but like so many suggestions presented here, part of a larger integrated strategy that could help environmental groups reduce the wasteful direct-mail appeals.

Merge and Purge. Environmental groups that do use direct mail can be more efficient by eliminating duplicate mailings. Brownie

Carson of the Natural Resources Council of Maine notes that the object of direct mail is to get people to open the letter, to read it, and to push the right buttons so that they write a check. But this approach doesn't wash with somebody who is already a member. In fact, it becomes irritating and creates hard feelings.

Wherever possible, state and national groups should merge mailing lists and purge duplicate names. Certainly, this isn't always affordable and it is not possible when a group receives preprinted labels. However, lists should be purged whenever possible to reduce the outflow of mail, save paper, and help us live more consistently with the values we espouse.

The U.S. Postal Service is developing a computerized list of names and addresses that direct mailers can use to determine the accuracy of their lists. It won't give groups access to more names and it won't help them purge lists. It just allows them to correct addresses, helping reduce undeliverable third-class mail. The service should be available in two to three years.

Credit Card Contributions

One of the more disturbing trends of late is the credit cards offered by conservation and environmental groups, such as the Nature Conservancy, the Environmental Defense Fund, and the National Wildlife Federation. From a marketing standpoint, it is a great idea. A small percentage of the purchase price of every item charged to a card goes to the environmental group that issues the card. The National Wildlife Federation, for example, is offering a Visa card with a credit line up to $15,000. They call theirs "the cards that make a difference." By the spring of 1989, NWF had already raised over a half a million dollars.

By modern marketing measures, it's a stroke of genius. Brilliant! Easy credit promotes consumption, however, no matter who offers it. Credit cards in the name of the environment make spending just a little more palatable. The small donation made possible by an environmental credit card promotes spending in much the same way that discounts on merchandise promote purchasing. Environmental credit cards generate more paperwork—in the form of carbons and copies and monthly statements and advertisement included with the bills. Moreover, it furthers the cash conscience—the idea that we can buy our way out of the environmental crisis.

Environmental credit cards are part of the unspoken philosophy that absolves the consumer of individual responsibility.

Proponents argue that people will use credit cards anyway, so why not use ours? The hardline answer is that it makes buying even more acceptable than a card from one of the major credit card companies. By profiting from credit and consumption, environmental groups become unwitting agents of unnecessary environmental destruction. The contribution may be small, but it all adds up. The environmental crisis is the sum of millions of careless and wasteful acts.

We can't spend our way out of the environmental crisis. By promoting consumption and waste, environmental groups only deepen society's troubles—even if it is for a worthy cause.

More Overconsumption

A staff member at the American Wilderness Alliance once argued that the AWA should shift its focus from protecting wilderness to ways to enjoy nature. People, he said, are tired of the preservation stuff. They care more about having a good time. A great many of us do venture into the wilderness to enjoy the quiet splendor. A great many of us are committed to saving it. Still, a surprising number of people have little to do with protecting the wilderness and wild rivers they so freely enjoy. They take, but they don't give back.

I think that for many the wilderness is a playground, exploited for what it can give, then forgotten. Joy Williams, novelist and essayist, wrote in an article in *Esquire*, "In your desire to get away from what you've got, you've caused there to be no place to get away to." A few environmental groups may be contributing to the problem.

One of the major culprits is the Sierra Club. Their books, says Dave Foreman, show pretty places, but don't talk much about the issues anymore. The Sierra Club should be a leader in promoting responsible lifestyles in the wilderness and at home but they're not. Making matters worse, the Sierra Club's magazine is nearly 50 percent advertising, and some of that is "pretty inappropriate advertising," according to Foreman. "If the ads in the magazine do not display the kind of lifestyle you think we ought to be moving towards," says Foreman, "then I think you've got a problem of in-

consistency at best or hypocrisy at worst." A great many will take
exception with this point. The Sierra Club is an organization that
has done much good work over the years. My point is that the
club is espousing one set of ideals and displaying another.

Many environmentalists fall into a similar trap. A case in point
is our love for outdoor gear. Advertising (much of it in environmental magazines) promotes the latest outdoor gear: tents, sleeping bags, mountain bikes, and outdoor clothing. And many of us
who champion environmental conservation run out and buy the
stuff as fast as it can be put on the shelf. Articles on the latest
greatest material for rainwear spur people to replace perfectly good
gear with the newest fad. What we had last year is no longer good
enough. There's nothing wrong with owning good camping gear.
The problem is that good or adequate isn't good enough—we
have to have the latest kayak gear or outdoor wear. Manufacturers,
of course, realize a significant portion of their annual profit by
dangling the new fashions and new equipment in front of people
who subscribe to the notion that whatever we had yesterday surely
can't be good enough today.

Environmentalists as a whole abhor the rapid turnover of goods
in our economy when it pertains to automobiles or kitchen appliances, but are blind to the same phenomenon when it involves
camping gear. In the final analysis, such spending patterns acceler-
ate the destruction of the very resources we're striving to protect.

Given the deteriorating state of the environment, it is becoming clear that we need to be more conscientious consumers and
move toward lower-impact lifestyles. But as I pointed out in Chapter 3, environmental organizations have not done nearly enough
to make this point.

Moreover, advertising in some of the magazines seems to suggest that we can have our cake and eat it too. Ads in the Sierra
Club magazine in particular do nothing to promote a simpler
lifestyle. Advertising from major auto manufacturers, which has
taken up more and more space in recent years, is totally inappropriate. The automobile manufacturers (except for Chrysler) have
systematically fought to weaken mileage standards, hindering efforts to reduce energy extraction, improve energy efficiency, and
cut pollution.

Michael Fischer, executive director of the Sierra Club, pre-
dictably disagrees with the notion that the Club is promoting over-

consumption. "We screen the ads relatively carefully," he says, "though . . . the automobile ads have been taking a larger proportion of our ad space. If you will look at many of the rest of our ads, they are for benign or environmentally sensitive investments and for other outdoor things."

Fischer adds: "We are attempting to make the most with a relatively limited set of resources." *Sierra* magazine "is expensive, and if we were as wealthy as the National Wildlife Federation is, we would absolutely do away with advertising. However, were we to do away with advertising, *Sierra* magazine would not be the attractive full-color snazzy document that it is." Fischer looks forward to the day when they can diminish and avoid advertising altogether.

The National Wildlife Federation has an annual budget of $87 million. One-third of the money comes from the sale of so-called "nature educational materials." All told, the National Wildlife Federation sells nearly $28 million worth of calendars, glass blankets, figurines, Christmas cards, and sweatshirts. For NWF, the justification is fairly simple: it's lucrative and the profits help support their work.

Greenpeace also has an elaborate catalog of sweatshirts, tee-shirts, shopping bags, and other trinkets for sale, and they sell millions of dollars worth of products to help support their work. The Sierra Club does its share of peddling as well, selling millions of calendars and Christmas cards annually.

One could argue that consumption in the name of the environment is permissible. But like any other unnecessary consumption it results in pollution and waste. The sale of such items is a contradictory expedient to an important end. To some, its an unjustifiable means that ultimately contributes to the destruction of the environment. The cotton used to make tee-shirts, for example, is grown on American farms liberally sprayed with pesticides or on Central American farms that receive 30 applications of pesticide a year. Cotton crops, like those grown in California's Imperial Valley where rainfall is under 5 inches per year, require 40 to 60 inches of rainfall or intensive irrigation. To irrigate the farmland of southern California, water must be impounded. Dams are thrown up on northern California's rivers and water is diverted from the Colorado River. The Sierra Club calendars are printed in Italy, a country's whose environmental policy is shabby at best and whose water and air pollution problems are some of the worst in the developed world. Sierra Club cards and calendars are not printed on recycled paper.

Arguably, the $28 million earned by the National Wildlife Federation and the millions other groups receive from the sale of products helps support legal and legislative work that offsets the damage the manufacture and distribution of such goods cause. There is no easy answer to the issue. At the very least, however, environmental groups should consider the following guidelines:

1. Emphasize essential products, such as environmentally sound cleaning agents, washable diapers, and low-flow showerheads.
2. Sell products made from renewable resources.
3. Sell only cards, books, and calendars printed on recycled paper.
4. Sell only products that are easily recycled.

The environmental movement has drifted a long way from its Earth Day roots. It is slowly being sucked into the modern consumer movement and is struggling to stay alive, like others, using some of the same logic that is responsible for environmental decline. Instead of becoming a mainstream concern, the environmental movement has softened, become mainstream itself. One of the founders of the modern environmental movement, John Muir, who strode against the stream of public opinion so often, would be shocked at what we have become.

Angela Medbery, an environmental activist and long-time Sierra Club member who lives in Colorado, tells a story of a conservation-minded cousin who went on one of the Sierra Club's international outings. Her cousin showed up at a campfire on a trip to Nepal ready to discuss issues, but found that everybody around the campfire was discussing stocks, bonds, how to make more money. He expressed dismay that those who can afford that type of an outing were not willing to discuss the issues. Medbery worries that "in the driving need to get more money so that we can hire people that will effectively lobby, and effectively put out newsletters and do all the things that need to be done . . . we're selling ourselves to the only people that can afford to join us, who are the ones who are probably a big cause of the problem."

The environmental movement needs everyone, but we need more than dues-paying members. We need people who live their lives in accordance with their beliefs. If the environmental movement, however, does not set a better example, it ends up putting a stamp of approval on the wasteful lifestyle that is a big part of the problems we face.

Aligning Environmental Goals and Actions

Environmental leaders agree that more progress needs to be made on the issue of recycled paper use. Peter Coppleman, vice president of The Wilderness Society believes that environmental groups should use recycled paper whenever feasible. Toward this end, the ten leading environmental organizations are jointly exploring ways to increase their use of recycled paper.

The publishers of *E Magazine* and *Garbage: The Practical Journal for the Environment* have proven that a classy, four-color magazine can be produced on recycled stock. To help stimulate market demand and to bridge the gap between ideals and practice the national environmental groups, such as the Sierra Club and the National Audubon Society, should switch to recycled paper for their magazines.

A wide variety of high-quality papers are available for book publishing as well. Sierra Club Books and others should make the switch soon. Environmental groups that publish through mainstream publishing houses should insist on recycled paper.

Using recycled paper is an important first step in aligning the movement with its goals. Recycled paper will cost more initially, but in the long run it's worth it. Paper recycling saves energy, reduces pollution, and helps slow down the rate of deforestation. A single ton of newspaper, for example, will save seventeen 40-foot Douglas fir trees, 7,000 gallons of water, and enough energy to heat an average American house for six months.

Wherever possible environmental groups should use recycled paper for direct mail and newsletters. Paper costs can be reduced through cooperative buying agreements between the major groups. Buying recycled paper in bulk cuts down on shipping and unit costs. Surely given the volume of direct mail sent out by the major environmental groups, recycled stock could be purchased at a price that is competitive with virgin paper.

As for eliminating ads from magazines and cutting back on wasteful mailings, don't expect significant changes in the near future. It's not until the membership rebels that the leaders will change, and the membership may be driving the process in the first place.

That's where you and I come in. Perhaps it is time for those of us who belong to groups, but have been reluctant to criticize them, to lobby our *own* organizations for policies that are more directly aligned with our principles.

Clearly, it's time for change. The messages the environmental movement is giving by the examples it sets are out of step with its own goals. National and local organizations could use more recycled paper. Those that promote excessive consumption can abandon such wasteful practices. We can counter the philosophy that says we can protect the environment by writing checks. Most important, we must align our principles and actions. If we say "use recycled paper," we had better use it. If we say, "cut waste," we had better set a good example. If we say "use resources wisely," then we need to find ways to do it ourselves. If we say "be conscientious consumers," we must not send a double message by filling our magazines with inappropriate advertisements. If we decry the spoils of junk mail and overconsumption, we must avoid sending out massive mailings filled with tons of unnecessary fluff.

Waste in the name of the environment is intolerable because it puts the ends above the means. It ignores the important advice of Gandhi, who said "take care of the means and the end will take care of itself." It is symptomatic of a society out of sync with ecological realities.

We are giving the wrong message but it may be just a sign of the immaturity of the environmental movement. Changing will take a lot of self-examination, and it will require a willingness to examine the spirit and intentions of our movement to bring our actions more in line with our principles. Our wilderness, our air, our water—indeed our planet—are imperiled by our lifestyles, but we can live responsibly and through responsible action make significant inroads into environmental problems. Ultimately, however, environmental groups and environmental educators have to get the message to people that their actions count.

"If . . . humanity is going to survive on the planet earth," says Paul Watson, there "will have to be a revolution in economic values, political values, cultural values and spiritual values." Accepting waste in the name of the environment is like building bombs for peace. Past a certain point, the logic falls apart and very likely becomes counterproductive.

*We must indeed all hang together
or most assuredly we shall
all hang separately.*

BENJAMIN FRANKLIN

7 | *Marshalling Our Forces*

The obstacles to a healthy environment are formidable: overpopulation, economic exploitation, and rampant technological development. Our problems are exacerbated by a bankrupt national ethic that puts personal interests above the needs of others. Progress against the environmental crisis has fallen short of the task at hand because the obstacles we face proved much larger than anyone could have imagined and because we have overlooked some important strategies.

Eliminating Duplication

This chapter focuses chiefly on environmental groups and examines several opportunities for their evolution. It examines ways the environmental community can reduce duplication while retaining diversity and increasing strength. It discusses ways we can support important state and local environmental work. Finally, it looks at the issue of leadership and discusses ways that the environmental community can be strengthened from the top down.

From the outside, the environmental movement appears to be a patchwork quilt of overlapping interests and activities. On wildlife issues, there's the National Wildlife Federation, Defenders of Wildlife, Fund for Animals, the Animal Protection Institute, and others. Wilderness issues have a similar constituency. The patches of the quilt appear to overlap so much that the public often complains that one group seems indistinguishable from another.

One would hope that the large number of groups working on environmental issues would provide a safety net that catches virtually all of the issues, but it doesn't. Important issues still fall through the cracks, contends Esther Edie, of the South Dakota Resources Council. According to Edie, one current issue that's receiving little or no attention is a proposal by the Nuclear Regulatory Commission (NRC) to downgrade the classification of some the nation's nuclear waste. If the NRC takes this action, one third of the low-level radioactive waste that is now being hauled to a disposal site in South Carolina would end up in local municipal landfills. Relaxation of the average automobile mileage standards in 1988 was another decision that few people in the environmental movement had much to say about. Raising the speed limit on interstate highway systems was another issue with profound implications, especially now that U.S. oil imports hover once again near the 50 percent mark and the end of global oil supplies comes nearer. Important issues are often left unattended while environmental groups flock to the flashy issues, often working toward similar, if not identical, goals.[1]

A Mixing and Matching of Talent. Overlap begins with issues. The recent upsurge of interest in solid waste issues, for example, has spawned a proliferation of small groups at the local level in many states. In Colorado, for example, at least seven or eight recycling advocacy groups sprang up in 1987 and 1988. Many of them are working on the same problem: promoting curbside recycling in Denver. Some of the "new groups" were offshoots of existing organizations, some were brand new. All in all, the groups were incredibly diverse; one was decidedly "new age," another drew its members from a local college campus, and still another had a definite religious following. To those of us who were interested in trying to solve Colorado's solid waste problems, it became clear that we could all benefit from the upwelling of interest. We met to explore common interests and ways of working together. The members of the new coalition were eager to accommodate the wide range of interests. Before too long, however, it became evident that everyone had a different idea about what our coalition should do. One person wanted to stage a protest on the steps of the mayor's office, another wanted to put together a slide show and speakers bureau, while still another wanted to mount a public letter-writing campaign to put pressure on the mayor and city council. The then-shaky coalition sought ways to encourage different interests while pledging to work together. All three ideas were given the green light. People who were attending the meeting gravitated to their respective interests. The upshot of all this was that some people shifted project allegiance, creating a healthy mixing of viewpoints and talents.

By sharing information and dividing up the task, we eliminated what might have eventually resulted in a substantial amount of duplication. One group happily "dissolved into" the coalition. By working together, everyone now has a clearer idea of who's working on what. We think that in the long run more will be done to further the cause of recycling in our state than had we pursued independent but overlapping paths.

Duplication occurs at local, state, and national levels and numerous coalitions have formed over the past several years in an attempt to reduce the problem. Coalitions have in fact been a part of the environmental response since the 1950s, when conservationists teamed up to fight a dam proposed in Dinosaur National Monument. The late Howard Zahniser of The Wilderness Society built a coalition that won passage of the Wilderness Act in 1964. The Alaska Lands Coalition, including many national, regional, and state organizations, fought successfully for the passage of the Alaska National Interest Lands Conservation Act. Regardless, the response of many leaders to the charge of duplication (and the challenge of coalition-building) is often automatic: "Sure we hear that a lot, but what do you want us to do? Form one megaorganization and get bogged down in bureaucracy?"

Strength in Union. Duplication is inevitable, even desirable to a degree.[2] But where it wastes resources—time, talent, and money—we should find ways to reduce or eliminate it. The most obvious benefit of eliminating duplication is that it can free up substantial resources that can be used for other projects, perhaps even easing funding needs. By aligning its forces when it can, the environmental movement can become a more effective agent for political, economic, social, and personal change.[3] Coalitions help create political muscle.

Except for a handful of national groups with multimillion-dollar budgets, most environmental groups are overworked, underfunded, and understaffed. These endemic problems provide a challenge and an opportunity to evolve creative partnerships. Eliminating duplication, however, will require leaders to step back from the battle for a moment and set aside the competition and turf battles that often pit one group against another. It will require leaders to forge unions that may seem threatening to their organization's own self-interest.

The main object in building coalitions, according to Suzanne Mattei of the Connecticut Fund for the Environment, is to learn how to connect with each other and divvy up the effort. The issues are always going to be so big that there will never be a lack of things to do. The Connecticut Fund for the Environment, for example, has started a farmland preservation coalition, helped found a clean air coalition, a clean water coalition, and a coastal coalition. This work takes time but in the long run pays huge dividends.

Unfortunately, groups often become competitive instead of cooperative. And invariably, some groups are better at one thing than at another. "The Connecticut Fund for the Environment," says Mattei by way of example, "is great at actually carrying out a public hearing, going through the legal process, submitting testimony, exhibits, evidence, questioning and cross-examining witnesses." But getting people to a hearing is not their forte. Another group may have more freedom to lobby than CFE, which is a nonprofit, tax-exempt organization. Working with the press or the governor's office might be better handled by someone else. These are some of the tasks that can be divvied up in a coalition. By understanding strengths and weaknesses and areas of interest, we can take what seems to be a duplication of efforts, and turn it into an asset. What you have is not duplication of efforts, but a united front with divided tasks. Such a division of labor allows environmental groups to attack a problem at many levels, optimizing the skills and expertise of two or more groups.

The key to creating a successful coalition is a unity statement—that is, a statement of areas of agreement. Inevitably, there will be some areas of disagreement, but areas of accord will become the operating guideline for a coalition. "There is a security in knowing that the coalition will not take a position that individual groups oppose," says Mattei. Once the unity statement is hammered out, groups can develop strategies and work collectively to reach their goals.

Coalitions are not the be-all and end-all. A working coalition, in fact, should *not* dramatically increase the overall workload. It should help to make the work more efficient.

Increasing Our Effectiveness. By setting aside turf battles, differences of opinion, and competition for members, environmental organizations can become a more effective social and political force. A plan from a unified coalition bears more weight than one from a single group. It shows public leaders and the community at large that there is broad interest in an issue and, more important, consensus.

Peter Coppelman, vice president of The Wilderness Society, says, "The environmental movement needs much more coordination and focused effort." Instead of spreading each of our workloads thinner and thinner, which is a natural tendency for many groups, we need to find ways to concentrate our efforts. That may be possible through coalitions. By mixing and matching talent, coalitions can assemble the best teams possible to work on an issue. But this will require us to enter into creative partnerships, formed in a spirit of cooperation and unity. That may mean uniting with interest groups not typically thought of as allies—like business organizations, labor groups, corporations, and educational groups.

Besides working on issues, statewide coalitions can maintain directories of state and local activists and environmental groups. These directories, listing contact people, projects, and resources of groups and activists, serve several functions. First, they help those in the environmental community to identify others who are working on similar issues, which provides a way to identify potential working relationships.[4] Second, they can help us identify areas of overlap. By so doing, environmentalists can uncover ways to eliminate wasteful duplication and thus allow the environmental community to broaden its response. Third, they can help us identify issues that are not receiving adequate attention.

Statewide coalitions may find it to their benefit to publish a directory of environmental organizations, which they distribute to environmental groups, individual activists, libraries, governmental agencies, and business organizations with similar concerns. In so doing, the environmental community becomes a resource to the entire community. Statewide coalitions that keep track of environmental activism can also serve a useful purpose by starting action networks that alert activists and environmental leaders of upcoming events, important hearings, and political decisions. An action alert center that accesses a ready group of people who are willing to write letters, make phone calls, and attend hearings to testify can make a big difference, especially in local politics.

In a move that is bound to increase our effectiveness, Renew America sponsored a nationwide competition called Searching for Success to find and publicize American environmental success stories. The contest was open to individuals, organizations, communities, businesses, and governmental agencies. Awards were presented on Earth Day 1990 for the three most effective programs in twenty-two categories, including air pollution reduction, forest management, growth management, soil conservation, and renewable energy.

All entries were published in the *Environmental Success Index*, which is available from Renew America (see Appendix D). The index is a showcase of effective environmental action, a fountain of creative ideas for individuals, environmental groups, businesses, and others interested in launching new projects or making existing programs more effective. Because of Renew America's project, a successful program in Boston can now serve as a model for a program in Tallahassee.

Creating a Network of Scientists and Attorneys. The environmental movement can benefit immeasurably at the state level by developing a strong network of lawyers and scientists who are willing to volunteer their time to help state and local citizen groups.

Scientists at universities around the state may not have a lot of free time, but often can spare an hour or two to explain issues or offer advice on solutions. That input could go a long way to help citizen groups in their struggles. Attorneys can offer legal advice in a free evening or two. The directory of environmental groups and activists might include a section on scientists, engineers, and attorneys who are willing to volunteer some free time.

Preserving Diversity, Building Strength. Some of the people I interviewed for this book down-played the merits of coalitions. Peter Berle, president of the National Audubon Society does not see a problem with duplication, and thinks that we need more players rather than fewer. "I'm not concerned about the fact that you've got groups that have somewhat similar objectives because they may go at it in different ways and I think that's helpful."

Without a doubt, diversity in the environmental response is useful. For example, diversity means that there are more groups and the more groups that are involved in an issue, the more individual members hear about it and take action. Groups often differ considerably in their viewpoint and their tactics, sometimes making it best for groups to work separately.

Clearly there's an important distinction worth making. Coalition-building does not have to be a process that eliminates diversity of opinion and action. Its goal is to eliminate duplicated effort while maintaining diversity. Coalition-building can, in fact, give us more players, rather than fewer. It does not diminish our presence and power in the political arena, but can augment it. It does not reduce the number of members that hear about an issue and take some action, but increases it. By splitting up the workload and working together for a unified goal, we widen and strengthen the foundation on which the environmental response is built.

Coalitions should not erase the differences between us. Coalitions must be tolerant of different viewpoints and tactics, and must resist the "we're right/you're wrong" approach. Let splinter groups form. Keep them under the protective wings of the coalition and keep in touch, but let them soar on their own if necessary.

Craig Sarbeck, writer and member of the Stewardship Community, notes that it wasn't too many years ago that you could hardly get an Audubon staff person to talk to a Sierra Club member. Even today, there's a lot of in-fighting over philosophy and tactics. These internal battles can rip coalitions asunder and create enemies among people working toward a common goal.

Many people I interviewed listed diversity as one of the environmental movement's main strengths. Unfortunately, within the ranks of the environmental movement diversity is sometimes viewed with contempt. Differences over tactics and philosophy have spawned considerable animosity, and can turn one group against another. This animosity keeps us from the essential work of environmentalism.

Talk of reducing duplication often raises legitimate fears and automatic defensive reactions, so it is worth repeating that I'm not suggesting the environmental organizations of the world merge into one gigantic organization, which runs the risk of becoming too big and tangled in bureaucratic red tape. Rather, I'm suggesting that we find areas of duplication and, wherever possible, seek ways to eliminate them, freeing up people to work on other issues or other aspects of the same issue, thus broadening the environmental response. Where the problem is national, we can form national coalitions. Where it falls within a state, we can pull the state organizations together. Where it befalls a region, such as the Pacific Northwest or the Southeast, we can form regional coalitions. Where it meshes with other interests, cross the lines.

The Convergent Evolution of Environmental Values. One note about merging with groups not typically viewed as allies: Tim McKay, coordinator of the Northcoast Environmental Center in northern California, a coalition and activist group, notes, "There are a lot of people with environmental awareness. Many of them . . . have gotten there from different starting points. A duck hunter is concerned about habitat . . . The person who fishes is concerned about the water quality or the in-stream habitat . . . People in the urban environment may become concerned about environmental health because they determined that they or their families are exposed to toxic or hazardous materials, or they may be totally disgusted with litter on the street and be concerned about wastes." The point is, environmental concern arrives by convergent evolution, starting at different points but ending with the same outcome, much the same way that mammals and birds evolved mechanisms of flight.

"A lot of these people come to a point where they realize that something is wrong," says McKay, "yet they may not have a real strong appreciation for the fact that some other person has a slightly different perspective, but also understands the problem." A good example is the extreme polarity between hunters and many environmentalists, who share several key values. The environmental movement could benefit from an appreciation of the fact that people's interests are sincere, even if they got to those interests by different pathways. Moreover, it is possible to make the common interest work to the benefit of all.

Redefining Solutions to Include a Broader Constituency. Part of the problem today in the environmental response is that many of us are often unable and unwilling (or don't have the time) to step back from our problems and look at ways of redefining them and recasting solutions that can involve everybody's interest. Speaking about the conflicting interests of environmentalists, loggers, logging companies, country residents, and the fishing industry in the Pacific Northwest, Tim McKay notes that many of the problems are similar from one area to the next. Anglers were interested in stopping the destruction of streams by clear-cutting, which results in excess sedimentation and debris buildup in salmon spawning grounds, killing eggs or preventing salmon from their upstream migration. Environmentalists were interested in setting aside more forest for recreation and habitat and were interested in seeing lands managed properly. Logging companies are interested in keeping their mills supplied with timber and many local residents were concerned with employment security.

"I've been working real actively here for the past few years trying to . . . get people to accept the possibility of something very large . . . a solution that encompasses all of these backyard issues so that all of these people can be working toward the same goal," says McKay.

Coalitions of environmentalists, hunters, anglers, and other infrequent allies can be drawn together to draft bigger solutions. Local residents and even business interests can also prove to be valuable allies. To do this, we must agree to disagree on certain issues, and find common ground where we can work together.

In the Pacific Northwest, conflict and litigation have often defined the management of public forests. Since the early 1970s, numerous battles have been waged between timber companies, environmentalists, anglers, Indian tribes, wildlife managers, and whitewater enthusiasts. Rivals fight over ways to harvest timber while protecting recreation, wilderness, fisheries, and other important environmental values.

In 1986, however, the warring factions paused to explore an alternative method of decision-making.[5] The process began when representatives from the Indian tribes and the timber industry decided to find a way to put differences behind them. They were hoping to discover creative ways to solve several thorny resource management problems. Two of the thorniest issues were timber-cutting near lakes and streams and construction of logging roads. Both practices can lead to excessive soil erosion that damages streams. The Forest Practices Board of Washington's Department of Natural Resources had been struggling for four years to draft rules for timber-cutting in riparian zones. The board had developed technical reports, sponsored workshops, and was beginning to arrive at some management recommendations when it was approached by a few individuals who were embarking on a new way to negotiate their own solutions to the same problems the board was grappling with.

Brian Boyle, Washington's Commissioner of Public Lands, liked what he heard and temporarily suspended the Forest Practices Board's activities to give the new proponents some time to see if they could hammer out an agreement.

The first step was for the various groups involved—the technical people, the researchers from the state of Washington, Indian tribes, environmental groups, and timber companies—to sit down and draw up some basic resolutions about these issues. This process helped delineate the interests of the individual groups, bringing greater understanding of the issue.

Within six months, the Indian and timber representatives, working with environmentalists, government agencies, and other individuals, had completed their historic Timber, Fish, and Wildlife Agreement. The TFW agreement established a new kind of management process called adaptive management. It calls for a procedure to monitor and evaluate forestry practices. Using the information from scientific studies, researchers will find out what works and what doesn't. This information is then evaluated and reviewed by a TFW policy group. If it is found wanting, the policy group can suggest changes in the regulations, which, if adopted, could improve forest management and better protect the environment.

To help the process along, certain ground rules were set up. First, there would be no votes. All decisions would be achieved by consensus. Second, each group would have all the time it needed to present its side. Spokespersons for fish, timber, water, wildlife, archaeological, and cultural resources were allowed time to outline their concerns. The group focused on ways to achieve win/win answers and solutions to a broad range of issues. Posturing and advocacy were set aside and old enemies found that they actually agreed on many issues.

The Forest Practices Board conducted public hearings and adopted the regulations recommended by the TFW participants, who then convinced the state legislature to appropriate $4.5 million, an unprecedented amount of money, to implement the agreement. The rules adopted by the state became effective January 1, 1988, and seem to be working well. When the program started, only 1.5 million acres of commercial forest land were placed under TFW management. Today however, at least 4 million acres are under the TFW program.

One of the benefits of the process is that it has given the environmental community unprecedented involvement in timber harvesting on both state and private lands. Adaptive management will help improve water quality in streams and lakes, could boost fish populations, and improve wildlife habitat. Decreased litigation and wider public involvement were also tangible benefits.

The TFW agreement was developed by the affected parties themselves—not a government regulator. During the process, new working relationships were formed that could eventually unite traditional foes in working for the common good. Those who participated in the project think that it worked because of a willingness on the part of the participants to go beyond confrontation to cooperation. The TFW agreement may provide a model for other conflicting groups throughout the United States, illustrating ways of redefining solutions that include a broader constituency.

Cynthia Wilson, former executive director of Friends of the Earth, argues that the large staffs of skilled members in today's national environmental organizations as well as well-organized grassroots members are finding it more difficult to deal with key environmental issues, such as acid rain. Part of this, she claims, stems from the fact that industries have learned how to block the environmental community's efforts more effectively. The Reagan Administration was a major impediment as well.

Although corporate polluters remain a major concern to the environmental movement, the environmental community may find it advantageous to build ties with business and other interests. When we put aside the posturing and rhetoric, we may be surprised to learn that we share many common interests.

Recently, Friends of the Earth worked to protect thousands of miles of river in the Pacific Northwest from hydroelectric projects. FOE worked directly with staff members of the Northwest Power

Planning Council as they created a four-state inventory of river resources. FOE provided information about the process to a variety of individuals and organizations and built a groundswell of public support. An impressive coalition of recreationists, Indian tribes, and environmentalists supported the protected areas program. This effort will eliminate the endless dam-by-dam battles that drain the resources of environmental groups, says Wilson. Wherever possible, we need to follow similar paths.

Supporting Local Efforts

National politics has been the arena for many environmental battles in the past twenty years. National lobbying has been a central preoccupation of most environmental groups for good reason. New federal laws and regulations were the victories we won. Unfortunately, in our efforts to change the national agenda in our favor, the environmental community may not be paying enough attention to state and local politics.

"During the 1980s," writes William Futrell, president of the Environmental Law Institute, "state environmental programs have blossomed; state and local enforcement programs have become reality." Some observers believe that by the end of the decade 90 percent of all environmental enforcement actions will take place at the state level.[6]

In the past ten years, momentum in the environmental movement has progressively shifted to more regional, state, and local focus. According to Suzanne Mattei of the Connecticut Fund for the Environment, more of the action is at the local level than ever before. For example, she argues that the states are now on the cutting edge in toxic air regulations and pesticide control. The states have assumed more and more control because the federal government is not doing the job.[7]

Unfortunately, many of the best-known environmental groups, which were effective in the sixties and seventies, seem to have become rigidly preoccupied with their own national and international agendas. Their work is essential to global ecological balance. However, opportunities for improving the environment today may lie in finding ways to address issues at the local and regional levels. By working more closely with local grassroots concerns, the national environmental groups could help increase the depth and breadth of the environmental response.

Nathaniel P. Reed and Amos S. Eno, former assistant secretary of the Department of the Interior and director of policy of the National Fish and Wildlife Foundation, respectively, write that "today, the real battle lines are no longer in Washington. The battles are being fought on myriad state and local fronts . . . where the national environmental groups are increasingly irrelevant to the political and social solutions being formulated to contend with resource conservation issues."

The authors are not pessimistic about the environmental movement, however.[8] They think that the progress and initiatives developed at the local level more than make up for the misdirected energies of the national environmental organizations. Other observers see encouraging efforts to find political solutions at the state and local level. Local and state lobbying has taken on an importance of its own.

"The environmental agenda needs to be crafted close to home, not in grandiose documents emanating from Washington, and it should incorporate the interests of the whole spectrum of local constituents and business interests," according to Reed and Eno.

Because of the cutbacks in federal programs and Reagan's new federalism, which puts considerably more emphasis on regional control, state and local groups are more important than ever. Throughout the nation, legislators unfriendly to environmental concerns are systematically working to dismantle regulations and to weaken pollution laws. They are aided and often led by business interests who are writing new bills to take the teeth out of state environmental laws or to weaken or cripple regulatory agencies. Unfortunately, however, state legislatures are often overlooked by the environmental community.

The exciting thing about local issues is that a small amount of attention can have a major impact. One Colorado state legislator recently stated that twenty letters on her desk alerted her to a problem and forty warned her of an impending disaster. State legislators hear far more from business lobbyists than from their constituency. By stimulating letter-writing and phone-calling campaigns directed to state legislators, local and state groups can have an enormous impact on local policy decisions.

As the states become one of the major battlegrounds for environmental protection, national environmental groups may find it advantageous to refocus their attention. National organizations can do a lot to help the local lobbying efforts, but they will have to give up some power and perhaps a little money to help out. Sam Hays, an active member of the Sierra Club in Pennsylvania, notes that the national groups want to keep their money for what they do. But, he argues, the state chapters have to say, "No, we're doing something important, too." Pretty soon, says Hays, the nationals will have to give a little bit.

Not everyone agrees that they will. Some think that the major environmental groups are too short-sighted about the value of funding regional offices and local chapters. Charles Callison, a fifty-year veteran of the environmental movement and a past executive of the National Audubon Society, points out that a few years ago the president of the National Audubon Society, with the approval of the Board of Directors, tried to cut the 400 Audubon chapters adrift. He abolished all of the regional offices, except one on the East Coast and one on the West Coast. The chapters rose in fury and, after several months of protest, succeeded in keeping nine of the ten regional offices open. The president and board, however, greatly cut their staffing. At the same time, says Callison, the chapters had to fight to keep Audubon's national headquarters from taking their share of joint membership dues.

What precipitated this was a perception that the field staff and chapters were financial burdens, and that Audubon could sell and keep as many members on the strength of the popularity of their magazine and through direct mail. Callison notes that the "centralization" of the environmental organizations results, in part, from self-interest on the part of home-office bureaucracies, which are headed by executives who draw six-figure salaries and who have generous retirement plans. They are flanked by highly paid deputies and department chiefs. As a result, according to Callison, the personal lifestyles of the executives motivate their management philosophy, which sees no advantage in sending money to local groups.

South Dakota's Esther Edie isn't bashful about pointing out problems in the environmental movement at the state level. "Our major weakness," she says, "is money. The grassroots people are starving for money." The South Dakota Resources Coalition has an annual budget that ranges from $4000 to $6000. It pays for a newsletter and assorted office expenses. But what South Dakota needs is a full-time, paid staffer to handle the dozen or so issues that keep the handful of overworked volunteers busy. The South

Dakota Resources Council is trying to get a grant to pay basic overhead, says Edie, but most funding agencies don't want to fund the nuts and bolts of the organization. They will fund a group for a special project such as a study of the possible relationship between groundwater contamination and cancer, but generally don't fund the day-to-day operations.

Edie feels that the environmental movement in South Dakota and elsewhere needs to be able to build a base of political power, but has been hampered by a lack of funding. By supporting local groups and local issues with modest grants, as well as expertise, the national groups can have considerable impact on state environmental policy.

A few thousand dollars can have an enormous impact on a local issue. It can allow local activists to reach a wide audience, sponsoring workshops and letter-writing campaigns. To a national group, a thousand dollars is petty cash. But to a local group, it may be a gold mine.

Besides continuing their important work on national and global issues, the National Audubon Society, the Sierra Club, and other major environmental organizations should find ways to support local organizations financially. Part of that challenge is for the national groups to be far-sighted enough to recognize the significance of local issues in the big picture.[9]

A sweater begins to unravel when the first strand comes undone. By focusing on the strands of our ecological fabric, the national groups can help protect America from the follies of blind economic development. They can play an important part in state politics, where money and power go hand in hand, and where business interests often pull the strings of legislators and local officials.

Local Liaisons. Tim McKay, coordinator of the Northcoast Environmental Center, complains of being isolated behind the redwood curtain, shut off from the national scene. Although the national organizations have worked successfully with the Northcoast Environmental Center, such local groups are often not consulted on important issues. The higher strata of the major organizations tend to discount the expertise of the grassroots organizations.

Of the Sierra Club, The Wilderness Society, and the Audubon Society, says McKay, "Each has its . . . own perspective and slant on achieving their overall objectives, and each has a different reason for being the way they are. . . . We have had very good cooperation over the years with our dealings with the Sierra Club, in part because we have a group of the Sierra Club affiliated with us." McKay goes on to say that not all national organizations communicate extensively with his group or the people working in the area. As a result, there is a perception on the part of some people who are working at the grassroots level that their interests are not being represented in Washington, D.C., or that there are tradeoffs being made without their knowledge and consent. Sometimes this is more a perception than reality, but it does occur.

One of the principal stumbling blocks to closer cooperation is turf—jealously guarded and assiduously protected. Turf battles, however subtle, exist at all levels in the environmental movement. The fear of losing power can pit one group against another in the fund-raising frenzy.

What can the national groups do to erase the boundary lines that hinder cooperation? What can they do to help local groups? In his case, McKay believes that where there are issues in common at both the national and the grassroots or regional level, the national organizations could do more to provide financial support. Moreover, says McKay, "It would be important for them to try and bring more people back to Washington, D.C., to involve them in a lobbying effort on legislation, the formulation of legislation, or meeting with the people who are involved with issues." Instead of relying solely on their own field reps, national organizations could call on local activists for information and assistance. The Wilderness Society and the Sierra Club both help send grassroots wilderness lobbyists to Washington, D.C. Expanding these efforts can help provide the local viewpoint, which is often missing in the national debate.

Cooperative relationships can be formed at the local level as well, between state and local groups and community activists. For some issues, such as toxic wastes, the most effective people are not necessarily those in the environmental community, but rather those who are personally affected. Local outrage over groundwater pollution throughout the nation, for example, has resulted in the formation of thousands of citizen groups directly involved in fighting hazardous waste dumps and toxic chemical production. Concerned about their own health and the health of their children, people are turning out in record numbers to halt the reckless disposal of hazardous wastes and to clean up existing sites.

"I'm not sure that the state environmental groups get into these little skirmishes," says Angela Medbery of the Colorado Pesticide Network. "I see them sort of standing aside . . . saying 'We don't have time for that.'"

Elizabeth Otto, a staff member for the Colorado Environmental Coalition, explains why. "In concept, we'll go to bat for that subject [hazardous waste control] in the legislature and at the federal level, but at the local level we can't always get involved." Many groups are already spread too thin and this keeps them from tackling every new issue that arises.

Even though state groups cannot get involved in every issue, they can lend support to the citizen groups and activists. State organizations, for example, can share their expertise and offer the use of meeting rooms, copiers, and phones. They can help activists contact other citizens and can offer advice on the political pressure points where their efforts will have the greatest effect. Although money at the state level is a major problem, small grants could help local groups; a seed grant of $500 could mean the difference between life and death to a project. State organizations might consider budgeting small amounts to help foster new groups.

Many newcomers, however, are often left to their own devices. Why? State organizations may be afraid of looking bad or losing credibility. They may be afraid of losing their grip on power. They may be nervous about a group or individual wanting to move into an area that might be viewed as their turf, even if they're not interested in being active on that particular issue.

Playing Fair. In building ties with local groups, state and national organizations must tread lightly and play fairly. "I think that citizens groups have much more sophistication than a lot of the formally developed environmental groups recognize. Many of them [state and grassroots groups] . . . do really excellent work," says Suzanne Mattei of the Connecticut Fund for the Environment. "I have seen national groups approach these groups as if they were children. 'Let us teach you how to run a meeting, let us tell you how to create your campaign . . .' State groups have done this too.

"Sometimes," says Mattei, "national groups use the labor of state groups and grassroots citizens groups in a way that is unethical. They do some really terrific project, get some great results, and then the state or national organization takes most, if not all, of the credit."

"But did they really accomplish it? Or did that citizen's group accomplish it?" wonders Mattei. "That citizens group was working with no staff, no funding, nothing. It was entirely a volunteer, getting up at 6:00 AM to write out a press release before their kids woke up type of thing."

When state and national organizations become involved in an issue they sometimes exert extraordinary pressure on local activists to do things their way. Long Island Sound, famous for the medical wastes washing up on its beaches, resembled Grand Central Station in 1988 and 1989. Many of the national groups flocked to Long Island Sound where they tried to align with local groups. In so doing, however, they applied a lot of pressure on local activists to convince them to do things their way. Local groups, however, have their own ideas about what ought to be done, and often resent the Johnny-come-latelys.

One of the concerns about the involvement of national organizations in local politics is that when the issue dies down they will be gone. The state and local groups will continue the battle, but they often do not get any of the money that the nationals received from foundations to "organize the local response." The nationals have a tendency to take the credit, then move on to another issue they can champion.

It isn't always this way, of course. The Connecticut Fund for the Environment, for example, worked with the Environmental Defense Fund to comment on a proposal to close a hazardous waste site. The Environmental Defense Fund submitted a joint proposal for funding, which they received. CFE and EDF worked well on the project, mixing and matching talents. But the important thing is that they both had resources to make it happen. "EDF realized how much work we would have to do on the project for it to be a success," says Mattei. "They made the effort to make sure that we had funding too."

This project underscores the value of cooperative relationships between national and state organizations. CFE shared its knowledge of state agencies and state regulations, and EDF brought to bear its considerable knowledge about what a hazardous waste dump closure plan ought to look like and its ability to obtain funding. "We were therefore able to combine our talents to make the project happen," says Mattei. "But nobody was using anybody." It was a partnership. "That is the kind of thing I like to see. It happens too seldom."

Leadership Development: A Role for the Nationals in Local Affairs.

National environmental organizations can do a great deal to help state and local groups build bridges with the public and potential volunteers. By assisting in staff training, in finding ways to motivate and recruit volunteers, the nationals can help build a stronger grassroots response. They can also help by offering training in leadership development. Workshops on collaboration sponsored by state and national environmental organizations may also help promote cooperative alliances at all levels—even with business and other traditionally unaligned forces.

Says Peter Berle of the National Audubon Society, at the local level there is "a dedicated group of leaders who are not particularly effective at ensuring their own replacement or generating a cadre of leaders to follow them." Speaking about Audubon chapters, Berle notes that many chapters have trouble finding people to assume a leadership position on issues. "Being a civic leader is tough. It takes time . . . you get harassed, all that sort of thing," he says. "But we've got to do better at generating more leaders at the local level and providing the support and the recognition and the kinds of things that inspire people to spend their time, and give up leisure time."

In short, we need to find leaders who can inspire, leaders who can endure the sometimes rough-and-tumble game of environmental activism. There are good activists throughout the United States, says Berle, who are dedicated and hardworking, but we need to greatly increase their numbers.

Weekend retreats cosponsored by national and state organizations might be a way to teach leadership and motivational skills for local leaders and activists. Leadership training can address a variety of important questions: What does it take to be a good leader? How do we inspire people? How can we tap into people's commitment? How do we recruit volunteers and new leaders? How do we maintain volunteers?

Leadership retreats or seminars sponsored by the environmental community could be hosted by people who have dedicated their lives to understanding leadership and commitment and who have devised inspirational presentations.

Local environmental groups recruit many really good people; for one reason or another, some of these people turn out to not be terribly effective leaders. Some may seek too much control and may not be able to bend to the majority opinion expressed by staff and board. Some can't seem to inspire other people, some lack commitment and fizzle out shortly after they're elected, and some can't delegate authority. Many of the good people move on to national organizations, leaving the state and local groups somewhat at a loss.

I pointed out in Chapters 3 and 4 that we need a legion of responsible citizens to help make things right. They become leaders by the example they set. But we also need more charismatic, articulate, and inspiring leaders in positions of authority and power within the environmental movement. That's a tall order for state and local groups. It can be done, however, through training and persistence. It can be achieved by finding ways to enlist new leaders who emerge in neighborhood battles over toxic wastes or other issues. By asking board members, staff members, and committee chairs to keep an eye out for activists emerging in the community, we can begin to spread our roots out into the community. When someone writes a strong letter to the editor, call him or her up and encourage them to join an existing committee, form a new one, or perhaps join the board of directors. That isn't something that occurs very often, says Berle. "I think that we have to be much more open about recruiting, finding, developing, encouraging leadership."

Bureaucratic Hurdles. Perhaps the most commonly articulated concern or criticism of the environmental movement is its tendency toward bureaucratization, our penchant to build complex, many-layered organizations, which often become roadblocks between the stimulus and reaction. Berle states, "I think we've got to beware of becoming too bureaucratic and too formalized, which is always one of the concerns about a big organization. I get worried about getting too stuffy and bureaucratic." One of the challenges in a large organization is being receptive to new ideas and being flexible. Rules and procedures stifle creativity. Maintenance of the bureaucracy becomes an end in itself, sapping strength and vitality, not to mention money, from an organization.

Clearly, organizations like the National Audubon Society with an annual budget of $32 million, can't be run on the back of an envelope. "You've got to be as good at managing or better than any private sector enterprise," says Berle. Donors have to be confident that, when they give to an environmental organization, the group is being managed professionally and efficiently.

One of the chief dangers of bureaucratization is wheel-spinning. "Unless you've got a team that's got a lot of hustle, you
spend a lot of time writing memos back and forth to each other
and sometimes that's easier than getting up and making things
happen," according to Berle.

Bureaucracies often take the power out of good ideas and important work. That translates into reduced effectiveness and invariably a slower response time. Clearly, the challenge is finding a way
to minimize the bureaucratic wheel-spinning and maximize effectiveness.

Paul Watson believes that the problem is that as organizations
get larger, they become less effective in achieving what they originally set out to do. Greenpeace is an example, he says, and as one
of the founding members of Greenpeace in 1971, he speaks with
considerable experience. "For the first eight years of the life of that
organization, much more was accomplished than in the years after.
From 1970 to 1977 we were an effective organization," he says.
"And on a very limited budget." In 1987, Greenpeace USA had a
budget of $26 million. "I would have expected to have seen a lot
more come out of that organization," says Watson. "Unfortunately, it, like many other large organizations, is bogged down in a
bureaucratic nightmare of paperwork and administrative details."

Another danger of bureaucracy is that it tends to stifle vision.
Because of this, some people doubt that the leadership needed to
help build a sustainable society will come from the mainstream environmental groups.

It may be a naive suggestion, but by sending back a larger percentage of a person's membership fee to the local chapters or by
supporting local groups that are unaffiliated with them, the national organizations could eliminate some of the need for some of
the potentially burdensome bureaucracy. Such a move would help
the state and local organizations as well in their struggles to address the burgeoning workload. It's an idea worth studying in
more detail. Decentralizing power, especially in an era when local
action is becoming more and more important, could strengthen
the roots of environmentalism.

If we imagine an organization as a wheel with a hub, says Angela Medbery, there are two decidedly different models of organizational dispersion of power. One involves a central hub with a
fairly weak perimeter. This is the model of groups like National

Audubon Society. Spokes emanate from the hub connecting the two parts, but the hub calls the shots.

The second model concentrates its strength in the wheel, the peripheral groups, the grassroots organizations where local actions are spawned. That's the model of the Green Party and the Pesticide Action Network. The hub is a facilitator. It provides information and guidance, but the real action is in the field.

There are at least two other models. The first is the one by which Environmental Action and the Citizens Clearinghouse for Hazardous Waste operate. These groups consist of a small, fast-acting core of facilitators who train and support local grassroots organizations that may have no formal affiliation with the core at all. The last model is one that dispenses with the local groups altogether, and is exemplified by groups such as the Natural Resources Defense Council, World Resources Institute, and Friends of Earth, in which the work is done by a central office.

There's no model that is right or wrong. They each have their benefits and no doubt will continue to be used in the years to come. The strong-hub approach, however, could benefit greatly by adding elements from the second and third models, given the growing importance of local issues and local decisions and the need to reach a wider audience and lobby individuals for personal changes.

Results, discussed briefly in Chapter 5, is an organization whose hub provides guidance and information. The action—the real power—exists in the thousand or so regional coordinators who do the phone calling and letter writing and make personal visits to legislators and aides. The Washington office of Results has an executive director and a small staff that sends information to people in the field. The goal of the central office is to help their regional representatives become more effective in dealing with legislators and newspaper editorial page writers. The central office works closely with the peripheral staff, but doesn't get in the way. They teach them a methodology and supply them with information, then let them do their own thing.

The Pesticide Action Network, which is an international organization, operates similarly. They have a number of offices worldwide, but their representatives in the Third World countries are the ones who push buttons. For opinions and judgement calls, they consult with the central offices.

I'm not suggesting that the Sierra Club and the National Audubon Society abandon their approach, only that they and others consider spreading money and power peripherally to the field. And by doing so, they will help make environmentalism at the state level more effective.

Earth in Transition: On the Threshold of Change

8

Psychologist and author Charles Kettering once wrote that a problem well stated is a problem half solved. If this were in fact true, the world would surely have made more significant progress in solving the environmental crisis. Unfortunately, between understanding our problems and solving them lies a huge gap.

Many of us have attempted to bridge the gaps through adversarial and compulsory means, as pointed out in earlier chapters. New laws and regulations or lawsuits, injunctions, and fines have been the methods of choice. These important actions, however, only address the symptoms of the disease. With few exceptions, they fall short because they do not remedy the root causes of our environmental crisis: rapid population growth, overpopulation, resource depletion, pollution, and the crisis of spirit manifested in large part by our adherence to the frontier mentality, a belief in unlimited resources and human dominance and control of nature.

Solving the wide range of environmental ills that besets our planet will require major shifts in politics, economics, technology, and human thinking. It will make the moon landing seem like a weekend fix-up job by comparison. Because of the enormous stakes at hand, the environmental movement has become a crucial thread in the fabric of modern society. Without the changes necessary, the cloth of our common existence might well begin to unravel, taking us along with it.

This chapter summarizes the changes recommended in this book—changes that could help us begin the process of reform required to build a sustainable society. The chapter concludes with some advice on strategies and pitfalls in the all-important task of building a sustainable society.

Visions of Sustainability

Despite the growing realization of impending ecological disaster, most people—especially our business and political leaders—remain aligned with outdated frontier notions. Regrettably, most environmental educators, environmental leaders, and others have made little progress in reversing the frontier mentality. In recent years, modern society seems to have given in to the logic that calls for continued economic development, thinking somehow that through this strategy we can work our way out of the mess we're in.

Many of us in the environmental field have been inclined to dwell on the present dimensions of the crisis—talking troubles instead of solutions. In so doing, the environmental movement has not yet developed and articulated a coherent image of a sustainable future.

Building a sustainable society will require changes in technology, industry, political institutions, leadership, economics, education, housing, and transportation. It will also require a fundamental change in our world view.

A sustainable society is based on three philosophical principles. The first is that there is not always more. The earth is *not* an unlimited supply of resources. The second is that "we are all one." Humans are a part of, not apart from, the environment. We are subject to its rules. Given the limits of the environment and our place within the system of nature, the sustainable ethic holds that the earth's resources are the common property of all species, and must be shared equitably. Heedless self-interest is an invitation to ecological (and economic) disaster. The third is that humans are not superior to other species, not the crowning achievement of nature, but another species. Our role is to cooperate not dominate.

A sustainable society is built on four pillars: conservation, renewable resources, recycling, and population control. It requires appropriate technology and appropriate policy. It requires flexibility—or adaptive management. It requires us to live within our means.

Sustainability is a tall order for a society whose economy has become increasingly dependent on nonrenewable resources and continual economic growth and material embellishment. To build such a society will require strong leadership from the environmental community to overcome daunting opposition to changing a system that, for many people, seems to be working just fine.

A sustainable society will result from a myriad of approaches. New rules and regulations can help reshape corporate and personal practices. A shift in attitude and lifestyle will help change society from the bottom up. But before we embark on the change we need a consensus for action. And we need an approximate roadmap for the journey.

Recommendations. The environmental community can help draw an approximate roadmap to sustainability. This task will require research and creativity to answer some key questions: What is a sustainable society? How will we transport people to and from work in such a society? What will happen to our cities? Where will we get our energy? How will we grow food? How can we learn to respect the rights of other species? We must study each aspect of modern society and propose sustainable alternatives to unacceptable modern practices.

After shaping a vision of a sustainable society, we must find ways to build it. The first task in making the transition to a sustainable society inevitably requires public outreach—articulating our goals to the general public, to government officials, to business interests and others. The broad environmental community can expound on the need for sustainable business, government, and personal lifestyles and ways of achieving them through speeches, classroom lectures, articles, interviews, television programs, and private conversations.

Through meetings of leaders at all levels, the environmental community can establish a blueprint for sustainability. State and nationwide conferences can be organized to discuss sustainable solutions and to build coalitions of like-minded individuals aimed at taking positive actions to build a sustainable future.

Tapping the Power of People

Modern society has, for the most part, failed to tap the enormous power of people to change their lives in ways that can help prevent and cure environmental problems. Too little attention has been focused on ways to encourage conscientious lifestyles. The time is ripe to unleash individual responsibility and action.

Unfortunately, society as a whole tends to discount personal caring. Unwittingly, we perpetuate the myth that people don't care or care only about things that affect them directly. Nothing could be further from the truth. Despite our apparent self-centeredness, most people want to make a difference. Most people would rather be a part of the solution. Although many of us dream of changing the world, we don't know where to begin. Many of us have grown cynical about the effectiveness of individual action.

Society as a whole also tends to discount individual action. Many people have taken themselves out of the cause-and-effect equation and have become content to pin the blame on others. With few exceptions, the environmental movement has not adequately drawn the connections between polluted skies and wasteful lifestyles. It's a message that we ignore at our own peril, for the belief that we are not part of the environmental crisis is a double-edged sword. It creates many of our problems and keeps us from solving them.

Environmentalism has helped to foster a somewhat superficial level of response—the cash conscience. "Fight money with money" is the unspoken motto of American environmentalism. We're fostering the notion that a cash donation is enough to solve the environmental crisis. Although we need money to wage legal and legislative battles, we need to travel down other avenues as well. We need people who are willing not only to donate money but are also willing to live their lives in accordance with the limits of the environment. We need people who will make changes, sometimes significant changes, in their lifestyles for the common good of the human family.

Recommendations. It's up to us in the environmental movement to delineate the connections between people and the emerging environmental crisis. But we must do it without evoking paralyzing guilt and despondency.

Carefully worded articles and advertisements can help us tap into the reserves of compassion. Newsletters, articles, television shows, classroom lectures, and conferences can serve as vehicles for discussing solutions that involve individuals.

We can publicize examples of individual actions that have made a difference. By so doing, we can focus attention on the changes possible when individual actions are multiplied many times over.

To help reach beyond our own tightly knit community of environmentalist friends, we may want to mount an outreach operation. Local, state, and national groups can ask members to spread the word to their friends, neighbors, and family. Environmental groups and others could sponsor the Decade of the Environment Campaign aimed at attracting broad public support for change. The campaign could focus on global climate change and ways individuals can work individually to help reduce greenhouse gases and other air pollutants. This campaign could involve businesses and governmental leaders, and can reinforce the idea that a clean and healthy environment cannot be achieved by occasional action, but will be achieved only by a lifetime of attentiveness and action. Earth Day must indeed be every day.

The Decade of the Environment could expand to an international effort aimed at healing the planet. Both programs can promote the idea of individual leadership—people who take action out of conviction.

Making Environmentalism Mainstream

The polls show that Americans are concerned about the growing list of environmental hazards now facing humanity. It's a concern that results in large part from widespread media coverage and the ever-increasing signs of environmental deterioration. But concern and the commitment to make the changes needed are two different creatures. Concern can deepen and become meaningful, but it will take time and concerted efforts on the part of the environmental movement to make this happen. Our key challenge today, then, is to capture the rising tide of concern and help transform it into a lasting public response that will help us build a sustainable society.

Public concern can be deepened but only if the environmental community articulates a vision for change and discusses appropriate solutions, especially those that engage individuals. These changes will help us reverse the gloom-and-doom image of environmentalists and will help us reduce the paralysis that can result from the view that our problems are too immense to be solved easily, or to be solved at all.

Many observers believe that the environmental movement must reach a much larger audience. If we can reach a larger and more diverse audience, we can build a base of support to reshape American society. Several barriers hinder this important task.

First, the environmental community has been typecast by business critics and others. We are often seen as elitists whose interest in wilderness, wild rivers, and endangered species conflicts with a broader human interest. Unfortunately, we haven't been successful in countering these criticisms. To draw on the sympathies of the general public, we must make it clearer that planet-care is self-care and that the wise use of resources and sustainability ultimately benefits everyone. Some observers complain that environmental activists are often too negative and self-righteous. This attitude, where it exists, prevents us from enlisting a broader constituency.

Perhaps one of the chief obstacles, though, is that our message is often a private one. Although we need to refine and expand our ideas and reach a consensus among ourselves, we also need to get our message to a broader constituency—we must begin to educate the public at large. Broadening public support will create the people-power we need to make environmentalism a mainstream value and lifestyle. For long-term success, however, we need to find ways to instill environmental values and appropriate lifestyles in our children.

The road to full public support of environmentally responsible lifestyles is long and difficult. It requires a transition involving five interdependent steps: awareness, knowledge, attitude shift, intention shift, and participation. Environmental educators, writers, publishers, and activists can be a part of this process, but so far most of our efforts have been focused on raising awareness and increasing the level of public knowledge.

Recommendations. To build a strong base of public support, we can find ways to be more positive and less self-righteous. We can counter the stereotype of elitism by explaining the connection between environmental protection and human well-being and by offering sustainable alternatives to costly and environmentally destructive projects.

Teachers, environmental activists, and others can begin to educate the public on the need for change. Environmental groups can produce and broadcast carefully worded television and radio advertisements or programs that help raise awareness and call for individual action.

To bring environmentalism into the mainstream, the environmental community must expand its efforts to reach minorities, the religious community, senior citizens, and children.

To reach minorities, we can build bridges with minority civic leaders, business interests, politicians, clergy, and others. We can help by pointing out the ways environmental issues directly affect the lives of minorities, if the connections are not already clear. We can provide information and technical support. We can help principally by reaching into the minority community to give.

To reach senior citizens, we may want to enlist the support of speakers who could tour the country talking to senior citizens on environmental problems, solutions, and the opportunities for them to get involved. To avoid unnecessary duplication, we may want to form a national coalition of groups that could pool resources.

Reaching the religious community is a task of extreme urgency as well. Environmental groups at all levels can work with local clergy to provide materials and advice as needed. A national coalition of environmental groups interested in working with the religious community might be created to avoid unnecessary duplication and could support on-going efforts of other groups.

For long-term success, we must find ways to better educate our children on the value of a clean, diverse, and healthy environment. Environmental education must expand considerably from a long-standing tradition that often focuses only on nature education to an emphasis on issues and solutions, especially those that involve individuals. Students can be taught ways to analyze conflicting viewpoints using critical thinking skills. Children must be encouraged to think about the results of individual choices. Ecological principles must be taught, along with the applications of these principles to our modern society. Ecological principles can be used to help promote the importance of a sustainable society.

Beyond Reactionism

Environmentalism has largely been a reaction to the ever-growing environmental crisis. Our chief response to governmental and corporate policies that threaten our environment has been the two Ls—legal and legislative. Not surprisingly, the lawyer and the lobbyist have been our chief operatives in this crucial battlefield.

The Reagan years forced us to continue our paperwork battles. By cutting funding to key agencies, by ending support of essential legislation and by relaxing (in some cases eliminating) important regulations, the Reagan administration forced environmentalists deeper into the trenches. The lawsuit enjoyed renewed interest. Lobbyists suffered no shortage of work.

The Reagan years, however, also forced us to assume an additional role as well—that of the nation's watchdog of regulation. It became painfully clear in those eight trying years of the Reagan administration that regulatory agencies weren't doing their job, so environmental groups stepped in to see that the laws were enforced. When it was necessary to sue businesses for violating regulations for hazardous waste, clean air, and clean water, we did it—and quite successfully. When it became necessary to sue a federal agency to get it to write regulations that it was required to draft, we did it.

The dependency on legal action has been forced upon us, many agree. While such actions are necessary and will continue to play an important role in years to come, we can do more. We can become a positive proactive force in modern society.

Recommendations. We can begin by proposing more sustainable alternatives to projects that are environmentally and economically unsound. In working with government and business, however, we cannot afford to lose our vision, or to compromise our future away.

To help build a sustainable economy we can promote economic health, rather than continual economic growth. The environmental community should eschew growth rhetoric and emphasize a view that sees economic and environmental health as parts of the same whole.

Environmentalists can find ways to promote businesses that cut waste. In other words, we can help local, state, and federal governments find ways to plug up the leaks in our economy, cutting the waste of water, energy, and other resources. Plugging up the leaks pertains to all sectors of society from transportation to housing to education.

We can also find ways to build businesses around our waste. We can help government and business find ways to put the waste to good use through reuse and recycling programs. We can help identify hidden economic opportunities with obvious environmental benefits.

Finally, let's encourage governments throughout the world to recruit or support clean and green businesses. That means businesses that don't pollute, or that produce minimal amounts of pollution; companies that reuse and recycle waste; companies that encourage carpooling or companies that locate near major mass-transit routes and encourage their people to use public transit; and companies that produce durable products that are necessary, not frivolous discardables.

To help green business, we can work with American colleges and universities to develop environmental courses for business majors. We may want to draft a Corporate Responsibility Act that allows CEOs of corporations to bypass opportunities for profit when they are environmentally destructive, without being sued by their shareholders. The law could also require environmental impact analyses for all offerings for investment, so that potential stockholders can screen companies and make a judgement of their environmental policies and impacts. Finally, the law could require an impact statement on all corporate takeovers. We can also work directly with corporations and small businesses through the Chamber of Commerce to find environmentally responsible alternatives.

To help build stronger working relationships with business and government, major environmental groups may want to establish a network of grassroots activists, following the Results model. Community activists can apply gentle but persistent pressure.

To help restore the earth's richness, we could mount a Green Century Project, similar to the Investing for Prosperity program in California. The Decade of the Environment could be the beginning of a 100-year program to restore the earth, replant trees, rebuild marshes, revegetate denuded landscapes, to reduce air pollution, cut hazardous wastes, and so on.

The Missing Connections

In our efforts to end waste and pollution, many environmental groups seem to have bought into Madison-Avenue sales tactics and their underlying logic. Environmental groups, for example, are flooding members and prospective members with direct-mail appeals. Until very recently, few were printed on recycled paper. Most have far more material than people care to read.

Opinions of excessive direct mail vary. Some think it's a necessary evil, others think it actually serves a useful purpose by educating members, and some think that it even gives a good message. But more and more people are growing dismayed at the constant barrage of appeals and the waste that they create. Many people fear that their donations are being eaten up by direct-mail campaigns. Many contributors want to see their money used more directly to do good work.

The environmental movement's growing dependence on direct mail promotes the idea that individuals can help solve environmental problems with cash. They promote the idea that new laws and regulations are all we need to solve the environmental troubles we face. Many of the environmental groups send appeals too frequently, include excess material that few people read, and ignore personal actions. They fight for conservation, recycling, waste controls, and cutbacks in pollution but are not taking their own message seriously enough.

Direct mail is part of an onslaught of advertising that is slowly desensitizing the public. To fight the desensitization, groups are finding new ways to catch people's eyes. One of the latest "inventions" of direct-mail advertising is the use of the large envelope, which stands out in the mailbox, apart from all of the rest. Although it may be a good marketing tool, it represents an unnecessary escalation in the practice of direct mail that increases the waste of paper and resources.

In their zeal to attract membership, some environmental groups have gone overboard in direct-mail campaigns. They recruit a lot of "soft members" who have a low renewal rate. To cater to them, say some critics, groups must soften their stand. One of the most disturbing trends is the "environmental credit card," offered by major groups. A small portion of the credit card company's profit is donated to the group offering the card. Credit cards, however, are another endorsement of excessive consumption. They generate more waste and encourage people to buy. By profiting from credit card purchases, the environmental groups become unwitting agents of environmental destruction.

Let's face it: we can't spend our way out of the environmental crisis. By promoting waste and consumption, we only worsen the mess we're in.

Recommendations. Environmental groups at all levels could re-vamp their outreach campaigns to find ways to cut back on waste, use recycled paper, and promote individual action. We can set a better example. Ultimately, we must live more consistently with our ideals.

Environmental groups could pass the equivalent of the government's Paperwork Reduction Act. Although most groups are convinced that what they put out is not wasteful, many individuals disagree. A waste-reduction initiative agreed to by the major mailers could go a long way in cutting back on the waste. Although many groups offer members an option that protects their name from being sold or traded and shelters them from appeals, it should be on all membership applications and renewal forms.

To help reduce resource-intensive direct-mail campaigns, environmental groups might consider increasing workplace solicitation. A national "Environmental Way" program could be formed to solicit money and to reduce direct-mail appeals. It should not become just another bureaucracy that wastes money and consumes vast portions of individual donations, however.

Groups can also start endowment funds that will provide money in the future to offset fund-raising. And groups can try to find ways to eliminate duplicate mailings. Wherever possible, state and national groups should merge mailing lists and purge duplicate names. Lists should be periodically updated with the U.S. Postal Service to reduce undeliverable mail. Finally, some groups may want to find ways to eliminate inappropriate advertising in their publications.

Marshalling Our Forces

Over the years, environmentalists have missed many opportunities to make the movement stronger and more effective. We often overlook opportunities to join forces with other environmentalists, business people, and others. We frequently fail in our efforts to recruit new and energetic leaders at the local level, creating unnecessary discontinuity. We often don't work hard enough to develop leadership skills that could help inspire people to action.

At the state and local level, many groups are crippled by a lack of funds and must therefore depend almost entirely on volunteers. Paid staffers are often overworked and underpaid.

Duplication of effort is another problem and is common at many levels. To an extent, some duplication is necessary. Where it reduces our overall effectiveness, however, it should be eliminated. Reducing duplication frees up time, talent, and money for other projects. Eliminating duplication will require leaders to form coalitions. This is not always easy, but the more successful we are at building new working relationships, the greater our strength and effectiveness. One of the secrets of building successful coalitions is to preserve diversity while building strength.

Keeping track of who's doing what in the environmental community is a bookkeeping task that needs more attention. Directories of groups working on various issues in each state, including contact people, current projects, and resources, can help us identify potential working partners. It could help groups share resources, time, and talent to build a stronger environmental voice in public affairs.

Part of the problem with environmentalism today lies in our frequent inability to define problems and solutions that involve the interests of groups and individuals from many different walks of life. Coalitions of environmentalists, hunters, anglers, and others can be drawn together to draft plans that satisfy a wider range of interests.

National politics has been the principal arena for political change in the past two decades. Recently, however, states have begun to assume more responsibility in environmental protection. Many groups have begun to focus their attention on local solutions. Local and state lobbying have assumed greater importance, but more effective state lobbying is needed. National groups can help strengthen the local response by working with groups, offering leadership training, and awarding small grants.

Local groups suffer from volunteer anemia, a lack of people to carry out their work. As a result, the ever-expanding workload is relegated to a handful of people. We need to find ways to enlist new people.

Perhaps the most commonly articulated criticism of America's environmental movement is the tendency to become bogged down in bureaucracy, which reduces our ability to respond quickly, if at all to fast-breaking issues. Bureaucracies may also tend to stifle vision, and waste money and resources that could be better spent on fighting issues. The environmental movement could benefit immeasurably at the state level by developing a strong network of lawyers, scientists, and other experts who are willing to volunteer their time to help local citizens groups.

Recommendations. To help build a stronger force for change, we can eliminate unnecessary duplication wherever possible. One way of eliminating duplication is through coalitions. Environmental groups can form coalitions around issues, find areas of agreement, outline goals, then divide up the workload.

State groups can publish directories of environmental organizations and activists, listing groups and individuals and their resources and activities. Directories can be made available to all groups and to the public so that citizens can find out who's doing what—and find ways to channel their interests.

To increase our strength at the state and local levels, environmental groups at all levels should encourage letter-writing and phone-calling campaigns to local officials. We can use the media more effectively to draw attention to local issues and solutions. National groups can help by financing state issue work and can also bring local experts to Washington, when necessary, to help with national issues.

To increase the number of active volunteers, environmental groups may find it advantageous to bring more newcomers into their organizations. The leaders and staff members of state and local groups can take a more active role in reaching out to community activists. Environmental organizations can find ways to train their people in leadership and recruitment skills. Environmental groups can also train leaders in ways to inspire people and learn to tap into individual commitment.

Some Parting Advice

One thing is certain. Environmental consciousness and support must grow considerably. For the most part, though, the broad environmental movement has been stuck in the trenches, caught under heavy cross-fire, unable to reach out to a broader constituency and to expand its approach.

A new era is dawning, though, and members of the environmental community are becoming a part of a proactive movement that seeks lasting change by plotting strategies that will transform society. This requires that we play smarter.

Strategies for Success. Too often environmental action is a matter of muddling through. We need to define objectives, set priorities, and plot ways to achieve our goals. But too often the flood of crises dictates our agenda. By strategizing more effectively we can become more successful in effecting change.

In 1988, the Natural Resources Council of Maine succeeded in tackling an issue that has baffled many environmentalists—local growth control. They overcame objections of developers, an organization of all the towns in Maine, and the governor. The Maine legislature passed a law that requires each town to develop a land-use plan that should help end the haphazard development pattern that is tearing the state into pieces.

Faced with a rapid influx of people, the Natural Resources Council of Maine outlined a detailed strategy with a three-year timetable, then systematically worked to see their plan through. They began by researching successful land-use planning programs in the United States. Brownie Carson, who heads the organization, spent ten days in Oregon talking with environmental leaders, political leaders, town planners, business people, bankers, and ranchers, criss-crossing the state to get a feel for how their program worked. When he and his colleagues returned to Maine, they talked with the governor's cabinet, business people, and newspaper editors. They convinced a major Maine newspaper to do a piece on the growth issue. NRCM members started writing editorials about it, and the group sponsored a conference on the issue as well.

"Essentially what we tried to do was to frame the problem and then propose a solution," says Carson. In 1987, they succeeded in convincing the legislature to form a commission to study the issue and the NRCM worked with the legislators on the commission. The commission sponsored a series of hearings around the state. The NRCM packed the hearings with people who were supporters of land-use planning by doing grassroots organizing around those hearings. The group drafted a proposal of the legislation, which, in essence became the bill. "We worked with the staff of the commission, which was the same staff of the committee that ultimately heard the bill and hammered out the final language," says Carson. This exhaustive well-conceived effort paid off and serves as a model of the approach that will help us become more successful in the future.

Avoiding Pitfalls. "Our doubts are traitors," wrote Shakespeare, "and make us lose the good we oft might win by fearing to attempt." The greatest barrier we have to becoming a more effective force is ourselves—our doubts and our skepticism about what we as a society can become. This is not an insignificant barrier. Can we overcome the widespread sense of hopelessness and despair? Can we strengthen the environmental response in a truly meaningful way—a way that will result in significant change, not more short-term stop-gap measures. Can we build a sustainable society?

Certainly. But these changes will require all of our resources. The transition to a sustainable society is the challenge and the opportunity far greater than any society has faced. Author Thomas Sancton writes in the Planet of the Year issue of *Time*, "Let there be no illusions. Taking effective action to halt the massive injury to the biosphere will require a mobilization of political will, international cooperation, and sacrifice unknown except in wartime." He goes on to say, "Yet humanity is in a war right now . . . It is a war in which all nations must be allies. Both the causes and effects of the problems that threaten the earth are global, and they must be attacked globally." Mobilizing our forces will require extraordinary leadership, of which the environmental community will be an integral part.

In rising to the challenge, environmentalists must avoid numerous pitfalls that may cause us to run aground. First, we must avoid the paralysis that stems from the attitude that we are doomed to perish by overpopulation, food shortage, war, or pollution. This paralysis will only keep us from thinking creatively and acting with determination to make necessary changes.

We must also avoid excessive optimism in legal and legislative solutions. While tighter controls on corporate pollution are surely needed, we must also go to the other roots of the problem: people and consumption, human lifestyles and the all-too-prevalent ethic that puts personal satisfaction above responsibility to the earth and others. We must avoid the attitude that someone else will solve the problem. The sustainable society comes closer to being a reality with each person's effort, no matter how small or large. Individuals can help by making changes that create a less resource-intensive lifestyle. Which changes we make are not as important as the decision to change and a lasting commitment.

We must also avoid outdated solutions and we must be careful not to overlook obvious answers. We must avoid narrow thinking and restricted imagination. All our creativity, cooperation, and patience will be called on to achieve a sustainable society.

In all of this, we must touch people's logic and their hearts. We must support our contentions with sound research and be honest with the facts. At the same time, however, we must encourage compassion for other living things. Our problems will not be solved solely in the minds of people but in our hearts as well. We must make our effort to transform the world a journey of the heart and mind, a fusion of reason and compassion.

Humankind is entering a period of unprecedented social change. Perched on this exciting threshold, we are being forced to rediscover connections and relationships—within ourselves, with the earth, and with the thousands of human and nonhuman inhabitants that share this planet with us, says David Lynch, president of the Stewardship Community.

We may have pushed our planet to the edge of environmental disaster. The only sensible thing to do at the edge of a precipice, says environmental writer Kirkpatrick Sale, is to step back.[1] Stepping back from the edge of disaster is the beginning of a long process of social transformation. The chief goals of the coming decade and the new century will be not to adopt fashionable new lifestyles or to bring the Green party into power or to "green" our presidents and legislators and corporate CEOs—although these are important steps.[2] Our goal will not be to continue our legal battles for imposed restraint, but to change our values and our culture. Our goal will be to create a stable presence on earth—a new social order in which men's, women's, and children's simple acts of love and kindness lead to profound change in the way we treat our endangered planet.[3]

The science of ecology has taught us that human beings are not visitors on earth, but part of the earth itself. The quality of the lives we lead and the quality of the life other living creatures can enjoy now and for generations to come depends chiefly on us. It depends on our willingness to learn to act in ways that strengthen and enhance, not tear, the fabric that binds us to our home, the earth.

Endnotes

Chapter 1: A Time for Change?

1. Richard Behar (1989). Joe's Bad Trip. *Time* 134(1): 42–47. Overview of the events taking place on March 24, 1989, before and after the Valdez oil spill.

2. Michael Satchell and Betsey Carpenter (1989). A Disaster That Wasn't. *U.S. News and World Report.* 107(11): 60–69. A shortsighted approach that attempts to add up the damage of the Valdez spill, but overlooks long-term problems.

3. Huey D. Johnson (1988). Environmental Quality as a National Purpose. In *Crossroads: Environmental Priorities for the Future.* Peter Borrelli, ed. Washington, D.C.: Island Press.

4. The United States banned CFCs used in spray cans in 1978. Canada, Sweden, Finland, and Norway took similar measures. By 1984 CFC emissions worldwide were 21 percent lower than they were in 1978 because of these and other voluntary cutbacks. The reduction in CFC emissions may have slowed ozone depletion somewhat, but would not stop it.

5. Christopher Flavin (1987). *Reassessing Nuclear Power: The Fallout from Chernobyl.* Worldwatch Paper 75. Washington, D.C.: Worldwatch Institute.

6. Oliver S. Owen (1989). The Heat Is On: The Greenhouse Effect and the Earth's Future. *The Futurist* 23(5): 34–40.

7. Barry Commoner (1989). Why We Have Failed. *Greenpeace* 14(5): 12–13.

8. In other words, you could not sue a company that polluted a river that ran through your property unless you suffered financial damage. If financial damage could be proved, you would have legal standing in court. This means that people couldn't sue to protect wilderness or keep rivers clean, unless they were directly affected. Thus, the environment had no standing in court.

9. As of January 1, 1989.

10. As of January 1, 1989, there were 9,260 miles of river protected by the Wild and Scenic River Act.

11. Richard and Joyce Wolkomir (1989). Landing the Deal. *USAIR* (July): 38–43. The Nature Conservancy buys on average 1,000 acres a day.

12. From 1975 to 1987 per capita declines in emissions were: 88 percent for lead, 33 percent for carbon monoxide, 25 percent for hydrocarbons, 43 percent for particulates, and 10 percent for nitrogen oxides.

13. Based on population data from the U.S. Census Bureau and the Population Reference Bureau and pollution data published in *Statistical Abstracts of the United States* (1989) and *National Air Quality Emissions Trends Report,* published by the EPA in 1987.

14. If abortion is made illegal and if immigration quotas are raised by Congress, U.S. population may not stabilize.

15. Nitrous oxide, chlorofluorocarbons, and methane are three additional greenhouse gases and all are produced from human activities.

16. There are ample resources that describe the environmental crisis and put it into a believable perspective. See Brown et al. (1989) *State of the World.* New York: Norton. This book is published annually. Read the introductory chapters to get an overview of the most pressing problems. Chapter 1 of Daniel D. Chiras (1988). *Environmental Science: Framework for Decision Making.* Second edition. Menlo Park, California: Benjamin/Cummings, describes the environmental crisis as well, giving a fairly broad overview of the major problems.

17. World Commission on Environment and Development (1987). *Our Common Future.* Oxford: Oxford University Press.

Chapter 2: From Futureblindness to Visions of Sustainability

1. Many politicians and business people continue to promote the notion of unlimited economic growth, and some citizens undoubtedly believe it is true. But most resource experts and responsible politicians regard this as untenable rhetoric, based on blind faith and ignorance of the real limits of many resources. A good many people know that we are heading down an unsustainable path.

For a good example of the cornucopian thinking see Julian Simon's *The Ultimate Resource* published by Princeton University Press in 1981. For the opposite view, one of the best sources is *The Limits to Growth* by Donella H. Meadows et al., published by Universe Books in 1974.

2. It is not my intention in this book to convince the reader of the seriousness of the problems facing the planet. Rather, I assume most readers understand this and are looking for ways to strengthen the global environmental response. For a review of the global environmental problems, see the September 1989 issue of *Scientific American* and the January 2, 1989, issue of *Time.* Four recent books may also be of assistance. They are *The Cassandra Conference: Resources and the Human Predicament,* edited by Paul Ehrlich and John Holdren and published by Texas A & M University Press in 1988; yearly editions of *State of the World,* by Lester Brown and colleagues at the Worldwatch Institute in Washington, D.C.; *World Resources 1988–89,* published by Basic Books for the World Resources Institute and the International Institute for Environment and Development; and the third edition of my college textbook, *Environmen-*

tal Science: Actions for a Sustainable Future (third edition), published by Benjamin/Cummings in August 1990.

3. See the Environmental Defense Fund's *To Burn or Not to Burn: The Economic Advantage of Recycling Over Garbage Incineration for New York City*, published in August 1985, for a good case study. *Waste: Choices for Communities*, published by Concern, Inc. in September 1988, is an excellent source of comparative information on recycling and incineration.

4. California's Metropolitan Water District, which supplies water to 14.5 million people in southern California, recently signed an agreement with the Imperial Irrigation District that will allow Metropolitan to pay for water conservation measures in the Imperial Valley. Water freed up by these measures will be delivered to San Diego and Los Angeles at a fraction of the cost of water supplied by new dams and diversions. Environmentalists see this approach as the new wave of water supply, replacing the old-style approach that relied on costly new dams and diversions.

5. Lynell Johnson (1987). Children's Visions of the Future. *The Futurist* 21(3): 36–40.

6. I am not arguing that technology is unnecessary, only that it cannot be relied upon as a principal means of salvation. It is one of the many tools at our disposal, but will probably not be the chief means of achieving a sustainable future.

7. See Barry Commoner's article, "Why We Have Failed" in the September/October 1989 issue of *Greenpeace* for a discussion of this point of view.

8. The list of problems is long. First and foremost is environmental contamination resulting from nuclear plant accidents, potential sabotage, transportation accidents, and waste disposal. Given the current number of reactors now operating around the world, a major accident can be expected every 18 years. Nuclear plants are costly to build and to decommission. They suffer from poor social acceptability and they are an expensive source of electricity.

9. Insect pests quickly become resistant to chemical insecticides, requiring new formulations or higher doses. Today, well over 400 species are resistant to one or more insecticides. Efforts to continue battling bugs through chemical poisons is ultimately fruitless.

10. Some exceptions are notable. Worldwatch Institute, for example, has been actively promoting sustainability since the mid 1970s. Lester Brown, president of the organization, published a treatise on the subject, *Building a Sustainable Society*, in 1981. The Fund for Renewable Energy and the Environment (now called Renew America) and the Rocky Mountain Institute are also doing important work on sustainability.

11. By reactionary, I mean characterized by reaction, especially in a political context.

12. Peter Borrelli (1987). Environmentalism at a Crossroads. *The Amicus Journal* 9(3): 24–37. Borelli traces the roots of environmentalism.

13. Samuel P. Hays (1987). *Beauty, Health and Permanence: Environmental Politics in the United States 1955–1985*. Cambridge: Cambridge University Press. Chapter 1 describes the fundamental differences between the conservation movement and environmental movement in greater detail.

14. Roderick Nash (1985). Rounding Out the American Revolution: Ethical Extension and the New Environmentalism. In *Deep Ecology*, Michael Tobias, ed. San Diego: Avant Books. For a comprehensive discussion of the evolution of environmentalism, see Roderick Frazier Nash (1989). *The Rights of Nature: A History of Environmental Ethics*. Madison: University of Wisconsin Press.

15. Peter Borrelli (1988). The Ecophilosophers. In *Crossroads: Environmental Priorities for the Future*. Peter Borrelli, ed. Washington, D.C.: Island Press.

16. Norman Myers (1985). *A Wealth of Wild Species: Storehouse for Human Welfare*. Boulder, Colorado: Westview Press.

17. Only a fool would propose that preservationist thinking could be divorced from considerations of our needs. What might be helpful, however, is a better balance between the two, fostered by a healthy respect for the rights of other species. Finding that balance remains one of the most perplexing problems facing modern society as it struggles toward sustainability.

18. It is important to point out that environmentalism, while still rooted in conservation ideology, has broader goals. When it arose, it embraced a notion of environmental quality. Conservation was concerned with efficient development of resources. Environmentalism, at the outset, was interested in securing a cleaner and more healthy environment. That included clean air, clean water, and recreation. As a result, as Sam Hays notes, the conservation ideology and the environmental movement did conflict a fair amount over rivers, forests, soils, and other resources. Efficient use of rivers meant damming them for irrigation and other uses. To the environmentalist, a healthier, more enjoyable environment often meant preserving rivers for recreation.

19. Bill Devall (1988). *Simple in Means, Rich in Ends: Practicing Deep Ecology*. Salt Lake City: Peregrine Smith Books. Chapter 1 describes some fundamental differences between the mainstream environmental movement and the deep ecology movement.   ·

20. Lester W. Milbrath (1984). *Environmentalists: Vanguard for a New Society*. Albany: State University of New York Press.

21. The New Amendment proposal reads: Each person has the right to clean air, pure water, productive soils, and to the conservation of the

natural, scenic, historic, recreational, esthetic, and economic values of America's natural resources. There shall be no entitlement, public or private, competent to impair these rights. It is the responsibility of the United States and of the several states as public trustees to safeguard them for the present and for the benefit of posterity.

22. Several other other proposals for Constitutional amendments are now circulating. Richard Cartwright Austin, a Presbyterian minister and environmental theologian, emphasizes the biocentric vision. Marshall Massey, a Coloradan who is on the Board of Directors of the Colorado Environmental Coalition and works on environmental issues through the religious community, has made (in my opinion) the best proposal. Although it is detailed and long, it takes a much more ecocentric approach than others.

Marshall Massey also publishes an Environmental Circular that outlines the proposals. Circular Number 3, available for $1.50 is the most recent and complete listing of proposed amendments. Copies are available by writing Marshall Massey at 4353 East 119th Way, Denver, CO 80233.

23. By reactive, I mean simply reacting to troubles that arise. This is distinct from a proactive government that seeks to find ways to avoid problems in the first place through preventive actions.

24. There are some notable exceptions. The Environmental Defense Fund, for example, has worked on many proactive plans with businesses and government agencies in an attempt to avoid problems. These examples are discussed in Chapter 5.

25. Charles E. Little (1987). Letting Leopold Down. *Wilderness* 30(177): 45–48.

26. Arne Naess (1985). Identification as a Source of Deep Ecological Values. In *Deep Ecology.* Michael Tobias, ed. San Diego: Avant Books.

27. Quoted in Oliver S. Owen and Daniel D. Chiras (1990). *Natural Resource Conservation: An Ecological Approach.* Fifth edition. New York: Macmillan.

28. Other ethics are unsustainable and bound to falter and disappear.

29. Daniel D. Chiras (1986). Lessons From Nature. *Colorado Outdoors.* May issue.

30. Sim Van der Ryn and Peter Calthorpe (1985). *Sustainable Communities: A New Synthesis for Cities, Suburbs and Towns.* San Francisco: Sierra Club Books.

31. This is the definition of sustainable development given by the World Commission on Environment and Development in 1987, in *Our Common Future,* published by Oxford University Press. The goal of meeting present needs without impairing future generations from satisfying their own needs strongly suggests the use of renewable resources now.

32. Kai N. Lee (1989). The Columbia River Basin: Experimenting with Sustainability. *Environment* 31(6): 6–11, 30–33.

33. Or should that be "cooperator's manual"? Kai Lee talks about this in more detail in his *Environment* article listed in Note 32.

34. Walter V.C. Reid (1989). Sustainable Development. Lessons from Success. *Environment* 31(4): 6–9, 29–35.

35. Energy Information Administration (1989). *Annual Energy Outlook: Long-Term Projections.* DOE/EIA-0383(89).

36. G. Tyler Miller, Jr. (1988). *Living in the Environment.* Belmont, California: Wadsworth. See Chapter 15 for a discussion of mineral reserves.

37. E.F. Schumacher (1973). *Small is Beautiful: Economics as if People Mattered.* New York: Harper and Row.

38. J.E. Lovelock (1979). *Gaia: A New Look at Life on Earth.* Oxford: Oxford University Press.

39. Peter Russell (1983). *The Global Brain: Speculations on the Evolutionary Leap to Planetary Consciousness.* Los Angeles: J.P. Tarcher. Russell was not the first to draw this analogy. Dane Rudhyar made the same point 12 years earlier. Christopher Stone picked up on the idea and published it in 1972 in an article entitled "Should Trees Have Standing?" which was published in the Southern California Law Review.

40. Russell describes Watt's views in more detail in *The Global Brain.*

41. The extension of the self I am talking about should not be confused with ownership. To say that I am one with what has traditionally been viewed as not part of me is not to say that I own it and can do with it as I please.

42. Lester W. Milbrath (1989). *Envisioning a Sustainable Society: Learning Our Way Out.* Albany: State University of New York Press.

43. Eisler's conclusions are not uniformly accepted. Some anthropologists question the evidence upon which she has based her conclusions.

44. Arne Naess (1985). Identification as a Source of Deep Ecological Values. In *Deep Ecology.* Michael Tobias, ed. San Diego: Avant Books.

45. William Tucker (1982). *Progress and Privilege: America in the Age of Environmentalism.* New York: Doubleday.

46. Cited from Daniel D. Chiras (1991). *Environmental Science: Actions for a Sustainable Future.* Third edition. Redwood City, California: Benjamin/Cummings. The original article was published by Greenpeace. See Bibliography.

47. Herman E. Daly (1987). *The Steady-State Economy: Alternative to Growthmania.* Monograph published by Population-Environment Balance, Washington, D.C.

48. Daniel D. Chiras (1991). *Environmental Science: Actions for a Sustainable Future.* Third edition. Redwood City, California: Benjamin/

Cummings. G. Tyler Miller, Jr. (1988). *Living in the Environment*. Belmont, California: Wadsworth.

49. One of the biggest challenges in my estimation is the shift needed to make the urban/suburban setting more sustainable.

50. That means going beyond the kinds of solutions presented in *An Environmental Agenda for the Future* and *Blueprint for the Environment,* two recent documents that outline a host of environmental strategies, requiring new laws, amendments to existing laws, tighter regulations, and more spending.

Chapter 3: Beyond the Chain

1. I'm not saying groups have not been involved in promoting conservation and responsible lifestyles. It's just that the effort has been too meager. It has not extended much beyond the environmental community itself.

2. The reader will note some significant changes in this respect in recent months. George Bush has taken an active role in promoting individual action in fighting drugs and environmental deterioration. In September 1989, while touring Montana and Wyoming, he called on Americans to plant a few trees to help reduce global warming. Environmental groups have also become more active in promoting individual action. The National Wildlife Federation published two articles in *National Wildlife* on individual actions in 1989. Also in 1989, the Green Party published a list of socially and environmentally responsible actions. The Greenhouse Crisis Foundation published a list of 101 do-it-yourself projects that could help reduce global warming. Greenpeace and other groups have published such ideas earlier.

3. A lot of this attention focused on energy conservation.

4. A push to cut electricity consumption by 10 percent or 20 percent through individual action might have resulted in an immediate decrease in acid precursors, sulfur dioxide and nitrogen dioxide, which are converted to sulfuric and nitric acid in the atmosphere. At this writing, despite a decade of political action, efforts to control acid deposition are meager at best. Some states have taken action, but there has been no federal action.

5. In April 1989, a coalition of environmental and civic groups, headed by Jeremy Rifkin, launched a campaign to publicize 101 do-it-yourself steps to curb greenhouse warming.

6. Christopher K. Leman (1988). Bringing Environmental Policy Home. *Environmental Forum* 5(4): 19–22. Leman argues that most of our environmental policy has centered on social intervention—modifying the behavior of corporations, municipalities, and other large organizations.

7. The key point here is that we have failed to reach a broader constituency. Most environmentalists, many teachers, and some government officials understand the connection between our wasteful lifestyles and the environmental crisis, but we have failed to get this message across.

8. John H. Adams et al. (1985). *An Environmental Agenda for the Future*. Washington, D.C.: Island Press. Excellent reading, but limited principally to legislative and regulatory solutions.

9. Quoted in Peter Borelli (1987). Environmentalism at a Crossroads. *The Amicus Journal* 9(3): 31.

10. Quoted in Peter Borelli (1987). Environmentalism at a Crossroads. *The Amicus Journal* 9(3): 30.

11. Wendell Berry (1977). *The Unsettling of America: Culture and Agriculture*. San Francisco: Sierra Club Books.

12. Not everyone in an urban setting can use mass transit, but there's little doubt in my mind that ridership could increase dramatically.

13. Christopher K. Leman (1988). Bringing Environmental Policy Home. *Environmental Forum* 5(4): 19–22.

14. See *National Wildlife* 25(3): 4–13; *National Wildlife* 26(4): 30–37 and *National Wildlife* 27(5): 4–11.

15. Amory Lovins spreads the word about individual action by promoting the use of energy-saving technologies and points out how using such products can make significant inroads. The Fund for Renewable Energy and the Environment, now called Renew America, also helps publicize ways in which individual actions can mount up. What I'd like to see is more proof of ways that conservation actions *have* added up. In other words, fewer projections and more hard fact.

16. Dr. Leon Swartzendruber, personal communication, January 8, 1989.

17. My personal theory is that we are stuck in the analysis phase because we are still trying to convince our audience that we really do have an environmental crisis. In the past few years several of the trends we have been concerned about have become evident, such as ozone depletion and global warming. Their manifestation is beginning to lead to action.

18. Individual action is not a panacea, but an important supplement to legal action. Legal action to control individual behavior can also be effective. For example, recycling programs that are mandatory generally have twice the participation of nonmandatory programs, even though there is little or no enforcement of the former.

19. Even here, though, we shouldn't barrage our audience with so many solutions they don't know where to begin.

20. Peter Steinhart (1989). Who Turned Out the Lights? *National Wildlife* 27(1): 46–49. Curtis A. Moore (1989) Does Your Cup of Coffee Cause Forest Fires? *International Wildlife* 19(2): 38–45. Curtis A.

Moore (1989). Will Changing Your Light Bulb Save the World? *International Wildlife* 19(3): 18–23.

21. For a discussion of the project, see M. McCoy-Thompson (1989). Saline Solution. *World Watch* 2(4): 5–6. For additional examples see John J. Berger's book *Restoring the Earth,* published by Knopf in 1985.

22. Denver, like many western cities, experiences numerous temperature inversions during the winter months, which prevent air pollution from dissipating.

23. In the first three years, studies showed that the Better Air Campaign cut driving substantially during the high-pollution season. But in the winter of 1989, a reporter uncovered an error in the initial mileage calculations. When the daily driving of Denverites was recalculated, researchers found that the program had not produced a measurable decrease in driving.

24. As it is now, the environmental message is largely a private one. Environmentalists are talking to one another, but not to our friends, relatives, and neighbors.

25. In our area, I have only seen EDF's advertisement once, and then at 5:00 AM, on one of the mornings I couldn't sleep. If the ads are being aired similarly elsewhere, they will obviously only reach a small audience.

26. James Gustave Speth (1989). Dedicate the '90s to the Environment: International Commitment Could Be Our Gift to New Century. *Los Angeles Times,* February 16.

27. The truth be known, many of our so-called leaders are really followers. They sit back and wait to find out what the people want, then act on it.

Chapter 4: The Minds of Many

1. Huey D. Johnson (1988). Environmental Quality as a National Purpose. In *Crossroads: Environmental Priorities for the Future.* Peter Borelli, ed. Washington, D.C.: Island Press.

2. Lois Marie Gibbs and Karen J. Stults (1988). On Grassroots Environmentalism. In *Crossroads: Environmental Priorities for the Future.* Peter Borelli, ed. Washington, D.C.: Island Press.

3. A similar peak in interest occurred in the 1970s.

4. Phone interview, January 8, 1989.

5. Dues-paying memberships in environmental organizations have tripled in the past five years. Some college teachers have witnessed a dramatic increase in the number of enrollments in environmental science courses. The course I taught in the spring of 1989 at the University of Washington had an enrollment 50 percent greater than expected.

6. Concern about the economy displaced much of the environmental concern in the late 1970s and well into the 1980s. Concern about drugs and crime may similarly divert American attention unless signs of environmental decay continue to be as obvious as they have been of late.

7. Ron Arnold (1987). *Ecology Wars: Environmentalism as if People Mattered.* Bellevue, Washington: The Free Enterprise Press. Arnold describes how some people view environmentalists. His arguments are a bit narrow and are tainted by a strong antienvironmental viewpoint, but he does help clarify the views of people who fear that environmentalism is threatening free enterprise and the American way of life.

8. Personal communication, February 1989.

9. Just a few days ago a mother complained to me about her daughter's teachers who are harping on the problems of modern society, and claiming society is doomed, thus offering little or no hope for solution. This may be an isolated incident, but I doubt it. It is most likely the result of educators who are confused about the solutions, and perhaps overwhelmed and pessimistic as well. They are a symptom of a long-standing tradition of uncovering problems without focusing on individual action leading to solutions.

10. By concentrating almost exclusively on environmental problems and ignoring solutions, environmental leaders, educators, and others may be facilitating denial. It is far easier to deny a problem than to come to grips with it.

11. Ron Arnold (1987). *Ecology Wars: Environmentalism as if People Mattered.* Bellevue, Washington: The Free Enterprise Press. William Tucker (1982). *Progress and Privilege: America in the Age of Environmentalism.* Garden City, New York: Doubleday.

12. Tucker attacks environmentalists as elitists out to protect their own interests at the expense of the working man and woman, much the same way America's aristocracy once fought to protect its wealth and way of life by attempting to thwart economic development.

13. Phone interview, December 1988.

14. Chapter 5 discusses several similar examples and carries this thesis further.

15. Personal interview, November 1988.

16. Phone interview, March 13, 1989.

17. Lois Marie Gibbs and Karen J. Stults (1988). On Grassroots Environmentalism. In *Crossroads: Environmental Priorities for the Future.* Peter Borelli, ed. Washington, D.C.: Island Press.

18. We must begin to create support that, ironically, could put some of us out of business. If we are successful in building a sustainable society, however, environmentalists could become the first "species" to go happily on the endangered list.

19. Quoted in Bill McKibben et al. (1990). How We Can Save It. *Greenpeace* 15(1): 4-8.

20. Phone interview, February 22, 1989.

21. Barry Commoner (1989). Why We Have Failed. *Greenpeace* 14(5): 12–13. Commoner argues that the poor are subjected to a more severe environmental burden than wealthier people.

22. *United States Population Estimates by Age, Sex, and Race: 1980 to 1987.* U.S. Department of Commerce, Bureau of the Census.

23. Some may balk at the thought of a large coalition, thinking instead that many hundreds of smaller groups could work more effectively. Action at both levels has its pros and cons and I wouldn't discourage either. My personal bias is to eliminate duplication chiefly because of the need for rapid change.

24. The Ecojustice Working Group recently put out a modified version of *101 Ways to Save the Earth: A Citizen's Action Guide,* produced by the Greenhouse Crisis Foundation (See Appendix D).

25. For more information contact Noel Brown at the United Nations Environment Programme. (See Environmental Sabbath in Appendix D).

26. The Interfaith Council for the Protection of Animals and Nature is a multifaith organization formed ten years ago. It is an all-volunteer organization that produces Christmas and greeting cards, contributes articles to magazines, and lobbies to get animals added to the endangered species list. Contact the Interfaith Council for the Protection of Animals and Nature at 2841 Colony Road, Ann Arbor, Michigan 48104.

27. Without this, we almost certainly guarantee a future racked with strife and hardship. We guarantee continued political and social conflict.

28. Personal interview, August 1988.

29. Ecology is a body of knowledge about life and the interconnections of all living things and the environment. It does not teach us lessons, but we can learn from it nonetheless. For example, by studying sustainability in ecosystems, we can consider ways that human society can achieve sustainability.

30. For an introduction to environmental ethics, you might want to look at Chapter 19 of my textbook, *Environmental Science: Actions for a Sustainable Future.* The third edition is slated for publication in August of 1990 (Redwood City, California: Benjamin/Cummings). The suggested readings section at the end of the chapter lists several additional references that might be of help.

31. I have published some models to help students develop critical thinking skills that might be of interest to the reader: Models for Evaluating Environmental Issues in the Classroom. *American Biology Teacher* 42(8): 471, 1980. Risk and Risk Assessment in Environmental Education. *American Biology Teacher,* 44(8): 460–465, 1982. Additional mod-

els are presented in my environmental science textbook listed in Note 30.

32. This does not negate my belief that people care, which I advanced in Chapter 3. People do care. They are concerned with wealth and material possessions, but underneath, most care about the quality of the environment and the future of the planet. That compassion has been suppressed and thwarted by social forces, but it is still there.

33. No one knows precisely how many registered environmentalists there are. The number is estimated from total paid membership, with some adjustment for overlap because many of us join several groups.

34. Lester W. Milbrath (1985). *Environmentalists: Vanguard for a New Society.* Albany: State University of New York Press.

35. Of course, this is much easier said than done. Many people are wary of talking to others for one reason or another. But reaching out to our friends and relatives can really help us broaden our base of support and make environmentalism mainstream.

36. Island Press editorial office address: Box 7, Covela, CA 95428.

37. *E Magazine*, 28 Knight Street, Norwalk, CT 06851.

38. I propose a new kind of capitalism that takes into account future generations, limited resources, and environmental protection, factoring in external economic costs of production.

Chapter 5: The Third Wave of Environmentalism

1. Douglas P. Wheeler (1988). A Political Handbook for the Environmental Movement. *Washington Post National Weekly Edition,* September 19–25: 25.

2. Membership data from *U.S.A. Today* article published on September 5, 1989, page 5D.

3. Growth within the movement, however, was a mixed blessing. Swelling organizations developed unwieldy bureaucracies riddled with organizational problems.

4. Cynthia Wilson (1988). A View from the Trenches. In *Crossroads: Environmental Priorities for the Future.* Peter Borelli, Ed. Washington, D.C.: Island Press.

5. On other issues, however, the environmental movement was not so fortunate. We had virtually no success in getting the EPA to set standards for pesticide residues on food.

6. Huey Johnson notes that groups such as Greenpeace, Earth First!, and Sea Shepherd Conservation Society have concentrated on "creative conflict," a kind of reactionary display that impresses on the public the need for wilderness and wildlife preservation. Through direct action and confrontation, Earth First! stopped a logging operation in Texas long enough for Friends of the Earth to get a court order to halt logging operations. If it were not for Earth First!, working in cooperation with

Friends of the Earth, the trees would have been chopped down long before Friends of the Earth had gotten through the maze of legal hurdles.

7. Environmental groups also work through other avenues, such as the purchase of property and education, but the chief avenues of action have been laws, lawsuits, and protests.

8. Frederic Krupp (1988). The Third Stage of Environmentalism. In *Environmental Science: A Framework for Decision Making*. Daniel D. Chiras. Menlo Park: Benjamin/Cummings. Krupp published this essay originally in the EDF newsletter.

9. Population stabilization is one of the principal goals of a sustainable society. The world population is projected to climb to 10 billion, twice what it is today, before stabilizing. Once global population is stabilized many people think that it will need to be trimmed by attrition—that is, holding the growth rate below the death rate. How many people the planet can support remains an open question. Estimates range from 500,000 to 40 billion. Given the present state of affairs it seems to me that the carrying capacity is probably well below 5 billion.

10. Romer quickly caved in to pressure applied by the Denver Water Board and public officials. When the EPA announced that it was going to veto the project, Romer objected.

11. Huey D. Johnson (1988). Environmental Quality as a National Purpose. In *Crossroads: Environmental Priorities for the Future*. Peter Borelli, ed. Washington, D.C.: Island Press.

12. Instead of making environmentalism a mainstream concern and way of life, we in the environmental community may be giving up on what we believe to work within the system. That is, we are becoming mainstream.

13. Joy Williams (1989). Save the Whales, Screw the Shrimp. *Esquire* (February): 89–95.

14. Lester W. Milbrath (1984). *Environmentalists: Vanguard for a New Society*. Albany: State University of New York Press.

15. Of course, many business people also end up in Congress, so the myth may be partly due to this phenomenon as well.

16. Given their druthers most environmentalists would prefer a healthy economy to an economy in shambles. But in much the same way that human health precludes constant growth, our economic health may depend on stability rather than constant, possibly unsustainable expansion.

17. Many of our critics pick up on this—William Tucker and Ron Arnold, for example.

18. Richard Kazis and Richard Grossman published an article in 1982 entitled "Environmental Protection: Job-Taker or Job-Maker?" in *Environment* 24(9): 12–20, 43–44. It describes how jobs are used to

blackmail us, to convince people of the need for a project. It points out that environmental protection creates far more jobs than it eliminates. It also notes that many companies that go under because of environmental regulations were marginal to begin with.

19. The argument gets tricky here. Economists and business people argue that we need continued growth to help the poor. But the benefits of continued economic growth are often illusory, and they never seem to make it to the poor. What is needed is a system that raises the standard of living of the poor, while the rich remain at the same level. It is naive to suggest, but CEOs and other wealthy people need to take less of the profit, so the many can have more. We need more equity in our economy.

20. Denver officials pushed for the new airport despite the fact that 25 percent of the gates at Stapleton International were vacant and despite the fact that two major airlines refused to endorse the project, feeling that it was unnecessary and invariably would raise rates.

21. William D. Browning and L. Hunter Lovins (1989). *Energy Casebook.* Snowmass, Colorado: Rocky Mountain Institute. Also see Barbara A. Cole (1988). *Business Opportunities Casebook.* Snowmass, Colorado: Rocky Mountain Institute.

22. Worldwatch Institute quoted in Janet Raloff (1988). Energy Efficiency Means More: Fueling a Sustainable Future. *Science News,* 133(19): 296–298. Two important papers on energy efficiency are: Christopher Flavin and Alan B. Durning (1988). *Building on Success: The Age of Energy Efficiency.* Worldwatch Paper 82. Washington, D.C.: Worldwatch Institute; W.U. Chandler (1985). *Energy Productivity: Key to Environmental Protection and Economic Progress.* Worldwatch Paper 63. Washington, D.C.: Worldwatch Institute.

23. Just ten years ago, many energy analysts predicted that energy efficiency improvements of 20 or 30 percent could occur, but would create enormous social change. People would shiver throughout the dark winters or abandon the family automobile. However, Christopher Flavin and Alan Durning of the Worldwatch Institute note that these improvements *have* occurred over the past decade, largely without notice. Between 1973 and 1985 most western European nations reduced energy consumption (as measured per dollar of GNP) by 18 to 20 percent. The United States and Japan saved even more: 23 percent and 31 percent, respectively.

24. Environmental Defense Fund (1988). *Coming Full Circle: Successful Recycling Today.* Washington, D.C.: Environmental Defense Fund.

25. John J. Berger (1985). *Restoring the Earth: How Americans Are Working to Renew our Damaged Environment.* New York: Knopf.

26. Unfortunately, in areas where trees are being replanted, like China, deforestation outstrips reforestation.

27. Described in Spectrum in *Environment* (1989) 31(1): 23–24.

28. Robert K. Anderberg (1988). Wall Street Sleaze. *The Amicus Journal.* 10(2): 8–10.

29. While other companies often overharvested their redwoods and firs, Pacific Lumber selectively cut theirs, under a policy that actually allowed new lumber to grow faster than trees were cut.

30. Rosalyn Will, Alice Tepper Marlin, Benjamin Corson, and Jonathan Schorsch (1988). *Shopping for a Better World. A Quick and Easy Guide to Socially Responsible Supermarket Shopping.* New York: Council on Environmental Priorities.

31. Described in the June 1988 *EDF Letter,* p. 4.

32. Many environmentalists believe that love and unity do not preclude criticism and statements of alarm. The trick is to find a way to act lovingly while still being adamant about your position. The trick is to push without angering and alienating those you are pushing. This may not always work and may not always be the fastest route to action. I can think of several examples where environmental and social change protagonists were downright rude. Without the rudeness, it is arguable that nothing would have happened.

33. Michael G. Renner (1989). What's Sacrificed When We Arm. *World Watch* 2(5): 9–10.

Chapter 6: In Thought and Action: The Missing Connections

1. Overconsumption is one of the chief roots of environmental decay in the United States. Americans use almost three times as much energy per capita as the Japanese and Western Europeans.

2. Please be careful not to misinterpret my intentions. I realize how important fund raising is and I recognize that direct mail is one of the chief access points we have to the general public. What I oppose, however, is wasteful direct mail—mailings that come too often, mailings packed with all sorts of inserts, and mailings that are not printed on recycled paper.

3. I haven't done a formal poll but have talked to a great many people about environmental direct mail. Almost without exception, environmentalists are growing irate over the issue.

4. This illustrates one of the trickiest issues in the American economy. To stay competitive, we think we have to keep upping the ante.

5. My personal view after having been in the textbook industry for ten years is that the extras may help sell a book, but teachers on the whole don't use much of them.

6. I think this assumption is true.

7. I'm not altogether convinced that the science of direct mail is very reliable.

8. I don't think many groups consciously shape their agenda around

the sexy issues. No one says, "This is hot, it will earn us lots of money, let's work on it." What happens is that groups are attracted to the startling or pressing issues. They become interested in helping solve the problem and thus mount fund-raising campaigns to support the kind of work they want to do. That's a little different than sitting back and consciously shaping an agenda around the hot issues.

9. Groups have to go after issues that the public perceives as important. Environmental organizations are caught in a Catch-22. They may want to work on the issues that are not as flashy, but can't find the money to do it.

10. Certainly, this is true in Colorado. But the lack of interest here also comes from a feeling that the issue is too big to solve.

11. Lester R. Brown (1989). *State of the World*. New York: Norton. In 1988, 5.5 billion tons of carbon dioxide were emitted into the atmosphere by fossil fuel combustion. Deforestation contributes 0.4 billion to 2.5 billion tons per year.

12. My work with the Colorado Environmental Coalition suggests that people will donate money for appeals that are made simply and succinctly.

13. One of the most common arguments I get when proposing that we all find ways to cut back on direct mail is the same one we hear when people talk about unilateral disarmament: If I cut back and my opponents don't, then where will I be?

14. I'm not suggesting that workplace donations are a panacea nor that they are without problems. I'm simply suggesting that we can reduce direct mail and offset any potential losses by workplace solicitation. Once the system is up and running, it provides a steady flow of money without the paper and resource waste of direct mail.

15. The New Alternatives Fund, which invests in energy conservation, insulation, cogeneration, photovoltaics, and other companies, earned 26 percent in 1989 and 23.9 percent in 1988. Its five-year average was 16 percent. New Alternatives Fund, 295 Northern Boulevard, Great Neck, NY 11021. Other "green" investments are also available through stockbrokers.

Chapter 7: Marshalling Our Forces

1. Global warming seems to be the issue everyone is flocking to now.

2. I think that diversity in the environmental movement breeds strength, but wherever possible we should find ways to merge efforts, freeing up individuals to work on other critical issues that might fall through the cracks.

3. Duplication can occur as well in education. School districts often work on curricula in isolation from one another, creating unnecessary duplication.

4. The Colorado Environmental Coalition's Environmental Health Committee, for example, has assembled a directory of state groups interested in chemical contamination issues—air pollution, water pollution, hazardous wastes, pesticides, radiation, and so on. They're publishing the directory and distributing it to all groups. The directory is keyed for easy reference, so readers can locate groups with similar interests. The preface calls on people to meet and discuss areas of duplication and to hammer out plans to work together. The Environmental Health Committee will help bring interested parties together by sponsoring meetings on areas where interest overlaps and is using the listing to identify issues that aren't being covered.

5. Timber, Fish and Wildlife. *Totem.* Washington State Department of Natural Resources. Fall, 1988. Contains a number of articles on the TFW agreement. Also see: Northwest Renewable Resources Center (1987). From Conflict to Consensus. *Timber/Fish/Wildlife: A Report from the Northwest Renewable Resources Center.*

6. J. William Futrell (1988). Environmental Law—20 Years Later. In *Crossroads: Environmental Priorities for the Future.* Peter Borrelli, ed. Washington, D.C.: Island Press.

7. In a number of programs, the federal government sets standards or offers technical advice, but it is up to the states to regulate. A good example is groundwater protection and surface mining reclamation work. In other areas, the federal government has played virtually no role whatsoever. Recycling and waste disposal are good examples. Municipalities have issued outright bans on plastic packaging and the states have passed their own bottle bills. Federal action on some of these issues could be more effective in the long run in meeting environmental goals.

8. Nathaniel P. Reed and Amos S. Eno (1988). Looking Backward. In *Crossroads: Environmental Priorities for the Future.* Peter Borrelli, ed. Washington, D.C.: Island Press. More and more national organizations are focusing their attention on international issues as well—and for good reason.

9. In the late 1970s, I wrote an article on the proposed Strontia Springs Dam. The dam is located downriver from the proposed Two Forks Dam and is a vital part of a huge and costly water diversion project in Colorado. I argued that if Strontia Springs were completed, the Denver Water Board would surely ask for Two Forks. Its approval was the Denver Water Board's foot in the front door.

Two Forks and the necessary water diversion projects that would shunt water from the western slope of the Rockies to the eastern slope, where the dam would be built, would have incredible national impact. I noted in the article that the Two Forks project would alter the water flow and water chemistry of the Colorado River, which, at the time, supplied water for more than 17 million people.

With local Sierra Club sponsorship and a covering letter from a high-ranking local member emphasizing the importance of publicity, I sent the article to the *Sierra Club Bulletin*. Some weeks later the editor wrote back saying they couldn't publish it because it wasn't an issue of national concern.

The Two Forks project has since made the national news. It was the central focus of a nationally broadcast special on PBS. As the story unfolds, critics are finding all kinds of national impacts—including threats to several endangered species. In early 1989, the EPA permit approval was bumped from the regional to the national level. It landed in the lap of newly appointed William Reilly of the Environmental Protection Agency. It no doubt occupied the mind of George Bush.

No editor can be counted on to assess every single issue's degree of importance correctly. If national organizations decide to become more involved in supporting local work, they will invariably have to trust the local groups to pinpoint issues of concern.

Chapter 8: Earth in Transition: On the Threshold of Change

1. Quoted from Bill McKibben et al. (1990). How We Can Save It. *Greenpeace* 15(1): 4–8.

2. Paraphrased from Sale's article above.

3. I am indebted to my friend and colleague David Lynch and his associates at the Stewardship Community and Sunrise ranch for for some of the thoughts expressed in these paragraphs and for the title of this chapter.

Appendix A: Building a Sustainable Future

What Is a Sustainable Society?

A sustainable society is based on three ethical principles: (a) the world has a limited supply of resources ("there's not always more"), which must be shared with all living things, (b) humans are a part of nature and subject to its rules, and (c) nature is not something to conquer, but rather a force we must learn to cooperate with.

A sustainable society is built on four pillars: (a) conservation, (b) recycling, (c) renewable resources, and (d) population control.

How Do We Build a Sustainable Society?

To build a sustainable society we must make profound changes. Some may come as a result of legal action, such as new laws and regulations that force us to rely more heavily on conservation, recycling, and renewable resources and to control population size to reach a stable, sustainable level.

Technological innovations will help us become a sustainable society. More efficient photovoltaics that produce electricity from sunlight, for instance, will help us make the transition to solar energy. Water-sensing computers can help farmers apply appropriate amounts of water to crops to prevent overwatering. Improvements in automobile efficiency can help us cut back on fossil fuel consumption and will help us clean up our air. But technological solutions are not enough. We need fundamental changes in consumption patterns. We need people like you to pitch in to help build a sustainable future.

What Can Individuals Do?

1. **Conserve**: Cut back on energy, water, and materials. Even a 10 percent to 20 percent cutback will have remarkable effects when added to the actions of millions of like-minded people.
2. **Recycle**: Return glass, aluminum, newspaper, office paper, computer paper, plastic milk jugs, plastic bags, plastic soda bottles, plastic shampoo bottles, and paper bags to recycling outlets.
3. **Renewable Resources**: Whenever possible choose renewable or abundant resources (wood, paper, glass, cotton and wool) over nonrenewable resources (plastics and synthetic cloth).
4. **Population Control**: Limit family size to two children and help support international groups working to promote family planning in less

developed nations. Help reduce the pet population by spaying and neutering cats and dogs.

Citizen Action

Write your governmental representatives. Promote the idea of a sustainable society and ask that they consider the principles and goals of a sustainable society in every bill they vote on.

Water Conservation

Lawn and garden. Water your lawn and garden early or late in the day or at night when the air is the coolest and evaporation is low—this can cut outside water use by 50 percent.

Don't cut grass too short. By leaving it a little longer, you reduce water demand and reduce stress on grass.

Avoid overwatering. Use a tuna fish can to measure water applied to each section. Watch for water running off your lawn—this indicates your soil is saturated. Avoid watering sidewalks, driveways, fences, and streets. Plant shade trees—they'll also save you energy in the summer.

Use xeriscape in arid climates. Plant low-water shrubs, grasses and trees. Or remove hard-to-water sections and replace with rocks and shrubs. For new lawns, dig in compost, straw, sawdust, and manure to enrich the soil. The more organic material in the soil the better it holds moisture. Save grass clippings for mulching shrubs, trees, flowers, and vegetable gardens.

Inside water use. Take shorter showers and install showerheads that reduce water use but still produce a strong spray. Turn off water while brushing teeth or shaving. Place bottles, rocks, or bricks in toilet tanks to reduce water loss with each flush. Salad dressing bottles work well and help maintain pressure—two fit nicely in the toilet tank. There's no need to flush each time, either. Replace faulty ball cock valves and install low-water toilets. When washing clothes, adjust water level for each load.

Energy Conservation

Automobile energy savings. Buy energy efficient vehicles. Reduce unnecessary driving. Car pool, take mass transit, walk or bike to work. Combine trips. Keep your car tuned and your tires inflated to proper level. Drive the speed limit.

Home energy savings. If you haven't already done so, increase your attic insulation to R30 or R38. Caulk and weatherstrip your house. Add storm windows and insulated curtains. Install an automatic thermostat.

Turn the thermostat down in winter a few degrees and wear warmer clothing. Replace furnace filters when needed. Lower water heater setting to 120 to 130 degrees. Insulate water heater and pipes, install a water heater insulation blanket, and repair or replace all leaky faucets. Take shorter showers. Use cold water as much as possible. Avoid unnecessary appliances. Buy energy-efficient appliances. Use low-energy light bulbs.

Reducing Waste and Resource Consumption

Recycle at home and at work! Avoid products with excessive packaging. Reuse shopping bags. Refuse bags for single items. Use a diaper service instead of disposable diapers. Compost all lawn and garden waste. Reduce consumption of throwaways.

Donate used items to Goodwill, Disabled American Veterans, the Salvation Army, or other charities. Buy durable items. Give environmentally sensitive gifts.

Appendix B:
Gifts of Environmental Consciousness

This year why not give a different kind of present—a gift that helps protect the earth: items made from renewable or recyclable resources, presents that help promote resource conservation or help raise individual awareness? Below is a brief list of ideas that may help you this Christmas and at other times as well in selecting presents.

Gifts Made from Recycled and Renewable Materials

Why not buy a friend or relative a box or two of Christmas cards printed on recycled paper for next year or a box of recycled stationery or some lovely recycled wrapping paper? Such practical gifts will save them a trip to the store and will help promote the use of recycled products and help save our forests. Some beautiful designs are available through: Earth Care Paper Company, 325 Beech Lane, Harbor Springs, MI 49740. Phone: (619) 526-7003.

For children, consider wooden—rather than plastic—toys. Wood blocks make an excellent present for youngsters learning to read. And there are many wood toys, such as animals and trucks (which are often handcrafted), for children of all ages in toy stores and area gift shops.

Gifts That Promote Conservation

For nature lovers, consider a bird feeder or a bird house. They're available locally in many hardware stores. But avoid redwood feeders and houses—there's no sense in cutting down a redwood to house a bird in your backyard. For a complete catalog of feeders contact: Duncraft, Penacook, New Hampshire 03303-0508. For energy-conscious relatives, or ones you want to encourage in that direction, consider a low-energy light bulb or two. They're expensive, but save enormous amounts of energy, paying for themselves several times over. Contact Seventh Generation, 10 Farrell Street, South Burlington, VT 05403 for a catalog.

Why not buy a gift certificate to upgrade friends and relatives' attic insulation? Your gift will pay huge dividends over the winter months, making them more comfortable and saving them money on energy bills.

A water-conserving showerhead or plastic dam for toilet tanks makes a perfect gift for the practical-minded. You can buy them at most hardware stores or through the Seventh Generation catalog.

Trees and shrubs make wonderful gifts and help provide shade in the summer, cutting energy bills and reducing lawn watering. A gift certificate from a local nursery will be a welcomed gift. You might even consider planting the tree as an additional favor.

How about adopting a zoo animal for a friend? Many people are thrilled to become the parents of a bird or mammal from the zoo or raptor rehabilitation program. Contact your local zoo. They usually have a wide assortment of mammals and birds up for adoption. Recipients of your gift usually will receive an Adoption Certificate and an information sheet on the animal. You can also adopt an injured eagle, hawk, or owl from the Florida Audubon Society's Adopt-a-Bird Program, 1101 Audubon Way, Maitland, Florida 32751. Recipients of your gift will receive a photograph of the bird.

Gifts That Raise Consciousness and Promote Good Stewardship

For the gardener, how about an environmentally safe, biodegradable chemical kit to treat common insects and fertilize house and garden plants? Check out local garden shops and the Seventh Generation catalog. Avid gardeners not currently using these environmentally beneficial products will welcome a chance to experiment to see that they really do work!

Or what about a gift membership in an environmental group or a donation to a worthy cause in the name of a friend or loved one? The National Wildlife Federation publishes a list of state and national environmental groups that is available in most major libraries.

And for children, why not give a subscription to *My Big Backyard* (preschoolers), *Ranger Rick* (elementary school age), or *National/ International Wildlife* (high school and older). These beautifully produced magazines can give many hours of pleasure, help raise awareness, and can promote reading.

Dover Press produces a variety of coloring books for children about plants and animals. They help youngsters become aware of the world around them, are wonderful gifts for little ones.

This is just a partial list. With a little imagination, I'm sure that you can find an incredible number of environmentally sensitive presents. If your friends and relatives are like mine, you'll find that most are delighted to receive a gift that helps preserve our environment.

Appendix C: A Primer on Critical Thinking

Perhaps one of the most obvious needs for improvement in environmental education is the need to develop critical thinking skills in our children. Critical thinking is one of the chief tools of a good scientist (and a great many other professionals). There's no single formula for critical thinking, but most critical thinkers would agree that several key steps are required for this important process.

The first requirement of critical thinking is a clear understanding of terms. Define all terms. Make sure you understand them and demand the same of others.

The second requirement of critical thinking is that individuals question the methods by which facts are derived. Were the facts derived from experimentation? Can they be verified? Was the experiment correctly run? Or is it a generalization derived from a single observation? How easy it is for a single event to make a lasting impression and taint our thinking. A newscast showing an angry mob in New York, for example, may give the impression that the entire country is in turmoil.

A third rule of critical thinking requires us to question the source of the facts—that is, who is telling them. When the American Tobacco Institute argues that the link between cigarette smoking and lung cancer hasn't been proven, a critical thinker would be skeptical. When a business says that its pollution isn't causing any harm, one might again question the assertion. Even environmentalists are prone to exaggeration. They're fair game for your critical thinking skills. Sadly, bias taints our views and creates a distorted view of reality.

The fourth requirement of critical thinking is to question the conclusions derived from facts. Do the facts support the conclusions? There's a surprising number of examples in which conclusions drawn from research simply are not supported by the facts. For example, one of the earliest studies on lung cancer showed a correlation between lung cancer and sugar consumption. A careful reexamination of the patients showed that the wrong conclusion had been drawn. It turned out that cigarette smokers actually consumed more sugar than nonsmokers. Thus, the link between sugar and lung cancer was incorrect. The real link was between smoking and lung cancer.

This example illustrates a key principle of science worth remembering: correlation doesn't necessarily mean causation. Just because the economy improves when a certain politician is in office doesn't necessarily mean that the politician and his or her policies had anything to do with it. Bias and assumptions taint how we interpret our observations. They're deadly enemies to critical thinking.

The fifth rule of critical thinking requires us to examine the big picture. In 1988, researchers at Monsanto announced that they had discovered a way to genetically alter wheat, making it resistant to a fungus that causes enormous crop damage each year. To control the fungus now, farmers often rotate wheat from year to year with crops not infected by the fungus. Crop rotation prevents the fungus from proliferating, keeping the pest in check. With the new genetically altered strain, researchers say, farmers will not have to rotate their crops. They can plant wheat in the same field year after year and can even plant larger crops. This may sound good at first, but when one considers the bigger picture, it is clear that the solution is an invitation to disaster. Why?

Crop rotation helps build soil fertility. Rotating beans, clover, and alfalfa with wheat, for instance, adds nitrogen to the soil. This helps maintain soil fertility. Crop rotation also prevents insect pest populations from getting out of hand, because their food supply is not constant. Eliminating crop rotation could result in an outbreak of insect pests, requiring more pesticide applications.

In solving the fungus problem, then, science may contribute to several more. A careful examination of the bigger picture—the ecological relationships—often throws into question the apparent wisdom of new actions.

These are some of the elementary tools of critical thinking. They are simple to learn and pay huge dividends in the long term.

Appendix D: Contacts

Environmental Books
Johnson Books
1880 South 57th Court
Boulder, CO 80301
(303) 443-1576

Island Press
Box 7
Covelo, CA 95428

**Environmentally Sound
   Products**
Earth Care Paper Company
P.O. Box 3335
Madison, WI 53704

Conservatree Paper Company
10 Lombard Street, Suite 250
San Francisco, CA 94111
(415) 433-1000

The Recycled Paper Company
185 Corey Road
Boston, MA 02146
(617) 277-9901

Atlantic Recycled Paper Co.
P.O. Box 11021
Baltimore, MD 21212
(301) 323-2676

Seventh Generation
10 Farrell Street
South Burlington, VT 05403

Environmental Organizations
Children's Rainforest
Florida's International University
Miami, FL 33199
(309) 554-3083

Citizens Clearinghouse
for Hazardous Waste
P.O. Box 926
Arlington, VA 22216
(703) 276-7070

Clean Water Action
317 Pennsylvania Avenue, SE
Washington, D.C. 20003
(202) 546-6616

Connecticut Fund for the
   Environment
152 Temple Street
New Haven, CT 06510
(203) 787-0646

Conservation International
1015 18th Street, NW, #1002
Washington, D.C. 20036
(202) 429-5660

Cultural Survival
11 Divinity Avenue
Cambridge, MA 02138
(617) 495-2562

Defenders of Wildlife
1244 19th Street, NW
Washington, D.C. 20005
(202) 659-9510

Ecojustice Working Group
National Council of Churches of
   Christ
475 Riverside Drive
New York, NY 10115

Educators for Social Responsibility
23 Garden Street
Cambridge, MA 02138
(617) 492-1764

Environmental Action
1525 New Hampshire Avenue,
NW
Washington, D.C. 20036
(202) 745-4870

Environmental Defense Fund
257 Park Avenue, S
New York, NY 10010
(212) 505-2100

Environmental Sabbath
United Nations Environment
  Programme
Two U. N. Plaza
New York, NY 10017

Friends of the Earth
218 D Street, SE
Washington, D.C. 20003
(202) 544-2600

Greenpeace Action
1436 U Street, NW
Washington, D.C. 20009

Global ReLeaf
American Forestry Association
P.O. Box 2000
Washington, D.C. 20013
(202) 667-3300

Household Hazardous Waste
  Project
901 S. National Avenue
Box 108
Springfield, MO 65804
(417) 836-5777

Institute for Local Self-Reliance
2425 18th Street, NW
Washington, D.C. 20009
(202) 232-4108

International Alliance for
  Sustainable Agriculture
1710 University Avenue, SE,
  Room 202
Minneapolis, MN 55414
(612) 331-1099

International Planned Parenthood
  Federation
902 Broadway, 10th Floor
New York, NY 10010
(212) 995-8800

League of Women Voters
8 Winter Street
Boston, MA 02108
(617) 523-2999

National Audubon Society
950 Third Avenue
New York, NY 10022
(202) 832-3200

National Coalition Against the
  Misuse of Pesticides
530 Seventh Street, SE
Washington, D.C. 20003
(202) 543-5450

National Recycling Coalition
1101 30th Street, NW, Suite 304
Washington, D.C. 20007
(202) 625-6406

National Toxics Campaign
29 Temple Place, 5th Floor
Boston, MA 02111
(617) 482-1477

National Wildlife Federation
1400 16th Street, NW
Washington, D.C. 20036
(703) 790-4321

Natural Resources Council of
Maine
271 State Street
Augusta, ME 04330
(207) 622-3101

Natural Resources Defense
Council
40 West 20th Street
New York, NY 10011
(212) 727-2700

The Nature Conservancy
1815 North Lynn Street
Arlington, VA 22209
(703) 841-5300

Northcoast Environmental Center
879 9th Street
Arcata, CA 95521
(707) 822-6918

Pesticide Action Network
P.O. Box 610
San Francisco, CA 94101

Population Reference Bureau
777 14th Street, NW, #800
Washington, D.C. 20005
(202) 639-8040

Rainforest Alliance
295 Madison Avenue, Suite 1804
New York, NY 10017
(212) 599-5060

Renew America
1400 16th Street, NW, Suite 710
Washington, D.C. 20036
(202) 232-2252

Rocky Mountain Institute
1739 Snowmass Creek Road
Snowmass, CO 81654-9199
(303) 927-3128

Save the Rainforest, Inc.
(A student/teacher group)
Dodgeville High School
912 West Chapel
Dodgeville, WI 53533

Sierra Club
730 Polk Street
San Francisco, CA 94109
(415) 776-2211

Union of Concerned Scientists
26 Church Street
Cambridge, MA 02238
(617) 547-5552
The Wilderness Society
1400 Eye Street, NW
Washington, D.C. 20005

Worldwatch Institute
1776 Massachusetts Avenue, NW
Washington, D.C. 20036
(202) 452-1999

World Resources Institute
1709 New York Avenue, NW
Washington, D.C. 20006
(202) 638-6300

World Wildlife Fund
1250 24th Street, NW
Washington, D.C. 20037
(202) 293-4800

Zero Population Growth
1400 16th Street, NW, Suite 320
Washington, D.C. 20036
(202) 332-2200

Government Agencies
Seattle Metro
821 Second Avenue
Seattle, WA 98104
(206) 447-5875

Clean Air Colorado
Better Air Campaign
Colorado Department of Health
4210 East 11th Avenue
Denver, CO 80220

Bibliography

Adams, John H., et al. (1985). *An Environmental Agenda for the Future.* Washington, D.C.: Island Press. Excellent reading, but limited principally to legislative and regulatory solutions.

Anderberg, Robert K. (1988). Wall Street Sleaze. *Amicus Journal.* 10(2): 8-10. Excellent view of the effects of junk bonds and takeovers on natural resource management.

Arnold, Ron (1987). *Ecology Wars: Environmentalism as if People Mattered.* Bellevue, Washington: The Free Enterprise Press. Scathing attack on environmentalism.

Berger, John J. (1985). *Restoring the Earth: How Americans are Working to Renew our Damaged Environment.* New York: Knopf. Superb and uplifting book on efforts to repair past damage to the earth.

Berry, Wendell (1977). *The Unsettling of America: Culture and Agriculture.* San Francisco: Sierra Club Books. Incisive look at some of society's weaknesses.

Borrelli, Peter (1987). Environmentalism at a Crossroads. *Amicus Journal* 9(3): 24-37. Broad overview of the environmental movement, including some of its history and major weaknesses.

Borrelli, Peter (1988). The Ecophilosophers. *Amicus Journal* 10(2): 30-39. An interesting look at the major philosophical factions of the environmental movement.

Borrelli, Peter (ed.) (1988). *Crossroads: Environmental Priorities for the Future.* Washington, D.C.: Island Press. A collection of essays on environmentalism well worth the reading.

Browning, William D., and L. Hunter Lovins (1989). *Energy Casebook.* Snowmass, Colorado: Rocky Mountain Institute. Exceptional guide for economic revival through energy-conserving actions.

Chandler, W.U. (1985). *Energy Productivity: Key to Environmental Protection and Economic Progress.* Worldwatch Paper 63. Washington, D.C.: Worldwatch Institute. Detailed treatise on energy efficiency.

Chiras, Daniel D. (1980). Models for Evaluating Environmental Issues in the Classroom. *American Biology Teacher* 42(8): 471-473. Paper that presents ways to help promote critical thinking.

Chiras, Daniel D. (1982). Risk and Risk Assessment in Environmental Education. *American Biology Teacher* 44(8): 460-465. Overview of the risk assessment process.

Chiras, Daniel D. (1991). *Environmental Science: Actions For a Sustainable Future.* Third edition. Redwood City, California: Benjamin/Cummings. Describes current environmental problems and solutions, emphasizing ways to build a sustainable society.

Cole, Barbara A. (1988). *Business Opportunities Casebook.* Snowmass, Colorado: Rocky Mountain Institute. Extraordinary publication showing communities ways to revitalize sagging economies with special emphasis on methods that are environmentally sound.

Commoner, Barry (1989). Why We Have Failed. *Greenpeace* 14(5): 12-13. Commoner questions deeply cherished views of risk assessment.

Comp, T. Allan, ed. (1989). *Blueprint for the Environment: A Plan for Federal Action.* Salt Lake City: Howe Brothers. A list of recommendations for federal reform.

Daly, Herman E. (1987). *The Steady-State Economy: Alternative to Growthmania.* Washington, D.C.: Population-Environment Balance. A good overview of Daly's views on the steady-state economy.

Devall, Bill (1988). *Rich in Means, Simple in Ends: Practicing Deep Ecology.* Salt Lake City: Peregrine Smith. A thoughtful discussion of environmental values and ways to put your values into action.

Durning, Alan B. (1988). *Building on Success: The Age of Energy Efficiency.* Worldwatch Paper 82. Washington, D.C.: Worldwatch Institute. Detailed discussion on energy efficiency.

Durning, Alan B. (1989). *Action at the Grassroots: Fighting Poverty and Environmental Decline.* Worldwatch Paper 88. Washington, D.C.: Worldwatch Institute. Excellent look at grassroots movements throughout the world.

Ehrlich, Paul. R., and John P. Holdren, eds. (1988). *The Cassandra Conference: Resources and the Human Predicament.* College Station: Texas A & M University Press. Collection of essays on the environment.

Elgin, Duane (1981). *Voluntary Simplicity: Toward a Way of Life That Is Outwardly Simple, Inwardly Rich.* New York: William Morrow. Superb coverage of a topic of grave importance to the building a sustainable society.

Energy Information Administration (1989). *Annual Energy Outlook: Long-Term Projections.* DOE/EIA-0383(89). Data on energy use now and in the future.

Futrell, J. William (1988). Environmental Strategic Leadership: Defining Objectives. *The Environmental Forum* 5(1): 20, 22-23. Insightful look at environmental leadership.

Futrell, J. William (1988). Environmental Law—20 Years Later. In *Crossroads: Environmental Priorities for the Future.* Peter Borrelli, ed. Washington, D.C.: Island Press. Good overview of gaps in environmental law.

Gibbs, Lois Marie, and Karen J. Stults (1988). On Grassroots Environmentalism. In *Crossroads: Environmental Priorities for the Future.* Peter Borrelli, ed. Washington, D.C.: Island Press. Describes the upsurge in grassroots support and the need to broaden it further.

Hays, Samuel P. (1987). *Beauty, Health and Permanence: Environmental Politics in the United States 1955-1985*. Cambridge: Cambridge University Press. Wonderfully written history of the environmental movement.

Johnson, Huey D. (1988). Environmental Quality as a National Purpose. In *Crossroads: Environmental Priorities for the Future*. Peter Borrelli, ed. Washington, D.C.: Island Press. Discusses some important ways to build coalitions with government and industry to heal the earth.

Johnson, Lynell (1987). Children's Visions of the Future. *The Futurist* 21(3): 36-40. Study of children's attitudes on their personal future and the future of the world.

Kazis, Richard, and Richard Grossman (1982). Environmental Protection: Job-Taker or Job-Maker? *Environment* 24(9): 12-20, 43-44. Describes how jobs are often used to convince people of the need for projects and how environmental protection often creates far more jobs than it eliminates.

Lee, Kai N. (1989). The Columbia River Basin: Experimenting with Sustainability. *Environment* 31(6): 6-11, 30-33. Instructive look at efforts to achieve sustainability.

Leman, Christopher, K. (1988). Bringing Environmental Policy Home. *Environmental Forum* 5(4): 19-22. Looks at the ways law can be used to affect individual behavior.

Little, Charles, E. (1987). Letting Leopold Down. *Wilderness* 30(177): 45-48. Examines society's failure to heed Aldo Leopold's advice.

Lovelock, James E. (1979). *Gaia: A New Look at Life on Earth*. Oxford: Oxford University Press. Early description of the Gaia hypothesis.

McCoy-Thompson, M. (1989). Saline Solution. *World Watch* 2(4): 5-6. Discusses how the Australian government is working with individuals to help put a halt to salinization.

McKibben, Bill et al. (1990). How We Can Save It. *Greenpeace* 15(1): 4-8. Excellent collection of thoughts on how to save the planet by leaders in environmental movement.

McPhee, John (1989). *The Control of Nature*. New York: Farrar Straus Giroux. Delightful account of human attempts to dominate nature and the often catastrophic backlashes that result.

Meadows, Donella H., Dennis L. Meadows, Jorgen Randers, and William W. Behrens, III. (1972). *The Limits to Growth*. New York: Universe Books. Classic study on the limits of exponential growth in a finite world.

Milbrath, Lester W. (1984). *Environmentalists: Vanguard for a New Society*. Albany: State University of New York Press. Interesting look at public attitudes and the role of environmentalists in reshaping American society.

Milbrath, Lester W. (1989). *Envisioning a Sustainable Society: Learning Our Way Out*. Albany: State University of New York Press. Candid discussion of the author's vision of a sustainable society and some ways to achieve it.

Moore, Curtis (1989). Does Your Cup of Coffee Cause Forest Fires? *International Wildlife* 19(2): 39-45. Traces individual contributions to global environmental problems.

Moore, Curtis A. (1989). Will Changing Your Light Bulb Save the World? *International Wildlife* 19(3): 18-23. More on individual contributions to environmental solutions.

Mosher, Lawrence (1989). Washington's Green Giants. Jay Hair and the New National Wildlife Federation. *Amicus Journal* 11(4): 34-39.

Myers, Norman (1985). *A Wealth of Wild Species: Storehouse for Human Welfare*. Boulder, Colorado: Westview Press. Comprehensive view of ways that wild species enrich our lives.

Myers, Norman (1989). Making the World Work for People. *International Wildlife* 19(6): 12-14. Well-written essay on sustainable development in the Third World.

Naess, Arne (1985). Identification as a Source of Deep Ecological Values. In *Deep Ecology*. Michael Tobias, ed. San Diego: Avant Books. Divulges the importance of expanding our concept of the self to include the world of which we are a part.

Nash, Roderick (1985). Rounding Out the American Revolution: Ethical Extension and the New Environmentalism. In *Deep Ecology*. Michael Tobias, ed. San Diego: Avant Books. Insightful look into the expansion of the realm of ethics.

Nash, Roderick Frazier (1989). *The Rights of Nature: A History of Environmental Ethics*. Madison: University of Wisconsin Press. The first comprehensive history of the concept that nature has rights, covering the development of environmental ethics in history, philosophy, science, and religion.

Northwest Renewable Resources Center (1987). *Timber/Fish/Wildlife: From Conflict to Consensus*. Report from the Northwest Renewable Resources Center. Describes how the TFW agreement came about and how it works.

Owen, Oliver S., and Daniel D. Chiras (1990). *Natural Resource Conservation: An Ecological Approach*. Fifth edition. New York: Macmillan. Introductory textbook on natural resource conservation.

Raloff, Janet (1988). Energy Efficiency Means More: Fueling a Sustainable Future. *Science News* 133(19): 296-298. Good summary of ways of achieving energy efficiency.

Reed, Nathaniel P., and Amos S. Eno (1988). Looking Backward. In *Crossroads: Environmental Priorities for the Future*. Peter Borrelli, ed. Washington, D.C.: Island Press. Interesting views on the upsurge in environmental regulation at the state level.

Reid, Walter V.C. (1989). Sustainable Development: Lessons From Success. *Environment* 31(4): 6-9, 29-35. Important reading on the nature of sustainability.

Ruckelshaus, William D. (1989). Toward a Sustainable World. *Scientific American* (September): 166-175. Excellent introduction to the importance of sustainability.

Renner, Michael G. (1989). What's Sacrificed When We Arm. *World Watch* 2(5): 9-10. Addresses the question of national security and shows ways to redirect our thinking.

Russell, Dick (1987). The Monkeywrenchers. *Amicus Journal* 9(4) 28-42. Superb look at the creative engagement groups like Earth First! and Sea Shepherds.

Russell, Peter (1983). *The Global Brain: Speculations on the Evolutionary Leap to Planetary Consciousness.* Los Angeles: J.P. Tarcher. Beautifully written treatise on the role of humanity in global affairs.

Sancton, Thomas A. (1989). What on Earth Are We Doing? *Time* 133(1): 24-30. Painfully sobering look at the planet in peril in the famous Planet of the Year issue of Time Magazine.

Schumacher, E.F. (1973). *Small is Beautiful: Economics as if People Mattered.* New York: Harper and Row. Classic reading on economics and appropriate technology.

Simon, Julian L. (1981). *The Ultimate Resource.* Princeton: Princeton University Press. Criticism of the basic tenets of environmentalism.

Speth, J. G. (1989). Dedicate the '90s to the Environment: International Commitment Could Be Our Gift to New Century. *Los Angeles Times,* February 16. Call for international action to heal the environment.

Steinhart, Peter (1989). Who Turned Out the Lights? *National Wildlife* 27(1): 46-49. Describes the benefits of conservation.

Tobias, Michael (ed.) (1985). *Deep Ecology.* San Diego: Avant Books.

Tucker, William (1982). *Progress and Privilege. America in the Age of Environmentalism.* Garden City, New York: Anchor Press/Doubleday. An attack on environmentalists as elite obstructionists who are subversive to progress.

Turner, Tom (1988). The Legal Eagles. *Amicus Journal* 10(1): 25-37. Excellent history of environmental law.

Van der Ryn, Sim, and Peter Calthorpe (1985). *Sustainable Communities: A New Synthesis for Cities, Suburbs and Towns.* San Francisco: Sierra Club Books. Important reading on sustainability.

Wheeler, Douglas (1988). A Political Handbook for the Environmental Movement. *The Washington Post National Weekly Edition* (September 19-25): 25. Offers important political advice to environmental organizations.

Will, Rosalyn, Alice Tepper Marlin, Benjamin Corson, and Jonathan Schorsch (1988). *Shopping for a Better World. A Quick and Easy Guide to Socially Responsible Supermarket Shopping.* New York: Council on Environmental Priorities. Important reference for consumers who want to make a difference.

Williams, Joy (1989). Save the Whales, Screw the Shrimp. *Esquire* (February): 89-95. A satirical look at human responsibility—or lack thereof. Important reading.

Wilson, Cynthia (1988). A View from the Trenches. In *Crossroads: Environmental Priorities for the Future.* Peter Borrelli, ed. Washington, D.C.: Island Press. Covers a wide range of topics on the environmental movement.

Index